Congress Scotch-Irish, of America Scotch-Irish Society

The Scotch-Irish in America

proceedings of the Scotch-Irish Congress

Congress Scotch-Irish, of America Scotch-Irish Society

The Scotch-Irish in America
proceedings of the Scotch-Irish Congress

ISBN/EAN: 9783744739306

Printed in Europe, USA, Canada, Australia, Japan

Cover: Foto ©ninafisch / pixelio.de

More available books at **www.hansebooks.com**

THOMAS T. WRIGHT.

The Scotch-Irish in America

Proceedings of the Scotch-Irish Congress

AT

COLUMBIA, TENNESSEE

MAY 8-11, 1889

PUBLISHED BY ORDER OF
THE SCOTCH-IRISH SOCIETY OF AMERICA

CINCINNATI
ROBERT CLARKE & CO.
1889

CONTENTS.

Part I.

Introduction, by Mr. Robert Bonner	1
The Scotch-Irish Congress	3
Officers and Committees of the Local Organization	10
Contributors to Expense Fund	12
Letters	13
Minutes, and Short Addresses	24
Officers and Committees of the Scotch-Irish Society of America	66
Action of Committees	69

Part II.

The Harp of Tom Moore	70

ADDRESSES BY

Ex-Governor Proctor Knott	72
Prof. George Macloskie	90
Rev. John Hall, D. D.	102
Hon. William Wirt Henry	110
Rev. D. C. Kelley, D. D.	132
Colonel A. K. McClure	178
Hon. Benton McMillin	187
Rev. John S. MacIntosh, D.D.	191
Hon. W. S. Fleming	202

To the Members of the Scotch-Irish Society of America.

In offering this compilation to the Society, and the general public, we do not pretend that it is a complete history of the Scotch-Irish people. That will require the systematic effort of years. As the initial volume of distinctive Scotch-Irish records, however, we believe that it will prove interesting and satisfactory. In the selection and arrangement of the matter contained, we have acted with the advice of the Executive Committee. For the convenience of the reader, the formal addresses, bearing directly upon the race, have been taken from their regular order in the minutes and arranged separately in Part Second.

The addresses are published as they were delivered, and we do not assume any responsibility for the views of the speakers. We bespeak for the volume kindly reception and consideration.

        A. C. Floyd,
        Lucius Frierson,
        Robert Pillow,
          Publishing Committee.

THE SCOTCH-IRISH IN AMERICA.

PART I.

INTRODUCTION.

BY ROBERT BONNER.

To Mr. Thomas T. Wright, a prominent citizen of Florida, belongs the credit of having suggested the formation of an organization to preserve the history and perpetuate the achievements of the Scotch-Irish race in America. Owing to the efforts of Mr. Wright, who was ably assisted by Mr. A. C. Floyd and other gentlemen, the movement was started which resulted in the grand and successful meeting of the Scotch-Irish Congress at Columbia, Tennessee, in May last, and which led to the permanent organization of the Scotch-Irish Society of America.

It does not come within the purpose, scope or object of this Society to cultivate or in any way encourage sectarian feeling, for people of all denominations are eligible to membership; nor is it the purpose of the Society to stimulate undue pride of race, although it is impossible to ignore the historical fact, so eloquently stated by William Wirt Henry, Esq., a grandson of the great revolutionary orator, that the Scotch-Irish in America have given five Presidents to the United States.

I have been requested to write an introduction to this volume, which gives a carefully prepared report of the action of the late Congress; but it appears to me that a formal or lengthy introduction would be superfluous. The eloquent speeches made during the session of the Congress, and the other proceedings of that body, tell their own story. They exhibit the cordial good will, the patriotic fervor, the indomitable spirit, the tenacity of purpose, and the stern integrity which have always characterized the Scotch-Irish ; and it is to be hoped that the Society so auspiciously inaugurated at Columbia will develop, as the years go on, into an organization of the highest usefulness.

THE SCOTCH-IRISH CONGRESS, ITS OBJECTS AND RESULTS.

BY A. C. FLOYD.

The Scotch-Irish people have been second to none in their influence upon modern civilization. Their impress upon American institutions has been especially strong. They have been leaders in every sphere of life, both public and private. They were the first to declare independence from Great Britain, and foremost in the revolutionary struggle; leaders in the formation and adoption of the Constitution, and its most powerful defenders; most active in the extension of our national domain, and the hardiest pioneers in its development.

The associations suggested by a few of the illustrious men of the the stock are sufficient to outline the extent of their influence. Among them were Patrick Henry, Thomas Jefferson, John Witherspoon, John Paul Jones, James Madison, John Marshall, Andrew Jackson, James K. Polk, James Buchanan, Abraham Lincoln, and Ulysses S. Grant.

That they have been no less conspicuous in the material development and intellectual progress of the country, is evidenced by the names of Robert Fulton, Horace Greeley, Robert Bonner, and the McCormicks.

These men are but types of the Scotch-Irish, and their achievements are but examples of the numberless illustrious deeds of the race; and yet no distinct and connected history of this people has ever been written. Their marked and distinctive impress upon the country and their proverbial race pride renders this passing strange, especially in this history-writing age, when the Puritan, the Huguenot, the Dutch, and every other class and nationality composing our population, have recorded their deeds with minutest care. In this, they have done nothing more than perform their duty, for it is the duty of all to study great examples and hold their virtues up for the emulation of on-coming generations. Thus is patriotism cultivated and every noble endeavor stimulated. Thoughtful men, indeed, knew the wealth of Scotch-Irish achievement and keenly felt the poverty of its recognition. Where else could nobler types of manhood be found? The hand of the historian, brushing away the dust of time, was alone needed to reveal the grandest figures of the world. The greatness of the fathers still lingered in the traditions of the children, but the delay of a few more years would consign them to an oblivion from which they could never be recovered.

If the work was ever to be done, it was necessary that it should be commenced without further delay. These facts were recognized and discussed, but the demand resulted in nothing definite until it took form in the Scotch-Irish Congress held at Columbia, Tennessee, last May.

The objects to be attained were not new; but the Congress, as a means of their accomplishment, was altogether original. The projectors of this gathering fully realized the extent of the work they had undertaken, and desired that it should be done in the most thorough and comprehensive manner possible. A convention composed of representative members of the race from all quarters of the country commended itself to them as the best means of beginning the work.

The addresses of the distinguished speakers, the historical papers submitted, and the reminiscences recounted would form a nucleus for the complete collection of data which it was hoped to accumulate in the course of time. Important as this meeting was expected to be, however, its promoters realized that it could only begin the great work. A permanent organization was necessary to continue it. Besides, a Scotch-Irish association was desirable for social as well as historical purposes. In this, as in the matter of history writing, they were behind all others. Every other people in America had banded themselves together for purposes of mutual pleasure and assistance. When properly directed, these societies had accomplished much good. Why should not the Scotch-Irish organize in a similar manner? Why should not their proverbial and well warranted race pride serve to focus their great energies upon purposes of common good? Among the many great objects to which this organized power could be applied was the collection of the desired historical data and the promotion of social intercourse.

The one would contribute in the highest degree to the cultivation of patriotism; the other would promote the warmest fraternal feeling. A better acquaintance between the northern and southern members of the race would bring a better understanding and a broader sympathy, binding the two sections together in the strong and enduring bonds of real friendship. To effect such an organization was the second great object of the Congress.

Among all the states of the Union, none could have been more appropriate for the gathering than Tennessee, both on account of her geographical position and the blood of her people. Pennsylvania, Maryland, Virginia, and North and South Carolina received the first great accessions of Ulster immigration; but swarms from these parent hives, moving westward since colonial days, now make Tennessee about the center of the blood in the United States. Besides, her intermediate position between the extreme North and the extreme South makes her people freer from sectional prejudice than either of these quarters, and, therefore, better fitted to promote the fraternal spirit which the convention was intended to foster. In no other state is the Scotch-Irish blood purer. They were the earliest and most numerous of her pioneers. On the banks of the Watauga, they made the first American settlement west of the Alleghanies, and it was they who led the vanguard in the march of civilization westward through her territory. They filled the armies that subdued the savages of the West and South-west. It was their stern, unalterable courage and determination which prevented Great Britain and Spain from confining the Americans to the Atlantic slope, and secured the Mississippi valley to the Union. Their numbers and valor in every war in which the country has been engaged has won for Tennessee the proud title of "The Volunteer State." They stamped their predominant characteristics upon their descendants, and gave the prevailing type to the character of the whole people. It was but natural that a convention called to do them honor should meet with warmest approval.

Columbia, the place chosen for the first Congress, lies in the very center of Tennessee, and her Scotch-Irish population, surrounded by a country widely known as "the garden spot of Tennessee"—a country unsurpassed for salubrity of climate, richness and variety of products, and advantages of geographical position. This heart of the Middle Tennessee Basin, now carpeted with a rich growth of blue grass, was originally covered by luxuriant cane-brakes, the infallible sign of a fat soil. It is not strange that the Scotch-Irish should have occupied it first. Always in the foremost ranks of the pioneers, the richest lands became theirs by right of discovery and first occupation, while the poorer country was left to the more timid people, who followed at a later and safer period. The advantages thus acquired, and the characteristic tenacity with which they have been held, go far to explain why the race has ever since been the wealthiest and most influential of the people in the countries first settled by them. The strength of their influence in Maury county is illustrated in Judge Fleming's sketch of Zion Church, and Dr. Kelly's address, published in this volume. Among the distinguished men of this stock whom Maury county has produced was James K. Polk, who went from Columbia to the President's chair.

Another thing that recommended Columbia was her railway facilities. These roads, running north, south, east, and west, make her easily accessible from every quarter of the country. Arrived here, visitors, especially those from the North, occupy an excellent vantage point from which to visit and study the best parts of the South. Within short reach by rail are some of the most famous battle-fields of the late war—Franklin, Nashville, Murfreesboro, Shiloh, and others. In easy communication, also, are Florence, Sheffield, Birmingham, and other manufacturing cities of the celebrated coal and iron fields of the South, affording the finest illustrations of the marvelous industrial progress which this section is now making. These advantages and associations rendered Columbia a peculiarly appropriate place for the gathering.

Having decided that the Congress should be held, and that Columbia was the place to hold it, the initial steps in the arrangements for it were taken in October, 1888. This action was prompted by Colonel T. T. Wright, now of Nashville, Tennessee. To him belongs the honor of having originated this, as well as many other great ideas, which have resulted in much public benefit. He not only originated the idea and inspired the first action for carrying it into effect, but gave the movement, at every stage, the invaluable aid of his advice, time, and means.

The date fixed for the beginning of the Congress was May 8, 1889, the most perfect season of the year in Tennessee. Arrangements for the Congress were vigorously and systematically pushed from the beginning. Some of the most distinguished men of the race accepted invitations to deliver addresses and to prepare historical papers. A thousand leading newspapers published the general invitation to the race issued by Governor Taylor and the Secretary; also, the reports sent them from time to time, as events developed, together with extensive and favorable editorial mention.

GOVERNOR TAYLOR'S INVITATION.

EXECUTIVE OFFICE, NASHVILLE, TENN.

To the Scotch-Irish Race:

Recognizing the Scotch-Irish Congress, to be assembled at Columbia, in this state, on the 8th of May next, as an event of international interest, Tennessee will welcome to it representatives of that lineage from all parts of the world. No political or sectarian significance attaches to the Congress. Its object is to revive memories of the race,

and to collect materials for compiling a history showing their impress upon modern civilization, especially upon American institutions. It promises to be one of the most notable meetings ever held in Tennessee.
ROBERT L. TAYLOR,
Governor.

Private invitations were sent to every representative man of the blood whose name could be ascertained. So unique and manifestly desirable was the gathering, that it met with hearty commendation from all to whose attention it was brought. Extensive correspondence was developed, and the interest became wide-spread. The latent pride of the race was at last stirred, and the enthusiasm which the call inspired evidenced its strength when once aroused. Reduced railroad fare was secured, and a large sum of money was readily and generously subscribed by the people of Columbia to defray the expenses of the occasion. The hospitable people vied with each other in their preparations for entertaining visitors.

When the day arrived, every detail of the arrangements was complete. The doors of every house stood wide open with welcome. The town was gaily decorated and thronged with visitors, representing every section of the Union. The weather was perfect throughout, and all the exercises were held in a great tent stretched in the oak-canopied, grass-carpeted grove of the Columbia Athenæum, kindly offered the management by Captain R. D. Smith, president of this fine old institution for young ladies. The Rogers Band, of Goshen, Indiana, rendered delightful music, consisting largely of Scotch and Irish airs, prepared especially for the occasion.

The initial proceedings were thus described by the *Nashville American:*

"The large canopy was beautifully decorated with flags and bunting of all kinds. Long streamers extended from the central post to the various points of the outer circumference, producing a most harmonious and beautiful effect. A large stage, thirty feet by twenty, and capable of comfortably seating fifty persons, had been erected under the south side of the tent. Arches spanned its front, and festoons of lovely flowers, from the rose to the evergreen, graced the arches in handsome designs. Vases of flowers were also conspicuously displayed.

"Upon the stage were placed a large painting of Jas. K. Polk and an old and historic "Harp of Erin," the hereditary property of Mrs. Emma McKinney, of the Athenæum.

"It was not long before the spacious audience-room, so to speak, was filled with a crowded mass of humanity. The *personnel* of the audience and of the visitors in general was especially good, and free from all the rougher elements. Then the visitors, the descendants of the Scotch-Irish, who had assembled to engage in the events of the day, lent great dignity and intellectuality to the meeting.

"The procession formed at the head-quarters on Garden street and in front of the Bethell House on Seventh street. It was led by the Goshen Band, of Goshen, Indiana, followed by the Witt Rifles, of Columbia, in full dress uniform; then the carriages containing the visitors and members of the Reception Committee, and at last a large concourse. In one of the front carriages was the harp of Tom Moore, in charge of Captain J. T. Craik, Major William Polk, and Colonel H. G. Evans.

"The large tent had already been crowded, even as to standing-room, and when the procession arrived, its proportions amounted to anywhere between 6,000 and 10,000 people."

There were two sessions of the Congress each day, morning and night. The tent was filled to its utmost capacity at every session by cultured and appreciative audiences. In the afternoons, many of the visitors repaired to the Fair Grounds at South Side Park, where they were entertained with exhibitions of speed by Tennessee's fastest horses, and by the display of other blooded stock, in which this country stands unexcelled. Others enjoyed driving over the numerous fine pikes which radiate in every direction from Columbia like spokes from a wheel, leading to the great farms and points of historical interest in the country.

Representatives of the race from every section of the country met in freest and most cordial social intercourse. Old friendships were renewed and new ones formed. Rich stores of tradition were brought to light and valuable historical reminiscences were recalled. Memories of the past were revived, thoughts of the present interchanged, and hopes of the future discussed. Among the attendants were many old Federal and ex-Confederate soldiers, attracted hither by the reunion of the blue and the gray, and a desire to revisit the surrounding battle-fields of the late civil strife. Upon these fields, but a few years ago, these veterans had met each other in deadliest conflict. Now they met with hearty hand-shake and the warm regard felt by men who have proved each other's true manhood in the severest ordeals.

The Congress was a complete success in every particular, but its crowning result was the organization of the Scotch-Irish Society of

America, which will take up and carry on in a systematic way the work so auspiciously begun.

The principal objects of the Society have already been outlined. Its purposes are social and historical. Through its members, sketches of the families represented and of the race in general, together with interesting relics connected with their history, will be collected.

Princeton College, New Jersey, has kindly offered to become custodian of this data for the present, but in the course of time the Society will have a permanent home for its reception.

The data thus obtained will be properly acknowledged, and the manuscripts filed in the archives of the Society for reference, or for use in the annual publications hereafter to be issued.

No partisan or sectarian significance attaches to the Society. Composed of a race thoroughly identified with all that has been most patriotic in our country, it is purely an American institution, and does not propose to concern itself with foreign affairs.

The social features of the organization promise large results. The Congress at Columbia gave earnest of the good fellowship which may be expected from the annual gatherings hereafter. The publications of the Society, and the development and extension of its organization, will promote correspondence among its members, increase their knowledge of one another, and draw them into closer relations of friendship and sympathy.

Though but a short time has elapsed since the conditions of membership were definitely settled, it has already reached gratifying proportions. Numerous applications for enrollment have been received from all parts of the country, from men occupying the highest positions in every sphere of life. Systematic plans are in operation, by which every member who joins becomes instrumental in bringing others into the Society. The membership is advancing by geometrical progression, and the present plans continued will in no great length of time bring a knowledge of the Society to every person of Scotch-Irish descent in America. There is practically no limit to its possible power and usefulness.

OFFICERS OF THE LOCAL ORGANIZATION OF THE SCOTCH-IRISH CONGRESS.

President.

COLONEL E. C. McDOWELL.

Vice-President.

HON. J. H. FUSSELL.

Secretary.

A. C. FLOYD.

Treasurer.

LUCIUS FRIERSON.

Executive Committee.

HON. W. J. WHITTHORNE, *Chairman.*
HON. J. H. FUSSELL,   T. B. KELLY,
E. E. ERWIN,   A. C. FLOYD.

Advisory Board.

COLONEL T. T. WRIGHT, *Chairman.*
CHAIRMEN OF OTHER COMMITTEES.

Finance Committee.

GEO. L. THOMAS, *Chairman.*
JAS. ANDREWS,   S. D. F. McEWEN,
A. BARR,   JOHN MOORE, JR.,
COLONEL H. A. BROWN,   B. S. THOMAS.

OFFICERS OF THE LOCAL ORGANIZATION.

Military Committee.

Hon. J. H. FUSSELL, *Chairman.*
COLONEL H. G. EVANS,   CAPTAIN H. P. SEAVY.

Transportation Committee.

COLONEL H. G. EVANS, *Chairman.*
DR. T. B. RAINS,   CAPTAIN H. P. SEAVY.

Committee on Music.

CAPTAIN J. T. CRAIK, *Chairman.*
DR. W. C. SHEPPARD,   CAPTAIN H. P. SEAVY.

Reception Committee.

CAPTAIN H. P. SEAVY, *Chairman.*
W. J. HINE,   JOHN C. DEXTER.

Entertainment Committee.

MAYOR ROBERT PILLOW, *Chairman.*
S. D. F. McEWEN,   W. C. TAYLOR.

Decoration Committee.

MISS COBY DUNNINGTON.
MRS. J. H. FUSSELL,   MRS. W. J. HINE,
MRS. JOE HENDLEY,   MRS. E. W. GAMBLE.

Badges and Mail.

MISS FLORENCE IRVINE.

CONTRIBUTORS TO THE SCOTCH-IRISH CONGRESS EXPENSE FUND.

Geo. L. Thomas,
John Moore, Jr.,
A. N. Dale,
James Andrews,
E. W. Gamble,
Bailey & Moore,
A. N. Akin,
Frierson & Titcomb,
Holding & Cochran,
Mrs. E. Jones,
Rev. Geo. Beckett,
E. E. Erwin,
W. P. Ingram,
Major Will. Polk,
T. N., C. T., and W. C. Jones,
S. T. Cook,
Dr. J. H. Wilkes,
Nichols & Fariss,
A. D. Frierson,
W. J. Howard,
W. F. Embry,
Street, Embry & Co.,
C. C. Gross,
Lamb & Smith,
J. D. Wright,
J. T. Craik,
E. H. Hatcher,
H. A. McLemore & Bro.,
Henry Gross,
A. Maxville,
H. A. Brown,
Lucius Frierson,
Mayes & Walker,
R. P. Russell,
McEwen & Dale,
A. Barr,
Bethell House,
Dobbins & Ewing,
Caperton & Taylor,
F. J. Hendley,
Figures & Padgett,
Geo. N. Sarven,
W. J. Webster,
John B. Ashton,
Geo. Childress,
H. G. Evans,
Joseph Towler,
Chaffin Bros.,
Rains & Son,
Dr. Robert Pillow,
J. P. McGaw, Jr.,
James Bros.,
Edgar James,
Satterfield & Church,
W. C. Sheppard,
Mrs. Ellen Mayes,
G. T. Hughes,
Andrews & McGregor,
G. P. Frierson,
I. M. Sulivan,

A. G. Adams, of Nashville.

LETTERS.

EXECUTIVE MANSION, WASHINGTON, *April* 1, 1889.
A. C. FLOYD, ESQ.,
 COLUMBIA, TENN.
  MY DEAR SIR:
   I am in receipt of your letter of the 20th inst., inviting me to be present at the Scotch-Irish Congress at Columbia, Tenn., on the 8th of May next. I regret that my engagements will prevent my acceptance; but beg you will accept for yourself, and convey to the members of the Association, my sincere appreciation of your courtesy, and my best wishes for the success of your meeting.
     Very truly yours,
      BENJAMIN HARRISON.

NEW YORK, *April* 13, 1889.
A. C. FLOYD, ESQ.,
 Secretary, etc
  DEAR SIR:
   I desire to acknowledge, with thanks, the cordial invitation I have received to attend the Scotch-Irish Congress, to be held at Columbia, Tennessee, on the 8th of May next.
   I regret that prior engagements will prevent my acceptance of your courteous invitation.
     Yours, very truly,
      GROVER CLEVELAND.

NEW YORK, *May* 3, 1889.
MR. A. C. FLOYD,
 Sec'y Scotch-Irish Congress,
  COLUMBIA, TENN.
   DEAR SIR:
    Upon my return from an extended trip through the South, I have the honor to acknowledge receipt of your favor, dated April 25th.

I regret exceedingly that business engagements, already made, so engross my time at the date of your Congress, that I shall not be able to give myself the satisfaction of attendance. I cordially appreciate your earnest invitation, though unable to accept it, and, as my best alternative, have taken pleasure in providing a car for the Rev. Dr. John Hall, Mr. Robert Bonner, and several other gentlemen, who will doubtless be at the meeting.

Regretting that circumstances forbid my being with you, I remain, Very sincerely, yours,

JOHN H. INMAN.

WAR OFFICE, LONDON, *February* 1, 1889.
SIR:

I have received, with much gratification, your Excellency's letter of the —— ult., inviting me to attend the Scotch-Irish Congress, to be assembled at Columbia, Tennessee, on the 8th of May next.

I regret very much that the pressure of my official duties precludes the possibility of my proceeding to the United States at that season of the year. I am compelled to decline the honor of the flattering invitation which your Excellency has conveyed to me in such courteous terms.

I have the honor to be, sir,
Your Excellency's obedient servant,

WOLSELEY.

HIS EXCELLENCY, R. L. TAYLOR,
Governor of the State of Tennessee.

PHILADELPHIA, *February* 21, 1889.

MR. A. C. FLOYD,
Secretary.
DEAR SIR:

I thank you for the invitation of February 16th, to attend the Scotch-Irish Congress to assemble at Columbia, Tenn., on the 8th of May next. I should greatly enjoy meeting the men and women whom your invitation will doubtless draw to your beautiful city, but regret that my engagements will not permit me to be present.

No racial element has had more important, and, I think I may say, healthful influence, in shaping the destinies of our Republic than the Scotch-Irish. This is especially true of the great belt of middle and border states. The very backbone of these commonwealths has been drawn from the heathered hills of Scotland and the green slopes of Ulster. The thistle and the shamrock have found the free Republic of the West a congenial environment, and have flourished here most vigorously.

I trust that, in the future, those chief characteristics, grace and grit, which have made them so valuable a force in the formation of our young commonwealths, may continue without enervation or waste.

I trace my lineage on my mother's side to a New England family of early settlement; but my paternal name and blood are drawn from a Scotch-Irishman of Ulster, who, with a Scotch wife, emigrated to America in the ninth decade of the last century. As such, I feel proud of my ancestral descent, and extend to you hearty sympathy, and through you to all whom you represent, in your effort to commemorate the worth, works, and imperishable influence of our Scotch-Irish ancestors. Very truly, yours,

HENRY C. McCOOK.

MEMPHIS, TENN., *May* 7, 1889.

MR. THOMAS T. WRIGHT.

DEAR SIR:

I regret very much that I can not attend the Scotch-Irish Congress at Columbia. Business engagements of an imperative character detain me in Memphis, and will keep me here during the days when it will be in session.

I am quite alive to the value of such a gathering from a historical point of view, and as a means of vindicating the high position in usefulness of the Scotch-Irish almost ever since the foundation of the American colonies. They came first into history as a result of the settlement of Scotch immigrants in Ireland during the reign of the first James, and from that hour to this have been distinguished, above all things, for the courage of their convictions. They have always been tenacious as Protestants and lovers of individual liberty. Even in the church organizations, as Presbyterians, while adhering to "the faith once delivered to the saints," they have, on occasions, openly declared dissent, and in a spirit that even the British government in dealing with them has always recognized, have been ready to maintain it to the death. Thus founded in protest against what they believed were "errors of faith and practice," contending for the right of private judgment, and asserting their opposition to prelacy, and, therefore, kingly government, they were practically republicans. King James himself acknowledged this when, in a moment of anger, excited by the demands of the Presbyterian divines, he said, "No bishop, no king." The Scotch-Irish, therefore, came to this country the ready servants of republican liberty. Hence, when revolution impended, they, on the 20th of May, 1775, at Mecklenburg, North Carolina, made the first and most daring declaration of independence.

In heart and conscience they had always been independent, and they valued liberty above life. The names of the delegates present at the convention that adopted that declaration are nearly all of them Scotch-Irish. Polk, Alexander, Barry, Downs, Graham, Irwin, Morrison, McClure, Wilson, and Patton, are all Scotch-Irish names.

Thus, the race whose deeds are to be celebrated at Columbia by the Congress held this week, were first in the race for liberty on this continent, and their subsequent bearing during and after the Revolutionary war has proven that they have been worthy of that liberty. The men of Mecklenburg were influential in the settlement of this state—were, indeed, its founders, and in celebrating the Scotch-Irish race, we also celebrate the men who established the government of the Watauga Association and made the Volunteer State. They fought under Sevier, were the companions and comrades of James Robinson in the Mero district, fought the Indians under Jackson from the Tennessee river to the Florida everglades, defeated the British at New Orleans, and compelled the Spaniards to give up Florida, thus ending forever the claims of Spain to the Mississippi river. They were subsequently conspicuous in the Texas revolution and in the Mexican war; and in the civil war, now fast becoming but a memory, they were among the first for gallantry, as the names of John C. Brown, Porter, Bates, McNeil, and others, attest.

Blended and fused with the great mass of a population whose power of assimilation is a marvel of our time, the Scotch-Irish are losing their distinctiveness on this continent. It is, therefore, well that their history should be recovered and eliminated from all other histories, and thus be held sacred by their descendants, for there is much of incentive in example. And what nobler example of high moral qualities, of courage and endurance, can be found anywhere than with the Scotch-Irish, who, believing in the right of private judgment, have always contended for a government resting on a basis of consent.

Very respectfully,
M. KEATING.

LIVERPOOL, March 30, 1889.

A. C. FLOYD, ESQ.,
    Secretary to the Scotch-Irish Congress,
      COLUMBIA, TENN., U. S. A.
    DEAR SIR:

I am in receipt of your invitation to attend the Scotch-Irish Congress in your city on the 8th of May next, and I very much regret I can not avail myself of it, as I am about to start for a trip to Australia, India, China, and Japan, and do not expect to reach America till next spring.

I am, dear sir,
Very truly yours,
A. McDOWELL.

"BATTLE HILL,"
JACKSON, MISS., <i>March</i> 2, 1889.</div>

MR. A. C. FLOYD,
    Secretary.
    DEAR SIR:

I beg to acknowledge receipt of your letter of the 23d last, extending invitation to the Scotch-Irish Congress, to meet in Columbia in May.

I am glad to see that such an organization is effected, and I am sure it will be of great use in keeping our *esprit de corps* among the members of a race which is exceeded by no other in the number of distinguished men in all lines who have made our country illustrious.

The characteristics of the race are of the best. Steadfast, stalwart, true to conviction, tough brained but tender hearted, the men have always been who are called "Scotch-Irish."

I have to say what I said in a published speech in Derry last summer: "I have always been proud to call myself an Ulsterman, proud that I am a born Derryman, a son of the men that starved and prayed and fought, but never surrendered."

I deeply regret the appointments for my work are such that I am unable to accept your invitation for this year. Meanwhile, I hope, at another meeting to come up with the tribes.

     Very truly, yours,
       HUGH MILLER THOMPSON,
         Bishop of Mississippi.

      UNITED STATES SENATE,
     WASHINGTON, D. C., *December* 28, 1888.
MR. A. C. FLOYD,
  Secretary,
    COLUMBIA, TENN.
    DEAR SIR:

Your letter, inviting me to deliver an address before the Scotch-Irish Congress on the 15th of next May, has been received. I am greatly pleased with the suggestion of this Congress and its purposes, and am honored by your invitation to address it. The political situation forbids my making any positive engagement so far ahead, but it is my intention to accept your invitation, should the calls of duty here not prevent.

When this session of Congress shall have expired, and I can see what the next year promises, I shall communicate with you again.

     Very respectfully and
      Truly yours,
        Z. B. VANCE.

     HOUSE OF REPRESENTATIVES,
    WASHINGTON, D. C., *April* 6, 1889.
A. C. FLOYD, ESQ.,
  Secretary,
    COLUMBIA, TENN.
    DEAR SIR:

I thank you for your cordial invitation to be present at the Scotch-Irish Congress, to be held at your city on the 8th of May next. It would afford me real pleasure to honor the memory of the Scotch-Irish emigrants who came to this country and did so much to elevate and strengthen the character of our people. In my remarks in the House of Representatives, February 2, 1886, on the death of Vice-President Thomas A. Hendricks, I referred to his father, and to his uncle, who was governor of Indiana and senator from that state in the U. S. Congress in 1822 to 1825 and in 1837:

"They were Scotch-Irish pioneers, belonging to a race of men of splendid physical form, courage, and endurance, and renowned for their mental vigor and strength of character. These pioneers were the ancestors of many distinguished families of the South and West. Wherever these brave men fixed their abode, the land brought forth abundance and the people prospered."

It is, therefore, with regret I am constrained to deny myself the pleasure of being with you on that occasion.

I hope you will have a successful meeting, and that its results may be beneficial to the welfare and glory of our common country.

Yours truly,
SAM. J. RANDALL.

BROOKLYN, *March* 19, 1889.
A. C. FLOYD, ESQ.,
    Secretary Scotch-Irish Congress.
    DEAR SIR:
        Only previous engagements could hinder me from accepting your kind invitation, for which I thank you. Had the invitation come a little earlier, I could have accepted it, but now I am harnessed for other service. Most appropriate is it that the people come together and celebrate the achievements of that wondrous and magnificent race, the Scotch-Irish.

Again thanking you for the courtesy of your letter, I am,
Yours, etc.,
T. DE WITT TALMAGE.

GERMAN THEOLOGICAL SEMINARY,
DUBUQUE, IA., *April* 6, 1889.
MR. A. C. FLOYD,
    Secretary of Scotch-Irish Congress.
    DEAR SIR:
        I find it impossible to avail myself of the honor and pleasure of attendance at the Scotch-Irish Congress, to convene

on the third prox., to which your favor of February 16th so courteously and cordially invited me.

At first, I had hoped to so arrange former engagements as to be able to attend, but I find this impossible. Few things would have given me such true and permanent pleasure as this first organization of a much-needed association. All classes and races have their racial organizations; but in this country, the greatest and most energetic race in the land has hitherto contented itself with the preservation of its identity and unifying power, which pertain to great achievements, in peaceful arts, the discoveries of science, moral leadership, and heroic deeds at the formative epochs of national history.

The Scotch-Irish race is, indeed, *sui generis*, if not altogether unique; for, while possessed of strongly marked individuality, it nevertheless freely coalesces with all who seek whatsoever things are true, honest, just, lovely, and of good report. This race has the strong will, religiosity, and shrewdness of the Hebrew, the philosophic profundity of the German, the political sagacity and conservatism of the English, and withal, when needs be, the audacity of the French. What wonder that such a race has occupied so large a place in the history of our country? When, in this land, were not the ablest of divines, the bravest of generals, the wisest of statesmen, not found among the well-trained families of this race? Surely, it is time that the sons of such a race confederate themselves in closer ties of visible kinship. With such an ancestry and history, justice to the storied dead, and self-respect of the living, demand such an organization of the Scotch-Irish race in these United States as your letter indicates.

That the forthcoming convention may prove worthy of the great occasion and of the thoughtful hospitality that invites it, is the sincere wish of

Yours, with much respect,

A. McCLELLAND.

PUBLIC LEDGER BUILDING, PHILADELPHIA.
MR. A. C. FLOYD,
Secretary Scotch-Irish Congress,
COLUMBIA, TENN.
DEAR SIR:

When I wrote you in March, it was under the impression that the date fixed for the assembling at Columbia, Tennessee, of the "Scotch-Irish" Congress, was May 15th inst., as printed on the official letter-head. Finding subsequently that the actual date is May 8th, I am obliged to forego the pleasure of accepting your welcome invitation, which I very much regret.

The occasion is one of exceeding interest in many states; but great as that interest is elsewhere, it can hardly equal that of the people of Pennsylvania, where the pioneers of the "Scotch-Irish" immigrants found their first resting-places in their adventurous movement, which led them later on to Virginia, North Carolina, Kentucky, Ohio, and Tennessee, as well as into the then almost unbroken wastes of Southern and Western Pennsylvania. Every-where along that southern line of our state, especially west of the Susquehanna and throughout the Cumberland, Juniata, and Ligonier valleys, they have left the indelible characteristic marks of their early presence, just as they have among the eminent families of Kentucky and Virginia, Tennessee and North Carolina. Their course as pioneers is traceable by a track across that broad expanse of territory almost as distinct, in an ethnological point of view, as are the rock strata that mark the coal and iron bearing veins across a geological horizon.

The characteristics referred to are well understood by all students of the course of migration into the wild forest lands of America by the streams of colonists—colonists of the widely varying sects and races from European countries in the early days of our history. Distinct as the Puritan, or the Pilgrim, or the Cavalier, or the Catholic, or the Quaker, or the German Lutheran and Moravian, or the Huguenot, were the "Scotch-Irish," or, as I would prefer to put it, the Irish and the Scots, who came into Pennsylvania to help to populate it and the adjacent provinces (now states) to the south and west. They were high-spirited people, moved by lofty motives—not so much proselytism in their particular religious faith, as by the purpose to find a region in the new world where they could assert their right to decide what form of government they would live under—the right to choose for themselves their own rulers, whether for their political security or the welfare of their souls. They were, to an uncommonly large degree, men—and women, too—with a robust vigor of intellect, in full keeping with the stalwart muscular development which was the physical characteristic of a large proportion of them. They were earnest and brave people, full of energy, of self-assertion of their own right to free thought and free action, and full of the energy and high purpose that make patriots; yet comparatively exempt from the fierce fanaticism of the mere propagandist. They were born pioneers of the wilderness and leaders of other men. In all of the five or six contiguous states south and west of the middle line of Pennsylvania, the names of these Irish and Scotch pioneers and of their descendants shine with luster in histories and annals as among their noblest patriots, statesmen, soldiers, scholars, and men of renown.

It would be to make a catalogue of leading family names in broad regions of those states to attempt to individualize, for it could not fail to be invidious if only some were named. Their history and their work and their enduring influence should be written in a large way; and if this should be an outcome of the Columbia "Scotch-Irish Congress," it will be a valuable result, and a most instructive history to the whole country.

I do not know, of course, what other reason there was than the promise of the most genial weather, that decided the choice of May 8th for the date of the assembling of the Congress; but either by intent or by happy coincidence, your committees have come close to a notable anniversary in the annals of the pioneers of the Scotch-Irish immigrants into the American colonies. It was on the ninth (9th) of May, 1729, that the good ship "George and Ann" set sail from Ireland to bring to Philadelphia the McDowells, the Irvines, the Campbells, the O'Neills, the McElroys, the Mitchells, and their compatriots, who penetrated to interior Pennsylvania, and thence went west and south. With these were the high-bred and brave Margaret O'Neill and Margaret Lynn. I am not so sure of the ship that brought the Breckinridge company, whether the one just named, or the "John of Dublin," or some other; but I find recorded that, on the 22d of May, 1740, fourteen heads of families went to Orange Court House, Virginia, under the leadership of Alexander Breckinridge; that Breckinridge there made oath that he "had imported himself from Ireland to Philadelphia," together with John, George, Robert, Smith, and Letitia Breckinridge; and thence to this colony (Virginia). Among these heads of families "imported from Ireland to Philadelphia" were John Trimble, David Logan, James Caldwell, and, I think, John Preston. In fact, Philadelphia and Pennsylvania furnished the gateway, the first resting place, and the course of "Scotch-Irish" adventure and enterprise, as they moved west and south.

We of Pennsylvania may, therefore, fairly ask the Columbia Congress to bear that fact affectionately in mind; and that, while you are celebrating the merits and virtues of distinguished and eminent western and southern families, that Philadelphia has her annals richly illustrated with Meades and Moylans, Breckinridges and Barrys,

Waynes and St. Clairs, Allisons, Armstrongs, and Fultons, McKeans, McClures, McKibbens, and McCooks; with Thomas Fitzgibbons, James Mease, Sharp Delaney, and stout old Blair McClenaghen, with others of the leaders of the "Friendly Sons of St. Patrick," renowned among Philadelphia merchants and patriots of the revolutionary days.

With great respect,
GEORGE W. CHILDS.

BRITISH EMBASSY,
ROME, *February* 13, 1889.

MY DEAR MR. WRIGHT:

I am very much gratified by the kind invitation which you have sent me to attend the forthcoming Congress; but as I am now on my way home, after four years' absence from England, it would, I regret, be out of my power to cross the Atlantic.

With renewed thanks for the honor you have done me, believe me, my dear Mr. Wright,

Yours sincerely,
DUFFERIN AND AVA.

MINUTES.

COLUMBIA, TENN., *May* 8, 1889.

MORNING SESSION.

The Congress was called to order at 11 o'clock by Colonel E. C. McDowell, President of the Local Organization.

Rev. Dr. John Hall, of New York, led in prayer, as follows:

O, God Almighty, our Heavenly Father: We are gathered together in unusual circumstances. We pray that we may have the help of the Holy Spirit; that with reverence and devoutness we may come together to speak unto thee. May thy divine spirit enlighten the understanding of each of us; may it guide our thoughts; may it raise our affections to heavenly things; may it be to us at this moment a spirit of grace and supplication.

We worship thee, O God; we magnify thy great and holy name. Thou art the King of kings, and the Lord of lords. Thou dost determine the lives of individuals; thou dost control the fate of nations; all things are present to thy holy eye; thou art from everlasting and to everlasting; thou hast been the God of our fathers, and our prayer is that thou wilt be the God of our children. May the way in which thou didst lift them from thralldom, and the blessings vouchsafed unto them, be ever a source of thanks and praises to thee. We pray thee that thou wilt continue thy goodness; that thou wilt maintain in the hearts of thy children regard for thy truth, deference to thine authority, and the spirit of a true and real brotherly love.

O Lord Jesus, the Savior whom we worship and adore, whom we hold as King in Zion, let thy presence be with us and help us to walk as becometh disciples. We invoke thy blessings and pray for thy favor in this Congress; direct its officers; bless all its exercises. Let the issue be the bringing of heart to heart, the tendering and expanding of sympathy, the continuance of brotherly love, the promotion of Christian education, the good of the people of this state and of neighboring states. God Almighty, bless those who are gathered together in this city at this time, and as they partake of the hospitality of its people, may they be enabled to seek what will be for the good of the people, for the welfare of the state, for the stability of the nation. Bless our nation, and the President of the United States; bless the governors of the states and territories; bless the judges of the land; bless and guide all those of our fellow citizens who have been called to places of trust; give them skill, wisdom, unselfishness, zeal, and fidelity; and, O God, establish in the hearts of the people reverence to their law and their constituted authority. Continue thy favor to these United States, and let the whole land be in subjection to thee through Christ Jesus. And, our Divine Father, we come to thee one by one; we beg the forgiveness of our sins, the continuation of thy holy spirit, the guidance of thy providence, and an entrance finally into thy heavenly kingdom and glory, through Jesus Christ. And to the Father, the Son, and the Divine Spirit, the God of our salvation, be glory and majesty, dominion and power, world without end. Amen.

Opening address, by Colonel E. C. McDowell:

The migration of the Scots, it is believed, was through Northeastern Europe, by way of Belgium and the north of France, to Ireland. There they certainly lived in the third century, and there they first received the light of Christianity.

In the sixth century, a colony of these Irish-Scots migrated to Northern Britain, and settling in what is now the county of Argyle, established a kingdom, subjugated the Pictish tribes that were before them, and ancient Caledonia was thenceforward the land of the Scots, and Scotland it remains to-day.

When James the First came to the throne of Great Britain, for reasons of state, he determined to discountenance the Roman Catholic religion in Ireland. Some of the nobles of the north of Ireland resented this, and conspired against the government. Their lands were confiscated and reverted to the crown. James peopled these confiscated estates with Scotch and English colonists. The Scotch settlers greatly predominated. Thus, after a lapse of one thousand years, the Scots whom Ireland had given to Caledonia of old, came back to their ancient homes, and the Irish-Scotch, as they were called in the sixth century, became the Scotch-Irish of the seventeenth century.

These first Scotch colonists were soon followed by other Scots, until the descendants of these Scots are largely in the majority in the north of Ireland, especially in the province of Ulster. The Scotch-Irish race was prolific of colonists to America. Prior to 1707, they migrated to America to better their condition. The historical events of 1707 gave a great impetus to the immigration of Irish Presbyterians. Then they began to see that an Irishman had not equal rights with other British subjects. The idea of equality and freedom which afterward took form of expression in the Mecklenburg Declaration of Independence, was so strong in them that they could not remain in Ireland.

These emigrants settled principally in Pennsylvania, Virginia, and the Carolinas. Their descendants spread into Kentucky, Tennessee, and the whole South-west. Tennessee was selected as the place for holding this Congress as the state most central to this population in the United States.

This race of people was of a different origin, and had many race characteristics differing from the New England Puritans. The New England Puritans were of Anglo-Saxon origin, unmixed with the Norman. The New England Puritan idea is to get the greatest aggregate good in the community. The individual and the family are subordinate to the community. With them, the state is the people, and the people belong to and are made for the state. With the Scotch-Irish, the people are the state, and the state is made by and for the people. Individualism and familyism seem to be at the foundation of the Scotch-Irish philosophy of life. They hold that the community or state, and its laws, are made by the individuals living in the state or community, and the individuals are not made for, or to be governed for the good of the state or community; but the state and its laws are the creation of the individuals for their benefit. Having to live in the community, they claim the right to make the laws of the community, and select those put in authority to enforce these laws. They surrender to the community only so much of their individual freedom as may be necessary for the protection of their property, life, and liberty, while living in the community. With the Puritans, individual good and freedom is merged in and lost sight of in the good of the community.

The New England Puritans have in a large part written the history of the United States. They did not act the principal history of the United States. Although in the popular histories of the United States, individuals of the Scotch-Irish race have received due notice and full praise, yet the influence of the Scotch-Irish as a people in obtaining our independence, forming our institutions, and maintaining them, has never been properly recognized in written American history.

The Scotch-Irish are a peculiar people in many respects. They have always been doers, rather than talkers or writers—holding that there are only two things worthy of man's ambition: one to write what is worthy of being done, and the other is to do what is worthy of being written, and the greater of these two is the doing. Our Puritan brethren have written as well as done. It is time we were putting on the pages of written history the impress of our race on the institutions of our country.

The proceedings of this congress will begin the written history of the Scotch-Irish race.

It was expected that the governor of Tennessee would be present to deliver an address of welcome. A special session of the state legislature convened yesterday, rendering it impossible for him to be present on this occasion. In his place, and in the name of Tennessee, I welcome you all. On behalf of the large Scotch-Irish population of this county, I welcome you. In the name of Columbia, I bid you thrice welcome.

For the purpose of organizing, I move that Joseph F. Johnston, of Birmingham, Alabama, be elected temporary chairman of the Congress.

Motion carried, and Colonel Johnston introduced to the audience by Colonel McDowell.

Colonel Johnston's address:

I can not be unmindful of the fact that the distinguished honor of presiding temporarily over this convention has not been conferred upon me on account of any personal merit of my own, especially when I look around me and see so many gentlemen distinguished in peace and in war, in the paths of theology, science, literature, and art, who are present. But I accept this great honor as a compliment to the young men of the South, whose humble representative I am on this occasion—these young men who, not forgetting the past, not putting aside the ancient landmarks, are now engaged in erecting upon the foundation of the tradition and memories of their fathers a civilization and an empire that will be the pride and the glory of all who come after us in all this great and magnificent land of ours.

I take it, my fellow-citizens, as an auspicious circumstance that the first Congress of the Scotch-Irish of the United States is assembled here in this beautiful city "in this most lovely land" rescued by our fathers from savage beast and more savage man, and made one of the garden-spots of civilization, of virtue and refinement, of all the country; and I congratulate you, my brethren of the Scotch-Irish race, wherever you come from, that upon this occasion, and in this presence, should any one inquire where are the jewels of the race, we can point to the fair women, whose virtues are only equalled by their beauty, and say, *these* are our jewels. (Applause.)

If there is any one characteristic that I think distinguishes more clearly than any other the Scotch-Irish race, it is their disregard of odds of power and influence in the pursuit of liberty and of right. It was this sentiment that led the Scotch-Irish of Charlotte, in the county of Mecklenburg, N. C., in this month, in the year 1775, regardless of whether their brethren would join them in the cause, to declare that they "were of right, and ought to be, free and independent people."

It is a fact, in regard to the Scotch-Irish race of the South, that, while many of them believed in the inherent right of secession, few believed in the exercise of that right. They were greatly attached to the Union which their fathers had liberally contributed to establish and develop by their blood and treasure. They wanted to see it yet more powerful and great, and in Tennessee, Kentucky and North Carolina, where they were most formidable in numbers and influence, they were largely instrumental in delaying hasty action. But when the issue was joined, when "wild war's loud alarm had sounded," when the gods of war had loosed their fiercest dogs, they united with their brethren in the unequal struggle. They believed it to be an unequal struggle; they doubted the policy and the result; but when it came for men to suffer and bleed and die, they answered every roll-call. It was supposed that, when this great contest was inaugurated, the cavaliers of Virginia and South Carolina would lead all the rest, and right nobly did they discharge their duties. Their sons have a proud heritage, and history has to some extent given them this prominence. But recently, a distinguished soldier of the Federal army, Colonel Wm. F. Fox, of New York, has published, in a remarkable book, statistics showing the results of the war; and I propose to cite a few facts from that book. The fighting population of North Carolina in 1861 was 115,000, yet she furnished to the Confederate army 125,000 men. North Carolina led all the southern states in the number of men that died in this great struggle. There were killed of her sons on the field of battle fourteen thousand, five hundred and twenty-two men (14,522). The number of her sons that died from wounds inflicted on the field of battle was 20,602, while the great commonwealth of Virginia lost a little over 12,000 in killed and died of wounds— about one-third. South Carolina had 9,187 men killed. On the other side, the great state of Pennsylvania led all her sisters in the splendor of her achievements, and she suffered the greatest loss of any northern state in the great battles between giants.

The greatest loss suffered by any one regiment during the war was inflicted upon the Twenty-sixth North Carolina at Gettysburg, which went into battle 800 strong, and lost in killed and wounded on the field over 580 men; and this great loss was sustained in fighting the One Hundred and Fifty-first Pennsylvania and Cooper's Battery. The Light Brigade at Balaklava lost $31\frac{1}{2}$ per cent of its men and officers, and they were immortalized in prose and poetry. The Twenty-sixth North Carolina at Gettysburg lost over 70 per cent of its men and officers, and was scarcely distinguished from the regiments that surrounded it.

I am not speaking of the war with any desire to recall any thing that every citizen of the United States can not recall with pride and pleasure, no matter where he hails from, because I take it that the prowess, the courage, and the heroic valor of any soldier, whether he hails from Maine or Alabama, is the proud heritage of every citizen of the United States. (Applause.) But I state these astounding statistics to show you that, in the great contest between the states, the two most largely populated by the Scotch-Irish race were the two that led all the rest in the splendor of their achievements (Applause); and that the greatest losses were inflicted when the iron soldiers of North Carolina and Pennsylvania, descendants of the same race and stock, met on the field of battle and locked arms in the embrace of death. It was the dogged obstinacy, the tenacity, the unconquerable will of the Scotch-Irish, that deluged these fields with blood and immortalized Pennsylvania and North Carolina.

I am here in response to your selection, to return to you my thanks for the honor you have conferred upon the young men of the South, and to discharge the duties you have assigned me; and I announce that this convention is now ready for further proceedings.

Mr. A. C. Floyd, of Columbia, was unanimously elected temporary Secretary of the Congress.

A motion by Colonel E. C. McDowell, that a committee on permanent organization, and one on constitution and by-laws, be appointed, was carried.

Mrs. Robert D. Smith recited a poem on "The Harp of Tom Moore," written for the occasion by the poet, Wallace Bruce, of New York. The harp had been kindly loaned the Congress by Mr. Geo.

W. Childs, of Philadelphia, and during all the exercises occupied a pedestal upon the platform.

(See Part II, page 71.)

A song, "Here's to Thee, Tom Moore," was sung by the young ladies of the Athenæum School, accompanied by Mrs. Emma McKinney on the harp and Hal Seavy on the violin.

The following resolution was introduced by E. C. McDowell, and unanimously adopted:

Resolved, That the thanks of the Scotch-Irish of the United States are due and are hereby tendered Hon. T. T. Wright, for originating this gathering and contributing to the successful organization of this convention.

Chairman Johnston:

It is my pleasing duty, in obedience to the resolution just adopted, to extend the hearty thanks of the convention to the Hon. T. T. Wright, whose merit is only equalled by his modesty. It is said that Ney fought a hundred battles for France and not one against her; the Hon. T. T. Wright has fought a hundred battles for the prosperity and advancement of his country, and not one for himself. A great man once stated that it was better to be right than President. Had our friend lived in that day, we would know that he was the Wright referred to.

The first speaker of the day was Hon. Proctor Knott, of Kentucky, who was introduced by the Chairman as follows:

I announce and introduce a gentleman who is known from Pennsylvania avenue to Duluth. His fame has extended beyond the confines of this country as one of the proudest sons of this great race whose deeds we are met here to commemorate upon this occasion—a gentleman whose fame has not only placed him in the front ranks of Americans of this century, but whose name, when conferred upon a horse, makes the latter worth $30,000. I take great pleasure in introducing to you the Hon. Proctor Knott, of Kentucky.

(See Part II, page 73.)

Chairman Johnston read the following telegram from Hon. Senator John MacDonald, of Canada:

TORONTO, ONT., *May 8th.*

HON. THOS. T. WRIGHT,
　　COLUMBIA, TENN.

Kindly accept congratulations and assurances of abiding friendship and good will on the part of Canadians for the peace and prosperity of your great nation.

JOHN MacDONALD.

The Congress adjourned to 7:30 o'clock P. M.

NIGHT SESSION.

The Congress was called to order at 8 o'clock.

The Chairman announced the following committees:

On Permanent Organization—E. C. MacDowell, Tennessee; Dr. John Hall, New York; T. T. Wright, Florida; Judge J. M. Scott, Illinois; Lucius Frierson, Tennessee.

On Constitution and By-Laws—Proctor Knott, Kentucky; Robert Bonner, New York; W. O. MacDowell, New Jersey; A. C. Floyd, Tennessee; A. S. Colyar, Tennessee.

The Chairman then announced that Rev. Dr. Wilson Phraner was requested to favor the Congress with an address.

Dr. Phraner's address:

I think this is unfair. I was asked if, some time during the meeting, I would say a word, and I consented to do so; but I had no idea that I would be called upon at this moment. Hence, I am confused, and hardly know whether I am here or not.

I am neither an Englishman nor an Irishman; only a plain American citizen. You see at once I have not the brogue. I find the Scotch and the Irish so much at a premium, that I hardly know whether I can take my place among them or not. I am reminded of a little story that I may tell in this connection. It was of three Irishmen in London. One of them remarked: "What a strange thing occurred to me the other morning. In Hyde Park, a gentleman came up to me and addressed me as Gladstone." "Oh," said another of the three, " that was certainly a compliment; but I have something a little better than that. I was the other day walking through one of the streets of London, and a gentleman addressed me as Lord Salisbury, the Premier." The third one said : " That is surprising, but I can beat that. I was passing through the Strand, and a fellow ran up to me and said, 'Holy Moses, is that you?'"

In my opinion, Moses outranks both Mr. Gladstone and Mr. Salisbury. I am, however, not likely to be taken for either of the three; but I have come down here at the kind invitation of Dr. Hall; and now I am glad to see this assemblage of Scotch-Irishmen. We are glad that you are here in this country to help do something that needs to be done.

One of the objects to be accomplished is to unify this nation. We have a great many elements entering into our national life, and we all know the consequences when a man takes in more food than he can digest. But this country never has any trouble in digesting Scotch-Irishmen and true Scotchmen. They agree with us perfectly. There are some others not so easily digested and disposed of; but these are at home here, and we rejoice that they are here to help in unifying this nation, which is one of the great problems before us.

There is a second thing to be done: to educate this nation. The Scotchmen come here as educators. You will hear from one of them to-night. The Scotch-Irishmen come ofttimes in the same way as did Dr. McCosh, of Princeton. When we want a president for one of our leading colleges, we send to Belfast for him. Through the country they are known as educators, and there is a great work to be done in elevating and uplifting the nation through genuine education of the people.

My attention has been called to another matter. There may be some poor relations of the Scotch and Scotch-Irish that would very properly receive a little attention. They are not to be overlooked. Some of them I have heard of in Tennessee, Kentucky, and North Carolina. There are some who might be helped in that direction, and I hope one of the things to come out of this organization will be to look possibly after some of our poor relations.

I will say one other thing. The value of this element that comes into our national life from Scotland is that they have brought Christianity with them in their hearts. What makes them so welcome to my mind is, that they have brought Presbyterianism with them to this land. We can stand all that; the more of it the better. Look at the condition of things in New York. A leading man in our pulpit is a Scotch-Irishman. When one of the oldest churches, and the one in which I was brought up, wanted a minister, it sent to Dublin for him. We have him here to-night—one of the biggest men in the land. You have heard a good many things said in these recent times about long haul and short haul, but one of the biggest hauls the Presbyterian Church ever made was when it got John Hall. (Laughter and applause.)

A very important church in Philadelphia became vacant, and nothing would do but they must have a MacIntosh, and they sent to Belfast for him. So it is, all over the country; and we need this help to unify, to educate, and to evangelize this nation.

Alexander De Tocqueville never made a wiser remark than when he said a nation never so needs to be theocratic as when it becomes democratic.

A few minutes ago, I had no idea of making a speech. I am in sympathy with this meeting, though I can not claim to be either an Irishman or Scotchman, but only a simple, plain American citizen, speaking the English language. (Applause.)

Chairman Johnston:

I think the audience will agree with me, that the Chair has shown great discrimination in calling on Mr. Phraner "unbeknownst" to him; because, if he had been given an opportunity to prepare a speech this evening, he would have left few good things for the distinguished gentleman who is to follow him.

I am now going to have the pleasure of introducing to you one of the most distinguished men of this country, a citizen of New York, who has kindly consented to say a few words to you—Mr. Robert Bonner. (Applause.)

Mr. Bonner:

I am not in the habit of addressing the public or of making public speeches. Any little reputation that I may have acquired has been achieved by the pen. But I will say a few words.

I have very pleasant recollections of a former visit to Columbia. On that occasion, when our party left New York, I was known simply as Robert Bonner, without any title or handle to my name; but in passing through Pennsylvania, I was saluted by one of the railway officials as Captain Bonner; further on, when we crossed over the

Ohio river into Kentucky, I was called by the title of Colonel; and when I reached this place, I was addressed by one of your prominent citizens as General. Do you wonder that, after such rapid promotion, I have pleasant recollections of that visit?

When you take half a century out of the middle of a man's life, you make a pretty big gap in it. It was just fifty years ago, the second of this month, that I sailed from Londonderry, Ireland, for New York. I came from the old town of Ramelton, in the county of Donegal. I hold in my hand the report of an address delivered by the Rev. Matthew Wilson, in March, 1839, in the Second Presbyterian church of that town, an extract from which I shall read, and which, I think, will be of some historical interest on such an occasion as this. The manuscript, as you can see, is somewhat faded, but that is not to be wondered at, as it is over fifty years since I copied the address from the Londonderry *Standard*. Mr. Wilson, after stating that there were spirit-stirring recollections connected with Ramelton, said:

"But it is far more agreeable to listen to the artless tale of a rustic Presbyterian, as he tells of the treasure of truth and of salvation which a Presbyterian minister from Ramelton carried across the Atlantic and planted in a foreign soil—small in the beginning as a grain of mustard seed, but since it has leavened all the land. Yes, sir, it was a Makemie, himself a treasure, but bearing with him the far more excellent treasure, even the incorruptible riches of Christ, who, in company with a few expatriated ministers from the Synod of Ulster, formed the first Presbytery, raised the first Presbyterian standard, and planted the germ of the Presbyterian church in America—a church which has been blessed with extraordinary increase, and can now boast of nearly three thousand congregations."

In the printed slip which your Secretary kindly sent me a few weeks ago, it was stated that one of the attractions here would be an exhibition of Tennessee's fine blooded stock. Clergymen often tell us that we can not reason from the finite to the infinite; but I think we can get a lesson from the lower animals that will lead us up to a true appreciation of the Scotch-Irish. It is well known that a change of clime has great influence in improving the speed and endurance of horses. For example, from stock sent from New York to Kentucky, the swiftest trotting horse that the world has yet seen was raised in the famous blue grass region. Now, I think it can be shown by a single illustration that, when the Scotch went over to Ireland, a similar improvement in the stamina and endurance of the race took place.

Sixty years ago, the Rev. Dr. McCartee was the most popular Presbyterian clergyman in New York City. The old gentleman once told me that, in his younger days, he had two prominent members of his church who were not on speaking terms. One was Scotch and the other Scotch-Irish. They had quarreled about some trivial matter, and the feeling became very bitter. The Doctor labored for a long time to reconcile them, but neither could be moved. At last, after a serious talk, the Scotchman consented to meet his Scotch-Irish fellow-member in a friendly way, and let by-gones be by-gones. The doctor then went to the Scotch-Irishman, but he was as firm as ever; he did not want to have any thing to do with "that man." .Finally, the doctor bore down on him pretty hard, urging upon him his duty as a Christian, and asking him: "How can you expect to be forgiven, if you will not forgive?" when the Scotch-Irishman, with great emotion, while trying to conquer his feelings, exclaimed: "Yes, yes; I'll forgive him, but I want to get one good crack at him first." (Laughter.) Gentlemen, this is the reason why I think a change of clime has increased the stamina and endurance of the race to which I belong. (Applause and laughter.)

Chairman Johnston then introduced Prof. McCloskie, of Princeton, as one of the most distinguished educators of this country.

(See Part II, page 90.)

After the conclusion of Prof. McCloskie's address, Chairman Johnston read the following telegram:

CARLISLE, PENN., May 8, 1889.

A. C. FLOYD,
        Scotch-Irish Congress.
                Accept congratulations and best wishes.
J. A. MURRAY.

The Secretary then submitted to the Congress the following:

HISTORICAL CONTRIBUTIONS.

T. R. Kornick, Sr., Knoxville, Tenn.: "The Scotch-Irish in the United States. Some of their Characteristics, and an Approximate Estimate of their Number in the Thirteen Colonies. September, 1774."

Hon. W. S. Fleming, Columbia, Tennessee: "Scotch-Irish Settlers in South Carolina, and their Descendants in Maury County, Tennessee."

Mr. Geo. Edwards, Worcester, Mass.: "The Early Scotch-Irish Settlers in New England."

Samuel Evans, Columbia, Penn.: "The Scotch-Irish of Donegal, Penn., with Interesting Historical Relics."

Miss Sara A. Leitch, Pittsburg, Penn.: "The Sharon Tragedy; An Incident of the Irish Rebellion in 1798."

Mr. Alex. H. H. Stewart, Staunton, Va.: "The Descendants of Archibald Stewart, of Virginia."

Rev. A. W. Miller, D.D., LL.D., Charlotte, N. C.: A pamphlet, "The Presbyterian Origin of American Independence."

Rev. J. G. Craighead, D.D., LL.D., Howard University, Washington, D. C.: "Scotch and Irish Seeds on American Soil." A bound volume.

The Congress then adjourned until 11 o'clock, Thursday morning.

Thursday, May 9th.

MORNING SESSION.

The Congress was called to order at 11 o'clock.

The Goshen Band played a musical selection, entitled "Robert Bruce Melodies."

Rev. Geo. Beckett, of the Columbia Institute, made the opening prayer.

Chairman Johnston:

Before announcing the regular proceedings as arranged for to-day, I wish to say, in behalf of the committee here, that this gathering of the Scotch-Irish of the United States is a gathering without reference to creed or politics or sect of any kind. This gathering is greater than any thing of that kind. (Applause.) Whilst, as we all know, the great majority of the Scotch-Irish of this country are Presbyterians, no man is excluded from this association, whether he be Catholic, or Presbyterian, or of any other denomination. It is as broad as our great country is. (Applause.) And, in fact, our distinguished friend, Bishop McCloskie, of New Jersey—he ought to be a bishop, if he is not—has told us that St. Patrick was the first Bishop of the

Presbyterian Church, and the Emperor of China a ruling elder. There never was a better church, though I don't have the happiness to be a member of it myself. But I wanted to caution our friends here to dismiss the idea that there is any thing local or sectarian or political about this great gathering of the Scotch-Irish of the United States of America.

Rev. Dr. John Hall, of New York, was introduced, and delivered an address. (See Part II, p. 102.)

Dr. Hall's address was followed by a song from the young ladies of the Athenæum.

Hon. Proctor Knott, Chairman of the Committee on Constitution and By-Laws, submitted the following report, which was adopted:

CONSTITUTION.

Article I. The name of this association shall be The Scotch-Irish Society of America.

Art. II. The purposes of this society are the preservation of Scotch-Irish history, the keeping alive the *esprit de corps* of the race, and the promotion of social intercourse and fraternal feeling among its members, now and hereafter.

Art. III. Any male above the age of twenty-one years, and who has Scotch-Irish blood in his veins, shall be eligible for membership in the association.

Art. IV. The officers of the society shall be a President, two Vice-Presidents at Large, a Vice-President in each state, territory, and the District of Columbia, in the United States, and each of the provinces in the Dominion of Canada; a Secretary, Treasurer, Registrar and Historian.

Art. V. There shall be an Executive Council, composed of the President, Vice-Presidents, and other officers mentioned in the last foregoing article.

Art. VI. The annual convention of the society shall be held at such time and place in May as may be determined by the Executive Committee.

Art. VII. The officers of the society shall be elected at the conventions by ballot; provided, however, that Vice-Presidents not elected at the present meeting shall be appointed by the President.

Art. VIII. This constitution may be altered, amended, or repealed only by a majority vote of the members of the association present at the annual convention, or at a special meeting called for that purpose after thirty days' notice in writing to the members.

Art. IX. The Executive Council shall have authority to establish by-laws, rules, and regulations for the government of the society.

Colonel E. C. McDowell, Chairman, offered the following report of the Committee on Organization, which was unanimously adopted:

For Permanent President—Robert Bonner, of New York.
Secretary—A. C. Floyd, of Tennessee.
Vice-Presidents at Large—J. F. Johnston, of Alabama; E. C. McDowell, of Tennessee; and Thomas Kerr, of Toronto, Canada.
Vice-Presidents for States—Kentucky, Dr. Hervey McDowell; New York, Dr. John Hall; Illinois, Judge J. M. Scott; North Carolina, S. B. Alexander; Pennsylvania, A. K. McClure; New Jersey, Wm. O. McDowell; Louisiana, Wm. Preston Johnston; Florida, T. T. Wright; Virginia, Wm. Wirt Henry; Tennessee, A. G. Adams; Montana, Rev. J. C. Quinn, Helena; Andrew T. Wood, Hamilton, Ontario.
Treasurer—Lucius Frierson, of Tennessee.
Historian and Registrar—Thos. M. Green, of Kentucky.

Mr. Johnston stated that he would turn over the position of Chairman to Mr. Bonner, who was introduced, and said:

Ladies and Gentlemen:—This is an unexpected honor. I think there are much abler and better qualified men here that you could have selected for this position. But I accept the office with thanks, and shall endeavor to fill it to the best of my ability.

This afternoon, our party is obliged to leave for New York, and, as Colonel Johnston has presided so ably, I shall request him to continue to keep the chair during this meeting.

Mr. Johnston said he would not disobey the orders of a superior officer, and read from the poem recited the preceding day the following:

"Manhattan and Plymouth and Jamestown
  Can boast of their heritage true,
But Mecklenburg's fame is immortal
  When we number the stars in the blue
The Scotch-Irish-Puritan fathers
  First drafted the words of the free,
And the speech of Virginia's Henry
  Is the crown of our liberty's plea."

I now have the pleasure of introducing to you the grandson of this illustrious hero, Hon. Wm. Wirt Henry, of Virginia.

Mr. Henry was greeted with great applause. He spoke as follows:

(See Part II, p. 110.)

At the conclusion of Mr. Henry's address, Mr. Johnston adjourned the meeting to 8 o'clock, as follows:

There was an old Englishman whose name was Johnson—the only place he did not take his tea was in his name—and he said to a Scotchman, that the Scotch fed their men on what the English fed their horses; and the Scotchman replied, that that was the reason the English had the best horses, and the Scotch the best men in the world. It is about time to feed the convention on a little oat-meal porridge, and a motion to adjourn is in order.

NIGHT SESSION.

The Congress was called to order at 8 o'clock by Chairman Johnston, who introduced the first speaker, as follows:

We shall have the pleasure of hearing a few remarks from a Scotch-Irishman of Illinois; a gentleman who has attained the highest rank in that state as a judge, having been several years on the Supreme Bench of Illinois; a gentleman who has endeared himself to those who have met him since he has been among us—Judge J. M. Scott.

Judge Scott said:

I come to visit you in this beautiful little city by the kind invitation of the committee having this Congress in charge. I come for the purpose of meeting with those whom I know, and those whose ancestors have added much to the civilization of our country. I come to you from one of the great states carved out of the North-west Territory, the State of Illinois. Although one of the younger states of the North-west Territory, it is now a great commonwealth, of which her sons are justly proud. The Illinois country itself has a history that is more than two centuries old. It was the seat of French dominion in the valley of the Mississippi, where it was the purpose of France to establish a government to control the richest portions of this country. Kaskaskia, which was then founded, and which is a most beautiful village, is nearly as old as Philadelphia. But the civilization the French attempted to establish in the Mississippi valley and elsewhere on this continent was not suited to this country, and was destined to have a brief but brilliant existence. After the treaty of Paris, in 1763, the North-west Territory came under the control of the English government, and remained there until 1778, when that bold, daring, and chivalrous band of men under George Rogers Clarke, organized and commissioned by the illustrious Patrick Henry, as governor of Virginia, conquered it, and held it as the rightful possession of that great commonwealth. In that little band of fearless and determined men, there were included a number of Scotch-Irishmen. Everywhere any thing great was to be done, there was to be found Scotch-Irishmen, or some of their American descendants. I do not know that there ever was a large percentage of Scotch-Irishmen in Illinois as a state, but during the time of its territorial existence there was. They came mostly from Western Virginia with the earliest colonists. No people of any race have left more of the impress of their character upon the institutions of Illinois, both religious and civil, than did that indomitable race of men and women. They taught there the first schools. They aided in establishing law and order, and they were among the first judges to administer the law they had ordained. In fact, the history of Illinois, in that respect, is the same as that of Virginia, of Tennessee, of the Carolinas, and of all the southern states, except, perhaps, Louisiana.

It would not be proper, were I prepared to do so, to speak of the general history of the people designated as the Scotch-Irish. That has been done, and well done, by the distinguished gentlemen who have prepared papers and submitted them upon this occasion. But there are some things that we all know concerning them. We all know, as we heard from Dr. Hall this morning, that these Scotch-Irish were a frugal and industrious people. It may be, as was stated by the distinguished orator, that they think a dollar five times as large as it is; but when a Scotch-Irishman got a dollar, it was the wages of so much honest labor, or something given of equal value in exchange. (Applause.) He had earned it by the sweat of his brow, and as it was wholly his own, he could regard it, if he chose, as large as a millstone. I venture to say, here to-night, that there are fewer Scotch-Irish in the charitable institutions of this country than any other race or people that dwell among us. I never knew myself of a Scotch-

Irishman who was the inmate of a county poor-house. I venture another remark, and that is, that there are more of this race in high places, legislative, executive, judicial, ecclesiastical, and educational, than of any other race in our country. They have taught the sciences and literature in our common schools, in our colleges and universities. They have preached our religion; they have fought our battles; they have commanded our armies; they have written our literature, both in poetry and in prose; they have led public thought in the direction of liberty, right, and justice; and they have impressed our habits and customs and manners in our home life, as well as in public. They have administered and declared our laws. It can be truthfully said, that our common country is freer, stronger, better, and more enduring because of the Scotch-Irish element in our people.

My friends, I have said all that I intended to say on this occasion; but I beg to be indulged in one single remark further, and that is, that if all the Scotch-Irish in our country are as hospitable as those found in Columbia, they are the most hospitable people found on the face of this round earth. (Applause.) One remark more: If the Scotch-Irish women are all like those of Columbia, they are the peers in beauty and loveliness of the best women of our country, and, in all that is true and good and pure, are excelled by no women on the face of this earth, of any race or nationality. (Applause.)

Miss Stoddard, of the Athenæum, sang "Kathleen Mavourneen," accompanied by Mrs. Emma McKinney, on the harp. After an *encore*, she sang "I Canua Leave the Old Folk Now."

Chairman Johnston then said:

In introducing to you the next speaker, I feel as an adopted son would in introducing a father to his own family. I don't refer to the age of my distinguished friend, for he is old only in wisdom and experience. He is young in heart, in energy, in zeal and affections. I refer to Colonel Colyar, of Nashville.

Colonel Colyar:

Ladies and Gentlemen:—That I should be placed upon this platform, in the presence of so many distinguished men from abroad, is one of the things that I don't understand. I suppose somebody wants a plea for Tennessee put in. In regard to the claims of the Scotch-Irish, Tennessee may well be heard. If I were to give you the history of the Scotch-Irish in Tennessee, I would give you substantially the history of the state. Briefly, the early settlement or settlements in this state were made by Scotch-Irishmen. Of the four men who so distinguished the early history of Tennessee, two were Scotch-Irish, one a Welshman, and the other a descendant of the Huguenots. I mean Colonel Campbell, Colonel McDowell, John Sevier, and Isaac Shelby. It is not exactly true, as was stated by one of the speakers to-day, that all who fought the battle of King's Mountain were Scotch-Irish. Sevier descended from the Huguenots, and Shelby was a Welshman. If I had the time and ability to properly present it to you, you would be interested in the early history of Tennessee. These four men, and, in some respects, one more important than any of them, James Robinson, also a Scotch-Irishman, settled on the Watauga. And in referring to this matter, I wish to speak a word in regard to what I consider the most remarkable instance of chivalry and courage in modern history. A few men had settled west of the Alleghany mountains. Boone, it is said, was the first person that ever settled west of the Alleghany mountains, except the French and the Spanish. James Robinson built the second cabin on Tennessee soil west of the Alleghanies. These settlers built forts in which to protect their women and children from the Indians, until quite a large settlement was formed. The British war came up. During the darkest period of the revolution, when Washington had passed through the winter at Valley Forge, when Gates had surrendered South Carolina, and when Cornwallis, with Tarleton on his right wing and Ferguson on his left, removed from South Carolina into North Carolina, Washington wrote to Baron Steuben, saying: "This is a dark hour; I don't know what is to become of us." At that hour, Ferguson sent word into East Tennessee, that, if the people did not cease fighting the Indians and stop the war, he would come to their country and destroy them. What did these seven hundred men do? When they received this intelligence, two young men, about thirty and twenty-six, respectively, sat down on a log and said: "What shall we do? General Ferguson has an army of two thousand men, many of them trained British soldiers, and he says they will come and destroy us." What I regard as remarkable is, that these two young men did not say they would stand in the mountain fastnesses and fight back. Nobody knows whether John Sevier or Isaac Shelby made the suggestion, but, in accordance with their decision, they called in their troops from the surrounding country, and in four days they were on the march, with their squirrel rifles, for Campbell and McDowell, in Virginia. When united, the entire force amounted to 1,900 men. Ferguson pursued them, but was defeated at King's Mountain, in the most successful battle, except that at New Orleans, that was ever fought by the United States armies. With one-half his force, they killed Ferguson and 180 of his men, and took every other man prisoner. According to Mr. Jefferson, General Washington, and all the other great men of that day, this battle was the turning-point in the war. From that day, the clouds were lifted away, and the cause of Washington became brighter and brighter, until Cornwallis finally surrendered.

But that is a little tedious. I do not propose to pursue that history. I wish to say a practical word or two. I say, nearly the whole of that army was Scotch-Irish. Doak was the Presbyterian preacher in the early settlement, and preached all the sermons and married all the people. Of the one hundred and forty of these early settlers who signed a petition to the legislature of North Carolina, all except two signed their names in clear, strong hands, indicating that they were men of intelligence. It was the courage and chivalry that accomplished what was accomplished at King's Mountain, and in defending the women and children nineteen or twenty years from the Indians, that gave to Tennessee the name of the Volunteer State. Jackson came to Tennessee a few years afterward, and settled among the people that had fought the battle of King's Mountain. Sam Houston came near the same time, and was educated among the people. Has Tennessee since done any thing to merit the title of the Volunteer State? She gave to the country a Jackson, who, considering his force and losses, fought at New Orleans the most successful battle ever fought by any general; Tennessee has given to this country the immortal John Sevier, who fought thirty-five battles and never lost one; Tennessee has given to the country that Wizard of the Woods, Davy Crockett, who, with every man of his command, fell at the Alamo; Tennessee has given Sam Houston, who, after he had risen to the position of Governor of Tennessee, went west, and gained from Santa Anna and the Mexican army that vast territory, worthy of an empire, and laid it down at the feet of the United States in the great State of Texas; Tennessee has given to the country a Polk, who, during his administration as the nation's chief executive, brought into our bounds all that territory comprised in New Mexico; Tennessee has given to this country another distinguished statesman and President, in the person of Johnson, whom many of you revere.

Now, a practical word: I want to say to this vast crowd of young men here to-night, that I would be glad if I had it in my power to introduce something new into our homes and our schools. As I heard a distinguished man say in New York City last week, "We are doing a good deal in the way of educating our young men; we are educating them intellectually, in charity, and in Christianity; but are we educating them in patriotism?" (Applause.) Are we training them in the love of country? I want to say here to you men who served with me in the Confederate Congress, who fought the battle of Franklin on the Confederate side, and the battle of Murfreesboro on the other, there is no hope for this country except in true patriotism, which is love of the country and love of the flag. (Applause.) Let me say to you young men here, when you take down these flags which now decorate the city, take them into your homes and your school-rooms, and let them aid in the efforts we should make to educate the young men, and the young women, too, in patriotism and love of country.

I have detained you longer than I ought to have done. I have spoken truthfully, earnestly, and, I trust, about the facts. I feel deeply upon the question that I have last spoken about. I read and hear constantly the statement that we are carrying elections with money. I hear it stated that the two great political parties in the last campaign spent $4,000,000. This is a sad picture, if true; and I am rejoiced to see every-where true men rising up and saying: "This has to be stopped. We can't afford to carry elections with money." Let such an idea become engrafted in the minds of our people, and this country is gone. It can not live except through a love of country, and that don't mean carrying elections with money.

The next speaker was introduced as follows:

Our next speaker is also from the great State of Illinois. I don't know whether he found Judge Scott or Judge Scott found him, but we are glad that both were found and both are here. I introduce to you Rev. Dr. Dinsmore, of Bloomington, Ill.

Mr. Dinsmore said:

Mr. President and Ladies and Gentlemen:—The Scotch-Irishman at last has got his voice. That we have heard. He has modestly and quietly been doing his work, and carrying out his great career in the progress of this country, until the meeting of this Congress. More has been said during yesterday and to-day in just praise of his achievements than I have ever heard or read before. I suppose the characteristic word of the proceedings of this assembly is brag, as mentioned by Dr. McCloskie last night; but after expressing sympathy with this drift of things, if any man is a Scotch-Irishman, I am more. I have some doubts about the blood of some of the gentlemen on the stage. Judge Scott is an Irishman—he has the blarney, and has it bad. He spoke so gracefully—and so appropriately, I think—of the ladies of this brilliant assembly, that a gentleman said on my left: "Is he married?" I suspect that inquiry arose in the minds of many persons present. I am bound, as a truthful man, to say that Judge Scott has a remarkably beautiful and a remarkably healthy wife. That is not so amusing as some things that have been said before. I am exceedingly gratified that I came here at this time. I do not know when I have so richly enjoyed myself in many ways as I have during my stay here. I have been across this state from Cincinnati to Chattanooga, and also over the M. & O. Railroad, but never through this section before. I may as well honestly confess that my impression of the country of Tennessee was not the most flattering. I was impressed that a great deal of the land was poor, and that her prosperity was not so great as has been reported. But I am delighted that I have seen what I have seen during the last two days in regard to this magnificent country in the midst of which we are now assembled. This is certainly a garden—picturesque, fertile, highly cultivated—in every way one of the most beautiful and interesting parts of the country, and I have seen nearly all of them.

I am glad for another reason that I have come here. I do not know what Mr. Seavy's purpose was, and I have no grudge against him, in suggesting that I should accept the courtesy and hospitality of my most excellent newly found friends, Captain and Mrs. Smith, at the Athenæum. I have thought myself peculiarly fortunate in this respect, and have suspected that some of our *confrères* have been a little green-eyed about it. I have been surrounded by a bevy of beautiful and interesting young ladies. My head, however, is gray, and there is nothing in that; but at the same time it has been peculiarly delightful to me, and has made me feel twenty years younger, to be in the same dining-room with them. I think all of us who are here from abroad must have been impressed with the importance of this splendid and venerable institution, in whose grounds we have had this meeting. Where can we find anywhere more noble trees, more beautiful grounds, more interesting associations? And is it not a great pleasure to all of us who love our country and rejoice in its prosperity, and especially in its educational growth, that we have in this handsome city of Columbia, itself so beautiful, such a work and such a school, with so large a gathering of pupils? It shall be my pleasure to speak of this hereafter, whenever I have the opportunity, and to point out this institution as one possessing great attractions to those who have daughters to educate in a place where the surroundings will be the most happy and delightful, and where all the helps and influences are of the highest order. I am glad because I have had my temporary home in the Athenæum. I am glad that I am here for another reason. There is no class of men in this country that I am so interested in meeting, and in whose faces I look with more pleasure, than the Confederate soldiers. I say that with perfect honesty and real feeling. I have, however, seen the time when a meeting with them was not so enjoyable. Although I am a radical Republican, and have been ever since I knew any thing, as well as my father before me, at the same time, I would be ashamed for the American who could not appreciate and rejoice in the valor of those heroic men who lie in nameless graves all over this southland. I have not been so thrilled during this assembly as I was by the remarks of Colonel Colyar. I am in full sympathy, as you all are, with the suggestion that the thing we need most is a genuine and all-pervasive patriotism; and I have sometimes thought that it would almost be a blessing if some foreign war might come—though I do not press that, as a Christian man—in which the bugle might sound, and these old men in the fire and mettle of youth might stand at their country's call shoulder to shoulder and side by side in the ranks, as they would do, and their sons after them.

I will not go into the history of the Scotch-Irish, for that has been dwelt upon. In all the ramifications of my family for generations, no other blood has appeared. I profoundly sympathize with this movement, and most earnestly hope that it may result in something permanent and useful, and that it may foster, not a clannish or narrow spirit, but self-conscious and aggressive power, and fraternal feeling of a great and noble race, which, in my judgment, has done more for civilization, in proportion to its numbers, than any other people that has lived since the Christian era began.

Miss Rosa Barnett sang "Lass with Bonny Blue Een," being introduced by Dr. D. C. Kelley, as follows:

I have the pleasure of introducing to the audience one in whose gentle blood flows the fiery torrent that once pulsed in the veins of Knox; in whose blood mingles the inspiration of the calm, determined voice that uttered for the first time on the American continent the tones of independence, in reading from the court-house door to the assembled country the declaration of independence of Mecklenburg;

In whose veins mingle, also, the same flow of blood that coursed through the veins of James Knox Polk, concerning whom a recent historian has said: "The most brilliant presidential career that America has ever had was that of the man who gave the Pacific slope to answer back to the calls of the Atlantic waves." In her gentle veins are their Scotch-Irish blood, and we do reverence to their patriotism as we listen to her.

Chairman Johnston:

The next address that will be made will be by our friend, Mr. W. O. McDowell, of New Jersey. We have them from Tennessee, Kentucky, and North Carolina, and this gentleman is from New Jersey. He is not very high, but he is all wool and a yard wide.

Mr. McDowell:

Ladies and Gentlemen:—As we have been listening for the last two days to the grand story of the Scotch-Irish, as told by a Knott, a Henry, a McCloskie, and other gentlemen, you and I doubtless, have been asking the question: What on earth have the rest of creation been doing for the last eighteen hundred years? (Laughter.) It has been suggested to me that, if the Scotch-Irishman had been around on creation day, he would have been able to make a good many valuable suggestions.

I have been inquiring around this town to-day for a little information. I want to know how it is possible that such a display of womanly beauty could be placed before an audience like this. I was speaking to two native Scotch-Irishmen, and they explained it to me. One of them said that the very industrious committee had been at work sending all the poor horses a hundred miles from Columbia, and had been gathering the beautiful women of this country and Kentucky and bringing them to the front seats in this audience, and had locked up all the homely ones. The other said: "Don't you know that there is not a poor horse or a homely woman in all the State of Tennessee?"

My friends, I feel peculiarly glad to be with you here at this time. At 9 o'clock in the morning of the 30th of April, I had the distinguished honor to stand in the room where, after the close of the revolutionary struggle, George Washington said good-bye to the soldiers of his army. Surrounding me were delegates from twenty-two states of this Union. We had met in this sacred place and hour at the call of our President, to formulate and organize the national Society of Sons of the American Revolution. We could not understand how it was possible that the sons of the soldiers of the revolution could have rested quietly a hundred years, leaving its memories to be celebrated only by the Order of the Cincinnati. That perpetuates on American soil the principles of primogeniture, against which our ancestors fought. Our meeting gave birth to the Democratic Society of Sons of the Revolution. Our officers were elected, and as vice-president of the society for France, we elected a descendant of that famous Frenchman without whom even our Scotch-Irish ancestors might have been unsuccessful, La Fayette. The various states represented nominated their vice-presidents. We had felt that there was a patriotic society that could be born on American soil that was not sectional, with no North and no South, but with one common glorious country.

The Scotch-Irish were immigrants to America before the day of the revolution, and when you gather them around you, you gather a society of the sons of the American revolution. When the Scotch-Irishman comes here to-day, you see him in peace, and his influence will be one of peace all along the line. Just as I left New York, a document was placed in my hands, that I did not have an opportunity to examine until I reached Columbia. It was the message sent to the soldiers of the revolution immediately after the inauguration of George Washington, congratulating the great chief. This I will read, together with his response. . . .

One hundred years have gone by since those messages were exchanged and sent out to the country, and it reads almost like divinity's production. A little while ago, I was brought into contact with some of the most intelligent men of China, and I asked them what they thought of a government like ours. The man to whom the question was directed gathered himself up, looked down to me, and said: "From the stand-point of our four thousand years of written history, we look upon your government as a mere experiment." I want to say to the young men and the young women that are listening to my voice, that the responsibility of government for the people, of the people, and by the people, rests as strongly upon our shoulders to-day as it did upon the men of the revolution. We should be far from sitting down with the idea that nothing remains for us to do but to enjoy the luxuries that our fathers secured to us. On last election day, I stood at the polls within fifty miles of the city of New York, and saw the employes of a large manufacturing establishment brought to the polls, where the roll was called, and each man was given a certain ticket to deposit in the ballot-box. The northern papers tell you that things of that sort occur in the South; I tell you of something that I saw with my own eyes. If a man touches human life, he must pay the penalty of the law. But there is something in this country beyond human life, and that is the sanctity of the ballot-box. If we would see this government continue, we must see that no ballot goes into the box that is bought or forced. (Applause.) Washington, in the worst day of his experience at Valley Forge, said: "Put none but Americans on duty to-night." I want to see Americans on duty now, seeing that the laws of the land shall protect the ballot-box. Kentucky, Massachusetts, and other states have passed the law which the best judgment of men has declared most efficient—the Australian system of voting. I am told that Tennessee has passed it; thank God for that.

Another thing: When these Scotch-Irish got into differences in this country, and all the rest of you took up those differences, the flag of the Union stood second on the waters of the ocean. England soon swept it by diplomacy and chicanery from the sea, and beat us again by the same means in the Geneva conference. It is the duty of our young men especially to see to it that the position we once held upon the ocean is regained. Whatever England does, let us beat her at it, until our flag again leads upon the sea. Our educational institutions are the very foundation-stone of liberty. During the last few years, legal provisions have been made, whereby each school district, each locality, each city, can take upon itself special taxes to establish free public libraries to aid the public schools, and I hope to see the time when the social center shall be, not the rum shop, but the free public library.

A short while ago, I was in a company where a distinguished German made an able defense of the English side of the home rule question. In that audience was another gentleman, who sprang to his feet and said: "When you speak of art, science, literature, theology, the whole world can bow in respect before the German character; but when you speak of human liberty, the German should bend in the dust, for where in the world has the call been made for liberty that the Scotch-Irish did not respond all along the line?" My brother who has just spoken has expressed the wish that a foreign war might come to secure unity among our people. I want to say, that peace has its victories even greater than those of war. If you want to make thrones tremble, make this government so successful that the benefits of freedom shall be known throughout all the world. I believe in the evolution of governments, and in the survival of the fittest. I believe there are two forms of government that naturally conflict—a government of the people for the people, and the government of the people for a few. That conflict will continue until the world is again enslaved or is free. If you want the institutions you love so well spared this fate, make this government so successful and its benefits so pronounced that it will shake every tyrant from a human throne.

Chairman Johnston introduced the next speaker, as follows:

Our friend, Dr. Hall, said there was one citizen of the United States that had come over here expressly to be born. We will now have the pleasure of hearing from this gentleman, Dr. John S. MacIntosh, of Philadelphia.

Dr. MacIntosh:

There was a Quaker once, who came across the sea and found a pleasant place for a city that is known as the City of Brotherly Love. When he had got it fairly well under way, the Scotch-Irishmen found that it was a very satisfactory place to live in, and on the universal principle of Scotchmen that Scotland is a good place to be born in and an excellent place to come from, they took possession of the Quaker City; and from the time that the Scotch-Irishman came there, it began to grow, until now it throws its arms from shore to shore. I come here to-night, not to make any particular address, but to convey to the Scotch-Irish Congress, to our most excellent chairman, who has conducted all the affairs of this convention with a facility that I have rarely seen equaled and never seen surpassed; to the Committee of Arrangements, who will permit a Philadelphian knowing a little about the arrangement and management of conventions, to say that I wonder how they have gathered together so remarkable a band of men, every man knowing his place, every man knowing his own work, never getting in his neighbor's way, but doing every thing so well that a glorious unity is the result; and to convey to the people of this remarkably beautiful and attractive city, the salutations of a very large body of Scotchmen and of Scotch-Irishmen who could not possibly be here on this occasion. I have been charged to present the salutations of a man who stands easily at the head of that profession which is so honorable and in many respects so sacred, which so closely concerns the Master's work, healing the sick and the suffering—Dr. Hayes Agnew, whose name is well known over this continent. I am charged to present to the Scotch-Irish Congress, not only his congratulations, but his hearty love; and if you knew, as some of us know, that heart of his, you would appreciate the expression of a man who carries with him the confidence of every man and every woman who knows him, and whose pain he has ever touched in suffering. A nobler and grander specimen of the Scotch-Irishman than he is I know not from pole to pole. (Applause.)

I am further charged to express and convey to you on behalf of my session—and I can do this with some degree of historic propriety, in view of the objects of this gathering—the hearty and earnest salutation of the mother church of the mother synod of Philadelphia, whose name stands high on that flaming roll of glory of those who took so wondrous a part in working out the great achievements that have received the admiration of the world, as having had no little part in formulating that marvelous document, which the greatest master of international law and statesmanlike thought, Wm. E. Gladstone, has declared to be among the highest monuments of man's genius and governmental achievement. I come to convey the salutation of that old church that keeps within its historic archives and its most precious treasures the picture of Tennant, one of those great men who moved the hearts of the world, and discerned, as the great object of Scotch-Irish chivalry and heroism, christianized patriotism and patriotic Christianity. I come to convey, on behalf of a large body of lawyers and physicians, engineers and conductors, all over the county of Philadelphia, and all over the proud Keystone State, our hearty congratulations. One of them, bearing the historic name of Rogan, said to me: "See to it that, if there shall be any organization established, that my name shall be among the first enrolled, as my ancestors were among the earliest of those that struggled for the independence of this country."

I come charged, also, with the salutations of a man who, in one department of our great national work, has, perhaps, done more than any other man that I know—a Scotch-Irishman, a friend of Scotch-Irishmen; a man whose generous heart and whose characteristic Christian patriotism showed itself at a hundred points along the line; a man who cared for the wounded and the suffering, wherever they were found; a man who has been the friend of all those who were distressed; a man who has continually watched and added to the progress of this country. I refer to my old Sabbath-school superintendent, Geo. H. Stewart. Now would be the time for me to present to this association the letter of my honored friend and revered teacher:

May 1, 1889.

Thanks for your thoughtful kindness in inviting me to the Congress at Columbia, which invitation I hasten to acknowledge. As to the nature of the approaching meeting, I am not fully informed, but I feel sure it is for some good purpose. The Scotch-Irish blood that flows in my own veins would enthuse with new life in joining hands with my brethren in their heart-felt and soul-stirring utterances, which are sure to characterize this gathering. The very title of the conference and the historic memories evolved guarantee that it will not be lacking in Scotch heart or Scotch warmth; and would God bless the Scotch-Irish Congress in drawing to itself the wise and the good from all parts of our common country, and in still further cementing the ties that bind us in mutual love and Christian fellowship. I would gladly be with you, but I have been a great invalid for over a year, and spend most of my time at Clayton Springs, to which I expect soon to return. GEO. H. STEWART.

There is another friend of mine, whose only deficiency is, I think, the deficiency of friend Phraner; that is to say, he made the mistake of not going to Ireland or the South of Scotland to be born. If that had been the case, he would be a man that would almost make me doubt my catechism; but I think that was just left out to make it evident that no man is born absolutely perfect, for otherwise he claims a good share along this line. This is my friend, John Wanamaker. I hold in my hand the following letter:

WASHINGTON, D. C., *May 2*, 1889.
DEAR SIR:
I am greatly obliged for your kind letter of invitation, and wish I were free to make the visit you propose, and renew our old-time friendship. I can not express the pleasure it would give me in joining with you in commemorating the deeds of the Scotch-Irish race, and the influences that have exalted our American institutions and given growth to universal brotherhood and love. I would also visit the favored section of the South in which the exercises of the Congress are to be held. I regret exceedingly that my duties at present are of such a nature that I can not leave again for some time, as the recent centennial celebration in New York took what little time I could spare from the work of this department.
Yours truly,
JOHN WANAMAKER.

This will show you the feelings of the old Keystone State, and how this meeting has awakened the interest and enthusiasm of the race.

I want to say one other word in concluding my quite extemporaneous remarks. It is to me a personal matter of the greatest possible gratification that, in spite of the hundred forces that have threatened to become insurmountable obstacles in my way of getting here, that I have been able almost to complete a chain of personal investigation that has been for me one of the delights of years. Beginning away back in those early days of plastic and expansive boyhood, when the heart of the chivalrous lad will respond like the harp that we have listened to this evening to the almost divine touch of a mother's finger, I have heard of the deeds of Scottish ancestors and Scotch and Scotch-Irish ancestresses; I have listened to the old tales of St. Andrews; I have heard of Edinburgh and Glasgow; I have, in imagination, walked along the spur of the cloud, and passed and repassed over that battle-ground of the old border territory; I have sat and wondered what these marvelous places must be like, and have wondered, when first I listened to these names and saw in fancy's eye these wondrous pictures, if the time would ever come that my own feet should tread these spots and my own eye should see those scenes that had grown hallowed by the thoughts of the covenanting dead and the early struggles in the plantation of Ulster. But the time came when the Philadelphia boy must pass across the sea; and from the time that sea was passed, home after home, hamlet after hamlet, county after county, church after church, college after college, has been visited by me, until I have traced in Scotland and in Ulster those magnificent springs of glorious light and consecrated blood out of which first flowed the streams that have converged upon our own shore and rolled into that great river of power that has carried on its breast God's truth and human liberty; and I have followed, in coming to this meeting, with a strange thrill of affectionate recollection, the stream along which came those of the Scotch and Scotch-Irish race, as they passed from my own dear native state along the Cumberland stretch, over the little rise into the pleasant valley of Virginia, down along the states east and west, down the Blue Ridge and the Smoky, until they came into the clear and pleasant regions of Carolina and Alabama. Then, strangely enough, I have discovered that, winding around at Decatur, I have come right up in the valley of this great old State of Tennessee. As along this path I have traveled with the speed of the iron horse, I have thought of the days of toil, weary day after weary day, of those great pioneer souls, who were made of God the breakers of the way, in opening the pathway through the trackless wilderness, and planted the garrison spots for the defense of the country in its most critical hours. It has been to me a moment of most gracious opportunity to see thus the old homes that I have known so well on the other side appear in wondrous resurrection on this western shore; and to know that in the land of my birth my ancestors and my ancestresses live again in their mighty sons and their God-fearing, noble, consecrated daughters. (Applause.)

Miss Minnie Holding, accompanied on the piano by Miss Camile Herndon, sang "Comin' thro' the Rye," and, as an *encore*, "I Know a Maiden Fair to See."

Colonel A. S. Colyar paid a compliment to the Committee of Arrangements which had prepared the Congress, and said that he desired to offer a resolution thanking Mr. A. C. Floyd for the prominent part in the work which he had taken.

Colonel Colyar said:

Such great assemblies and such perfection of arrangements are the results of no ordinary effort or ability. Behind it all, oft times unknown, is always some thoughtful mind which devises plans, and some skillful hand which executes them. The moving and directing spirit on this occasion is a quiet but forceful gentleman, whose worth and efforts should command the recognition and the unqualified thanks of the whole Scotch-Irish race. I therefore move the resolution, that to Mr. A. C. Floyd, more than to any one else, is due the success of this Congress, and that we tender him our thanks for the work he has done.

The resolution was seconded by Mr. McDowell, of New Jersey, who remarked that Mr. Floyd, in doing this work, had builded wiser than he knew.

The resolution was unanimously adopted, after which the meeting adjourned.

Friday, May 10th.

MORNING SESSION.

The Congress was called to order at 11 o'clock by Chairman Johnston.

Dr. John S. MacIntosh led in prayer.

Chairman Johnston introduced the first speaker of the morning, as follows:

The first speaker this morning is a gentleman who rightly acquired fame in the service of the gods of war; and after the war ceased, he took up the sword in behalf of the God of Peace—Dr. D. C. Kelley.

(See Part II, for the historical address on "The Scotch-Irish in Tennessee.")

Upon the conclusion of his regular address, Dr. Kelley, who had been a colonel of cavalry in the C. S. A., at the request of the committee, spoke for the southern soldiers in the reunion of the Blue and the Gray, General John C. Brown, who was to have represented them, being kept away by grave illness.

The following is a synopsis of his warm and impressive words:

Already, in the course of what I have had to say, allusions have been made to many men of Scotch-Irish birth, who, as Tennesseeans, became foremost in the late war. Bishop and General Leonidas Polk, high in sanctity, learning, and patriotism, showed a courage surpassed by no soldier of the war. Lieutenant-General N. B. Forrest, the genius of war, and Alex. Stewart, the genius of discipline, with Major-General Jno. C. Brown and Brigadier-General Alex. Campbell, knights of untarnished honor, supported and illustrated the soldierly virtues of the race. To these, allow me, as we stand near the spot in Tennessee which was for a time glorified by the temporary grave of Pat. Claiborne, the loving and the brave, to add him, as a star of the first magnitude, to our galaxy, at whose zenith glows the name of Stonewall Jackson. If we turn to the other side and judge by name and places of birth, we have a right to claim Lieutenant-Generals Scott, McClellan, Smith, Wallace, and a score of other illustrious soldiers, conspicuous in the Union ranks. If you will allow us to add another criterion to name and place of birth, viz., the great size and tenderness of his heart, then, by every token, we would write at the top of all these the name of Abraham Lincoln. He could love as tenderly as an Irishman, and hold by principle with the tenacity of a Scotchman; no more can be said for man, while yet mortal. His birth in Kentucky, and name, link him with the race. As we found in Douglass and Bell, at the beginning of the political contest out of which the war came, Scotch-Irish representatives of love of the Union and conservative statesmanship, so, from beginning to end of the strife, until the autonomy of the states had been restored, we find this stick-to-rights race foremost in all that ennobled these years of bitterness and conflict.

Many of us of the South did not believe in the doctrine of states rights to the extreme of secession; many of us longed for the day when the negro and the white man would be freed from the curse of slavery. We did not believe in the methods adopted by the North to test the one doctrine or to accomplish the other fact; so, when driven by the call to arms to decide for the one side or the other, we stood by our people; we saw no other star of duty, so followed our hearts, which clove to our people and to the weaker side in its appeal to our courage. On both sides, men did what they believed right, and died in testimony of their faith. With reverent memory and uncovered heads, we hold forever as our equal heritage the sense of duty and the deeds of sacrifice and courage which illumined the years of strife.

The southern poet will, in the glad day to come, tune his harp to a major key, as he shall celebrate the courage, tenderness, and truth of the northern soldier, and historians from the granite hills will do justice to the statesmen and soldiers of the South. All shall thank God that we are one people.

Will our northern friends be patient while we work out our race problem in love to the Union, with tenderness for our brother, and faith in God's providence?

We bear no hatred to the negro; he has none for us. Time is the only solvent of our difficult problem. Give us time, your confidence, and your prayers, and in the end you will say of us, well done.

To Columbia, the heart of old Maury, which is God's paradise, the home of the Scotch-Irish, this convention bids me offer one word of good-bye. These days we have spent here, this gathering of the fairest women and the knightliest men, this first hand-shaking of kindred blood—as we think of you in connection with it, the memory will be treasured in the same heart chambers with the first kiss of our sweethearts and the last kiss of our mothers.

At the conclusion of Dr. Kelley's remarks, he was presented with a handsome bouquet of flowers, with the following remark by the Chairman:

I am requested to present to you these northern daisies, from a northern lady. You captured northern soldiers during the war; you are capturing northern daisies now; and I hope you will keep them longer than you did the soldiers.

Dr. Kelley accepted the flowers with the following words:

These daisies bear the name of my first-born daughter, who is now a missionary in Japan. I accept them for a token of northern love, and treasure them for the name they bear.

The next speaker was introduced by the Chairman as follows:

We are now going to enjoy the pleasure of hearing a representative northern soldier, who has kindly come a long distance to speak to you upon this occasion. His is a very English name. I don't know where he got his Scotch-Irish blood, but it is supposed from his mother; and as we get the best of every thing we have from our mothers, he got it in the right place. There has been a suspicion somewhat general throughout the country, that our distinguished friend, the Corporal, has a tendency to be a little prodigal with the people's money in certain lines. I know that the whole country will be deeply gratified to find that he has some Scotch-Irish blood running through his veins, which will tend to make him a little parsimonious in that line.

Mr. Tanner was received with applause. His first sentence secured the sympathy of the audience, which, with attentive ear and great applause, followed him through his amusing allusions, his forcible and eloquently expressed ideas, and his references of friendship, respect, and honor for the South and her people. His address was a fine effort.

Prefacing his remarks with some allusions to the many incidents that American history affords of the magnificent manner in which, on American soil, the representatives of the Scotch-Irish race have upheld the reputation of their nationality, and pointing out the fact that they were notably conspicuous on both sides in the late war, both for numbers and prowess, Mr. Tanner spoke as follows:

Friends and Countrymen:—We thank God and congratulate ourselves as we assemble here to-day, that there is so much in our possession, and so much in prospect for us in common as citizens of this great republic. And without regard to the boundaries of any particular state which we designate as our own, we look back over a hundred years that are passed and gone, and we see much of struggle, much of creation, much of bitter sectionalism, and all too much, we will all agree, in the last quarter of a century, of bloody strife. Thank God we can contemplate it as of the past, and we firmly believe, forever past. Standing to-day upon the shining uplands of prosperity and peace, we sweep the world with our gaze, and contemplate with pride the fact that the American nation stands secure; its position unchallenged in the face of the civilized world, the glory of its citizenship respected and honored in the four quarters of the earth. But a peculiar combination of circumstances encompass while they do not embarrass me to-day, and seem to indicate that there are some lines of thought and speech to which my mind should fitly turn.

Within the time of those of us who are now of middle or elder age, this country has been shaken from center to circumference by the rude shock of bloody war; of war in its most horrible form; a death struggle between brethren of the same household. We stand to-day on ground that for a long time was debatable, and we have gathered here to-day, representatives of both of those mighty armies that met in the shock of battle, to testify by our presence, by the greeting given, by the sentiments felt and expressed, that, however high the hopes of the past, however dear the ambitions which were swept aside in the smoke of battle, to-day we are proud above all other things, of the fact that we are citizens of the United States of America, that in our common possession lies the domain of this mighty republic, and the prestige of its citizenship wherever in foreign clime our paths may lead, that before us in our common destiny for weal or woe, and that we are one people, and that over our heads there floats to-day one flag.

Search all the history of the nations of the past, and among them you can find no such exhibitions of the unification of a people so recently and apparently permanently rent asunder and engaged in such a mighty and sanguinary strife.

Here to-day are assembled many men who, in the struggle of 1861 to 1865, contested on the one side for the disruption, and on the other for the preservation of the Union. If there be any fitness in my appearance on this platform to-day, it rises from the fact that in the days of that struggle I stood in the ranks of that mighty column of blue. If there are any words to which my tongue can most appropriately turn to give utterance to-day, they should formulate themselves into a message which I feel I can honestly, conscientiously and consistently bring from my comrades of the North, who in the years of our strife, in answer to the defiance of the old-time and never-to-be-forgotten rebel yell sent ringing back to the extent of our lung power the Yankee hurrah. If there be any class of citizens over the whole country with whose sentiments I am familiar above that of any other class, it is the veterans of the Union armies, who, from 1861 to 1865, when health was in their faces, and vigor in their steps, belted the country across with a line of blue, and beat back the mighty hosts of the South; and I am proud of the fact that I can bring from my comrades of the Northland a sentiment in perfect harmony with the peace and pleasantry and good feeling which is such an adjunct on this occasion to-day. If I may be pardoned a personal reference, then permit me to say that I am proud of the fact that the sentiments of my heart are, and for long, long years have been, entirely in accord with the unification and homogeneity of the exercises of this hour.

Very many years ago I stated, have repeated it many times since then, meant it every time I repeated it, and mean it to-day no less than ever, that if there should walk into my office the very "Johnnie" who pulled the lanyard of the gun which sent the shell which crippled me for life, and I was satisfied that he stood with us to-day, for the honor of our common institutions and the glory of our common flag, this right hand would reach way out across the so-called bloody chasm, and I would say, "Put it there, Johnnie, you and I will go out and take dinner together, and talk over old times."

The sentiment of no one class of men in this country has been more thoroughly misunderstood, or, if understood, more misrepresented by the citizens at large than the sentiments existing in the two columns that were led by Grant and Lee. The fact of the business is that when Lee surrendered to Grant at Appomattox, no two classes of men were more nearly together, not only physically but mentally, than the two lines of men who stood there dressed in gray and dressed in blue. They had met in the shock of battle; they had fought it out man fashion, and I call every soldier here present as witness, no matter on which side he fought, to this fact, that if at the time of the surrender, the settlement of the questions at difference between the two great sections of the country could have been left to those two lines of blue and gray, those questions would have been settled honorably, amicably and lastingly, and the politicians would have been out of business during the whole of the reconstruction period.

Grant epitomized the whole idea, when in the hour of his mighty triumph he turned to the leader of the "lost cause" and said to him: "General, tell your men to take their horses home with them. They will need them to do the spring's plowing with." Did you ever let your thoughts run out in contemplation of the beauty of that sentiment, springing from the heart of that man? He had been vilified and wickedly misrepresented in all the civilized sections of the globe; he had been pictured as one who delighted simply in scenes of carnage; who had no love for his fellow men; no regard except for his own ambitions, and yet in that hour instinctively his heart, as did the hearts of the veterans he had led to victory, welled up with the desire that the wasted and devasted places of the South might be made to bloom and blossom again in the shortest possible space of time. It was not so strange a thing when you come to think of it. All true men know this, that no matter how earnestly you may fight a man, no matter how utterly you may condemn the principles for which he contends, when you find that man so terribly in earnest that he offers his life in behalf of the principles for which he combats, a respect grows up for that mighty earnestness in spite of our utmost antagonism to the principles he contends for.

Borne out by my own experience in the years of peace which have followed the close of the struggle, I declare it to be a thoroughly enjoyable time when a lot of old comrades get together and live again in the memories of the past—calling to mind the rich associations of the days gone by; but when the feast of reason and flow of soul is to soar to its utmost altitude, then mix them up—the blue and the gray —and then as we gently remind one another of the days of the past when with the varying fortunes of the strife we could have played checkers upon each other's coat-tails, then time flies unheeded by.

You will bear in mind I am speaking of the men who fought. I am not speaking of those men of whom we have all too many, who never fronted the shock of war, and did not get mad until all opportunity to do battle had passed away, who were the invisibles of war, and are the invincibles of peace. I presume you have them here and farther South, among those who claimed to support the fortunes of the Confederacy. We have plenty of them in the North. They are the fellows who yelled themselves into an advanced stage of bronchitis, inquiring, "Why don't the army move," who were such superlative military tacticians that they could lay out more plans of campaigns in a night than the generals on both sides would see fit to fight in a year, but who, notwithstanding all the art and science of war, no sooner heard the cry for three hundred thousand more, than they at once came to a position of "rest," with a draft-list in one hand and a time-table of the nearest route to Canada in the other, ready to skip across the border if their names showed up in the list of those who were called. The man who stood before me on the other side and gave me, in relation to him, what he had in relation to myself—the chance of life for life—stands a thousand degrees higher in my estimation than the snapping, snarling and yelping curs and whelps who did not have courage enough to be soldiers in the time of war, and who can not turn their foul tongues to any thing venomous enough to say of veterans in time of peace.

. . . .

I congratulate you, and I congratulate myself no less that in these piping days of peace we have reached this high altitude where, from the uplands of long continued, and I trust never to be interrupted prosperity, we can gaze back, as though we were recalling a hideous dream, upon that bloody past.

God speed the day when in the hearts of all the people, North and South, there may come that same splendid feeling which permeates the breast of every one here assembled, and who in the olden days, with unflinching heart and undaunted mein, marched and met and fought as bitter foes, and who to-day and for the days to come are friends, and will be until those better days, when the call shall be sounded for the last assembly on that further shore, where all our services will be in the ranks commanded by the Prince of Peace.

When he had finished his remarks, Mr. Tanner was presented with flowers by Mr. Johnston, as follows:

I am requested to present to you, as a representative northern soldier, these southern roses, from a southern lady; and notwithstanding you are in the heart of Tennessee, you need have no apprehension that the soldiers of Jackson or Forrest will attempt to recapture this trophy.

The meeting adjourned to 8 o'clock.

NIGHT SESSION.

The meeting was called to order at 8 o'clock.

The Chairman introduced Mr. John Moore, of Columbia, who delivered a short, humorous address.

Colonel Johnston announced that he would be compelled to leave the city on the night train, having come with the intention of staying only one day. He said he wanted to come and meet with his Scotch-Irish friends from all parts of the country, but had met with so much kindness and courtesy, and had formed so many pleasing acquaintances, not only in the fair city of Columbia, but among the distinguished visitors, that he had been detained longer than he had contemplated. He said he wanted to return his thanks to the people of Columbia, and to the Congress, for the uniform kindness which had been shown him on this visit, which he should treasure as one of the happiest of his life.

Colonel E. C. McDowell took the chair.

Mayor Robert Pillow offered the following resolution:

Resolved, That the thanks of the Scotch-Irish Congress are hereby tendered to the Hon. J. F. Johnston, for the perfect manner in which he has presided over our deliberations, and that we, the citizens, as well as those who belong to the Congress, do esteem it a privilege thus publicly to express our appreciation of the very valuable services rendered.

The resolution was unanimously passed.

The next speaker was introduced by Colonel Colyar, as follows:

Ladies and Gentlemen:—I don't know when I have had a more agreeable task to perform than in introducing to you to-night the distinguished speaker. There is something peculiarly agreeable to me in introducing him to a southern audience, and I will in a very few words tell you why. We have had in the South a long, hard struggle; our great effort for the last twenty years has been to build up our industrial interests, and develop our great resources. I don't say that we have had but few friends in the North. Many men in the North have stood by us warmly, energetically, and have given us the right hand of fellowship on all occasions; but one man above all others has been the friend of the South in all our efforts, and that man is Colonel A. K. McClure, of Philadelphia. Wherever I have met him in the last fifteen years, whether in the South or in his home in Philadelphia, I have found him talking about the South and the southern people, sympathizing with them in their misfortunes, and using his great paper, read by all the better people of the northern states, in helping us along, and holding up our hands, and giving us a word of encouragement. Again I take pleasure in introducing to you my distinguished friend, Colonel McClure.

(For Colonel McClure's address, see Part II, page 178.)

Colonel Colyar made a statement concerning the exercises of the Tennessee Chatauqua, and the Mineral and Metallic Exposition, to be held in Nashville, in 1890, and said he would like to have Colonel McClure open the proceedings of the latter.

The Congress adjourned.

Saturday, May, 11th.
The Congress was called to order at 11 o'clock by Chairman McDowell.

Dr. Jerry Witherspoon led in prayer.

The audience joined in repeating the Lord's Prayer.

The first speaker of the day was introduced by Chairman McDowell, as follows:

Hon. Benton McMillin has consented to deliver a short address. His remarks will be almost *ex tempore*. To Tennesseeans it is almost unnecessary for me to say who Mr. McMillin is; to our guests I will say that he is a member from Tennessee to the United States Congress.

(See Part II, page 187.)

At the conclusion of his address, Mr. McMillin was presented with a bouquet of flowers.

The next speaker was introduced by the Chairman, as follows:

Your long-delayed desires are about to be satisfied. We reserved Dr. MacIntosh's address for the last, because it is one of the best. I now have the pleasure of introducing to you Dr. John S. MacIntosh, of Philadelphia.

(See Part II, p. 191.)

Mr. McDowell said it seemed to him that this address had been an inspiration, and one sent through the heart of a pure soul. From this day forward, the Scotch-Irish race will no longer be without a written history. A hundred years from now, or sooner, when the principles of that people and a belief in a government of the people, for the people, and by the people, shall be the fundamental principle of every civilized government, we will still be mindful of that race which gave to the world the principle that man has the right to govern himself, subject alone to the Almighty God. (Applause.)

Mr. Floyd read the following resolution, which he said had been left with him the previous night by Chairman Johnston just before he left:

Resolved, That the thanks of this Congress are eminently due, and are hereby tendered, Dr. Robert Pillow, for his constant attention upon, and his uniform courtesy and kindness to, every visiting member of the Congress.

Dr. MacIntosh seconded the resolution, as follows:

I want, on the part of myself and my wife, and all of us here, to second that motion. I don't know what would have become of us if it had not been for the considerate magisterial government of our honorable Mayor.

The resolution was adopted, and Dr. Pillow responded, as follows:

Ladies and Gentlemen:—As you well know, I am no speaker, but I express my thanks for this resolution, and say that it has been my pleasure to contribute to the advancement of this cause, in which I have had my whole soul.

Mr. Floyd said, on behalf of the several committees, that the people of Columbia felt proud that they had such a flattering attendance upon the proceedings, and that they had had the honor to entertain so distinguished a body of visitors.

Mr. W. O. McDowell said that, as the representative of one of the most distant points represented in the meeting, he wanted to move a vote of thanks to the citizens of Columbia for the magnificent way in which they had received the visitors. He said:

There is only one fault that I have to find, the warmth of your hearts has even affected the atmosphere. Would that my tongue was as gifted as that of a Henry; would that I had the eloquence of the Scotch-Irish race, that I might put in words our appreciation of your elegant entertainment. I must say, in addition, that never on American soil, or throughout the world, has there been held outside of official halls, a meeting more important in the progress of the human race than is this gathering after a hundred years of experience on American soil of the Scotch-Irish race.

Dr. D. C. Kelley said:

We desire to offer old Maury, the center of physical beauty, and to Columbia, the center of Maury, our voice of thanks, our words of joy, and the promise to keep in our memory these days as we would treasure the first kiss of our sweetheart, the last of our mother.

The audience united in singing "Auld Lang Syne," after which the Congress adjourned *sine die*.

OFFICERS OF THE SCOTCH-IRISH SOCIETY OF AMERICA.

President.
ROBERT BONNER, New York.

First Vice-President at Large.
JOSEPH F. JOHNSTON, Birmingham, Ala.

Second Vice-President at Large.
E. C. McDOWELL, Nashville, Tenn.

Vice-President at Large for British America.
MR. THOMAS KERR, Toronto, Canada.

Secretary.
A. C. FLOYD, Columbia, Tenn.

Treasurer.
LUCIUS FRIERSON, Columbia, Tenn.

Historian and Registrar.
THOMAS M. GREEN, Maysville, Ky.

Vice-Presidents of States and Territories.
REV. Dr. JOHN HALL, New York.
COLONEL A. K. McCLURE, Pennsylvania—Philadelphia.
HON. WM. O. McDOWELL, New Jersey—Newark.
MR. MATTHEW ADDY, Ohio—Cincinnati.

OFFICERS OF THE SOCIETY.

JUDGE JOHN M. SCOTT, Illinois—Bloomington.
HON. WM. WIRT HENRY, Virginia—Richmond.
HON. S. B. ALEXANDER, North Carolina—Charlotte.
COLONEL T. T. WRIGHT, Florida—Pensacola.
HON. WM. PRESTON JOHNSTON, Louisiana—New Orleans.
MR. A. G. ADAMS, Tennessee—Nashville.
DR. HERVEY C. MCDOWELL, Kentucky.
*HON. A. T. WOOD, Ontario, Canada—Hamilton.
REV. J. C. QUINN, Montana—Helena.

---

* A Vice-President for each of the remaining states and territories of the Union, and each province of Canada, will be appointed by the President as fast as selections can be made.

EXECUTIVE COMMITTEE.

ROBERT BONNER, *Chairman*, New York.
A. C. FLOYD, *Secretary*, Columbia, Tenn.
LUCIUS FRIERSON, Columbia, Tenn.
HON. J. F. JOHNSTON, Birmingham, Ala.
COLONEL T. T. WRIGHT, Nashville, Tenn.
REV. DR. JOHN S. MACINTOSH, Philadelphia.
PROF. GEO. MCCLOSKIE, Princeton College, New Jersey.
DR. ROBERT PILLOW, Columbia, Tenn.
COLONEL H. G. EVANS, Columbia, Tenn.

ACTION OF COMMITTEES SINCE THE CONGRESS.

At a meeting of the Executive Council, in New York City, on the 11th of July last, requisites for membership was one of the matters considered.

Article III of the Constitution is as follows:

"Any male above the age of twenty-one years, who has Scotch-Irish blood in his veins, shall be eligible for membership in the Association."

In addition to this, it was decided that each member should be required to pay annual dues of $2.00 upon entering the Society.

The payment of his dues entitles each member to a copy of this volume, in paper covers; thirty-five cents additional being required for a cloth-bound copy.

An Executive Committee of nine members was appointed, and to them were delegated all the powers not exercised by the Council.

At a meeting of the Executive Committee, in New York City, on the following day, A. C. Floyd, Lucius Frierson, and Robert Pillow were appointed a Committee on Publication. The name of this volume was chosen, and plans for its publication discussed.

The Secretary was instructed to accept the cordial invitation of the Scotch-Irish of Pittsburg to hold the next annual Congress of the Society in that city.

PART II.

THE HARP OF TOM MOORE.

AT THE SCOTCH-IRISH CONGRESS, MAY, 1889, COLUMBIA, TENN.

BY WALLACE BRUCE.

The top of the morning to Ireland
   And the Scotch-Irish Congress to-day!
All hearts respond to the banquet
   When the Harp of Tom Moore leads the way.
The bells of the Shandon are ringing
   Their music from over the sea,
But sweeter the Harp of her poet
   In the mountains of old Tennessee.

The sons of the Shamrock and Thistle
   Still cherish the visions of yore,
And the Harp of old Tara awakens
   Again to the voice of Tom Moore:
Each string, with memories sacred,
   Is tuned to Liberty's key;
And the songs that float down the ages
   Are always the songs of the free.

It sings of the "Exile of Erin,"
   But her exiles are exiles no more,
For the Isle of old Erin has drifted
   Close under Columbia's shore.
"Where Liberty is, is my country,"
   Has guided her over the way,
And Columbia holds in her borders
   The heart of old Ireland to-day.

Manhattan and Plymouth and Jamestown
   Can boast of their heritage true,
But Mecklenburg's fame is immortal
   When we number the stars in the blue;
The Scotch-Irish-Puritan-Fathers
   First drafted the words of the free,
And the speech of Virginia's Henry
   Is the crown of Our Liberty's plea.

The sons and the grandsons of heroes
   Who fought for freedom and right
With joy hail the dawn of the morning—
"Mavourneen!" Awake to the light!
The maidens of Lorne and Killarney
   Are swelling the chorus to-day,
For the castles of Oban and Blarney
   Are only just over the way.

Then welcome, a thrice hearty welcome,
   To legendry, lyric, and lore,
With a pledge and "Guid Hielan' welcome"
   To the voice and the Harp of Tom Moore;
A toast to the Shamrock and Thistle,
   And sunshine both sides of the sea,
As Erin clasps hands o'er the ocean
   With Columbia in fair Tennessee.

ADDRESS DELIVERED BY EX-GOVERNOR PROCTOR KNOTT, OF KENTUCKY.

Mr. Chairman, Ladies, and Gentlemen:—As we are assembled to honor the memories of our Scotch-Irish ancestry, and to devise, if possible, some means of gathering up, and crystallizing into the more enduring form of written history, the legendary memorials of their deeds, it has occurred to me that the proceedings of the present Congress might be appropriately prefaced by a brief inquiry into their origin, the characteristics which distinguished them from other people, and what they did to entitle them to the respectful recollection of coming generations. That office I will, therefore, attempt to discharge; and, in undertaking it, I will endeavor to do precisely as I think they would have me do, if they could come to me to-day from their consecrated graves and dictate the present utterances of my tongue—speak of them as they were; tell the truth, as I understand it, of their frailties, as of their virtues;

"Nothing extenuate,
Nor set down aught in malice."

When Agricola marshaled his legions on the north bank of the Firth of Solway, eighteen hundred years ago, he looked out upon a country lying beyond the parallel of latitude which forms the southernmost boundary of Alaska, and embracing about thirty thousand, five hundred square miles of territory, as cheerless, perhaps, in all its aspects, as any that ever provoked the ambition or tempted the cupidity of a Roman conqueror.

Directly in his front, and as far as the site of the present city of Dumfries, stretched a tangled labyrinth of swampy woods, interlaced by a matted network of creeping undergrowth. To the westward, as far as St. Patrick's Channel, lay a rugged and almost inaccessible district of roughly wooded, rocky hill lands, trenched by turbulent streams, and abounding in lovely lakes. Northward, beyond the present limits of Dumfries, to the narrow isthmus of low lands lying between the Firths of Clyde and Forth, and eastward to St. Abb's Head, extended a similarly broken region, covered with a growth of scrubby timber, interrupted here and there by barren ridges and dreary moorlands. What are now the fertile and flourishing counties of Ayr and Renfrew, was then a sterile and uninviting waste, while the unbroken umbrage of a primeval forest shut out the sunlight from the rich plains of Berwick.

North of the isthmus of Clyde and Forth, lay the vast sea-girt wilderness of Celyddon, the Caledonia of the Romans, extending away to the wave-washed rocks of Cape Wrath and John o' Groats— a bleak, inhospitable region, with its craggy shores fretted by firths and lochs, and its surface corrugated by an interminable maze of misty mountain ranges, with their barren crests and towering cliffs, interspersed with rushing torrents and roaring lynns, lonely tarns and solitary glens, desolate corries and densely wooded straths, while its eastern boundary, from the mouth of the Tay to Moray Firth, was a succession of extensive marshes and sterile hills, made more forbidding by the icy blasts which swept over them from the northern ocean.

Yet some of the remote ancestry of many of the courteous and cultured audience before me, as well as some of my own, had made their cheerless homes in this rude and repulsive region for centuries before the foot of the Roman invader first pressed its indigenous heather; while others of them might have been found, perhaps, in the wandering clans which went over from the northern part of Ireland in the earlier centuries of our era, as allies of their Caledonian kindred in their predatory inroads upon their southern neighbors, and finally settled along the western coast, from Cantyre to Sutherland.

They were not as elegant in manners, nor as elevated in morals, however, as might possibly be inferred from the intelligence and refinement of many of their descendants of the present period. On the contrary, they were as savage as their surroundings were wild and inhospitable, and were regarded by their neighbors not only with a well grounded terror, but with far more disgust and abhorrence than we do our thieves and tramps. The very names, indeed, by which their nationality has been designated in history were never assumed by themselves, but were mere terms of reproach applied to them by the victims of their rapacity, who, out of revenge for the manifold injuries they had suffered from their predacious hands, denounced the fierce and truculent tribes who occupied the eastern, as well as the greater portion of the interior and southern sections of the territory, as *pictich* or *pehts*, while they called the roving bands who went over from the north of Ireland *scuite*, signifying, respectively, in the vernacular of the early Briton, robbers and vagabonds, the two terms being subsequently latinized by the Romans into *Picti* and *Scotti*.

Nor was the country occupied by them known by its present

name for many generations after their first appearance in authentic history; not, in fact, for over two hundred years after the nominal union of the Scots and Picts under Kenneth McAlpine in 843, when the centuries of sanguinary strife between those two branches of the Celtic race in North Britain finally terminated in their complete coalition, and the united kingdom was called Scotland, after the dominant power. And even then, its inhabitants, notwithstanding the introduction of Christianity among them as far back as the middle of the sixth century, were still as barbarous in many respects as their fierce forefathers, who, more than thirty generations before, in a heroic struggle for their wild independence, met hand to hand the trained legionaries of imperial Rome upon the bloody slopes of the Grampian Hills.

Their lack of progress was not so much their fault, however, as their misfortune. Their history during that long period, as it was for centuries after and had been for generations before, was that of a constant, unremitting, and perilous contest for sheer existence. Compelled to supplement their meager domestic resources with the precarious spoils of the chase, they were obliged, in order to eke out their scanty means of subsistence, not only to encounter the dangers of a capricious and tempestuous climate, but to pursue their quarry frequently through hostile territory, across mountain torrents, through guarded passes, and along the treacherous brinks of precipitous cliffs hundreds of feet in height. Besides, they were in a perpetual state of war, when pillage and arson went hand in hand with slaughter, and the sword of the victor knew neither age nor sex. Harried by sanguinary feuds with neighboring clans, which hereditary hate or a mutual desire for plunder or revenge frequently kept alive from generation to generation, and almost constantly engaged in defending themselves from the cruel incursions of the powerful and rapacious nations around them, they had no time for intellectual culture or moral improvement.

Under such circumstances, their advancement in the scale of social being was necessarily retarded to the lowest possible degree. It is a marvel, indeed, that even the lowest grade of civilization could have existed among them at all, for without some settled assurance of the permanency and peaceful enjoyment of the acquisitions of individual industry, popular progress is an impossibility. With no feeling of certainty, on leaving his home in the morning for the perilous avocations of the day, that he would not return in the evening to rescue the charred remains of his butchered family from the smoldering ashes of his ruined dwelling, the savage Celt had neither the incentive nor the opportunity to accumulate more than was necessary for a squalid subsistence from day to day, or, at most, a beggarly account of portable chattels, which might be readily removed on the approach of danger. Wealth was, consequently, a thing unknown among them, and commerce, the great evangelist of civilization, a stranger in their midst. For centuries, they knew of but two methods by which property might be transferred—robbery and barter—approving as well as practicing the principle that—

> "He may take who has the power,
> And he may hold who can."

While of any thing like a standard of value or medium of exchange, they were so utterly ignorant that there was not so much as a word in their language signifying *money*, until they had learned the names, as well as the uses, of current coins from the Anglo-Saxon. And it is a singular fact that, even down to the present generation, many of their descendants seem to have acquired no true conception of the value of a dollar, as we rarely meet with one of them who does not appear to think it is worth about five times as much as it really is.

To such apparently inauspicious surroundings, however, may be plainly traced the development of those peculiar characteristics which have distinguished the Scottish race from all other people, and which, though modified in many respects by the intermingling of other blood, as well as by a more enlightened intelligence and a broader civilization, are still discernible, to a greater or less degree, in their descendants of the present day.

The constant exposure of the hardy Gael to privation and peril of every description, naturally tended to develop his physical courage to the highest pitch of savage heroism, as well as the habit of self-reliance, under the most trying exigencies, whether in the chase, amid the dangers of his native solitudes, or steel to steel with his dearest foe upon the battle-field. These as naturally inspired him with a confident pride in his own manhood, and an indomitable spirit of personal independence, which impelled him to the instant resistance of any encroachment upon his individual rights, and rendered him peculiarly impatient of all governmental restraint imposed upon him without his own consent. *Nemo me impune lacessit*, became the controlling sentiment of his being, and the guiding principle of his conduct, as it has since become, with singular propriety, the motto on his national coat-of-arms. While he may have been taught that royalty was hereditary in the blood, he nevertheless had a vague sort of notion, even in the hazy twilight of barbarism, that the ultimate repository of political power was in the people, as is clearly evident in the ancient Celtic custom of meeting in popular assembly upon the death of the ruler and electing his successor from among his sons, or some collateral branch of his family, as the public interest might seem to require.

As the legitimate outgrowth of these strongly developed traits, we find that there has always been less respect for self-assumed authority, and, consequently, more frequent rebellion against the hereditary claims of kingly power among the Scotch, than any other people on the face of the globe, as well as the still more striking fact that throughout their hundreds and hundreds of years of sanguinary warfare, they were never completely conquered. A clan might be exterminated, but it fought until the stiffening hand of its last expiring warrior was not able to strike for freedom or revenge. Overrun they might be, as they often were by the superior force of an invading foe, but upon the slightest removal of the immediate pressure, they were in arms again, reasserting their wild traditional liberties.

But the same causes which made them brave and self-reliant, also made them cautious, cunning, suspicious, and selfish, while the cruelties they so often suffered themselves, not only rendered them indifferent to the sufferings of others, with whom they had no connection by blood or affinity, but stimulated a disposition to revenge which frequently manifested itself in acts of the most cold-blooded and brutal atrocity. Nevertheless they were human, and felt the same yearning for society and sympathy, which universally pervades the human breast, however savage or depraved.

For the gratification of that sentiment, whether influenced by their own inclination or not, they were compelled by the circumstances surrounding them to resort mainly to their own hearthstones. There the mother and children, under an ever-present sense of their dependence upon his protection and counsel, gathered around the husband and father, as their hero and their oracle, with mingled emotions of love, gratitude, veneration, and pride; while he, in return, regarded the protegés of his prowess with those feelings of tenderness natural to the sacred relation he sustained toward them, deepened and intensified by a realization of their absolute dependence upon his strength and their confidence in his courage.

The strong feeling of domestic affection thus naturally engendered, strengthened by time and the constant necessity of mutual assistance, ripened, at length, into a degree of filial and fraternal attachment rarely witnessed outside of the ancient Gaelic household. Cherished by each member of the family through life, and sedulously inculcated around the fireside of each offshoot from the parent stem, to be again transmitted under similar surroundings to a still remoter generation, these ties of consanguinity eventually became the common bond of the clan, whose chieftain exercised his prerogatives by common consent, as the lineal representative of the original stock, or was chosen, if occasion required, from the worthiest of their blood.

In the light of such circumstances, it is easy to see how that peculiar sentiment of clannishness, which bound the ancient Celt to his kindred of the remotest degree, and which has brought us together to-day, became hereditary in our blood. Nor is it more difficult for us to explain that apparent paradox in the character of our earlier ancestry, namely, the passionate fealty of the clansman who esteemed it a privilege to die for his chief, while his lax allegiance to royalty suggested nothing improper in the murder of his king. His chieftain was of his own tribe and kindred, bone of his bone and flesh of his flesh; the embodiment of the dignity of his family, and the defender of its honor; the cheerful companion of his hardships, and the grateful partaker of his humble hospitality; the friend whose dirk was at his service in his private feud, and the leader whose flashing claymore was his beacon in the red storm of battle—ever first at the rendezvous and the foremost in the foray.

The king, on the other hand, was frequently a stranger to his blood, the descendant, perhaps, of some hereditary foe to his house, claiming authority over him without his consent, and by a title contrary to the traditions of his race or repugnant to his own sense of right. He consequently entertained a much higher regard for the sovereign of any other nation, who would let him alone, than for the ruling monarch of his own, whose reign was generally turbulent and disastrous, frequently terminating in the tragic death of the prince himself at the hands of his rebellious subjects. It has been indignantly asserted, indeed, by an English writer, though with evident exaggeration, that the Scotch had barbarously murdered forty of their kings, while half as many more had made away with themselves to escape the pains of torture or perished miserably in strait imprisonment. But however that may have been, it is quite safe to assert that, whenever they espoused the cause of one of their princes, a large majority of his followers were generally influenced by other motives than loyalty to his person or partiality to his government.

When, by whom, or in what manner, feudalism, with its various ranks of nobility, was introduced among the Scottish people, is a matter about which there has been considerable controversy among historians, but the weight of authority seems to support the opinion that it was inaugurated in the latter part of the eleventh century by Malcolm Canmore, when, with the aid of Edward the Confessor, he recovered the scepter of his father—immortalized as "the gracious Duncan" in the sublimest pages of dramatic literature—and extended from time to time by his successors, as opportunity presented, until it became finally established throughout the entire kingdom. But whatever may be the facts in that regard, it is quite certain that, while the introduction of the feudal system produced many and marked changes in the political constitution of Scotland, the power exercised by the nobility in the administration of public affairs was never due so much to their legal rank as to the influence of the strong feeling of clannishness among the masses of the people with whom they were immediately connected by the ties of blood or marriage, and which, from repeated inculcation and long heredity, had become inherent in their very natures.

But while their politics—if we except their unvarying fidelity to the leader of the clan—seems to have set as loosely upon them as their tartan plaids, their religion appears to have been ingrained with every fiber and tissue of their being; and their singular veneration for ecclesiastical authority, when compared with their lack of reverence for political power, especially when disassociated from the ever dominant influence of the family tie, has frequently been regarded as a striking inconsistency in their character. A little reflection, however, should satisfy us that an inconsistency in national characteristics is, in the very nature of things, an impossibility; and it is by no means difficult to see how this peculiarity sprung naturally from the same surroundings which developed the traits I have already mentioned.

Compelled by the necessities of their condition to be much alone amid the solitudes of their native hills, where the dark and lonely dells around them, and the craggy cliffs towering away into the far blue lift above them, with their fantastic shadows mirrored in the deep, still tarn below them, constantly conspired to incite in them the profoundest feelings of superstitious awe; their rude imaginations became impressed by the viewless presence of a vast, invisible, intangible, mysterious being, whose character they invested with the same savage attributes as their own. They saw his terrible chariot in the black mass of whirling clouds, and heard his angry voice in the roaring storm. They caught the gleam of his vengeful weapon in the lightning's bolt that shivered the gnarled oak, and saw the outpouring of his omnipotent rage in the rushing torrent that dashed the granite buttress of the mountain from its base; and when the wintry night wind shrieked its wailing dirge around their lonely hovels, they told their children, in the subdued tones of ignorant awe, of his wrath which they could not appease, and his power which they could not withstand. It is not at all wonderful, therefore, that when St. Columba came to them with the priceless truths of Christianity, they should hail him with joy as the messenger of peace from their fierce, mysterious deity, nor that they should seize with savage avidity upon the promises of the Gospel, while understanding little or nothing of its doctrines.

Nor is it any more remarkable that the Culdees, who embraced the earliest ecclesiastics among the converts of St. Columba, speedily spread throughout the whole of Caledonia, where they maintained an unquestioned supremacy in all matters of religious faith and practice, and, perhaps, preserved many of the traditionary customs and articles of belief common to an earlier period of the Roman Church until centuries later, when they were reformed or suppressed in a more advanced state of civil and ecclesiastical government. For it should be observed that these rude ministers of religion were not a body of foreign clergy thrust upon the people against their will and contrary to their prejudices, but were of their own kith and kin, often as actively engaged in the secular affairs of the clan as in the offices of their more sacred calling, the functions of chieftain and abbot of a monastery being not infrequently united in the same person.

Described as a kind of presbyters, who lived in small communities, elected and ordained their own rectors or bishops, and traveled over the adjacent country preaching and administering the sacraments of their religion, some claim to have discovered in their crude system of ecclesiastic polity the protoplasm from which the Presbyterian Church of Scotland was ultimately evolved. But be that as it may, being educated at home, understanding no language but their own, and having but a limited intercourse with other nations, they retained not only the traits and prejudices peculiar to their own race, but much of the plainness and simplicity of the primitive ages in their forms of worship, mingled, no doubt, with much of their former superstitions. They consequently obtained an unbounded influence over the minds of their savage parishioners, who were not only bound to them by the ties of blood and familiar association, but who confidently expected, through their ministration, to secure the never-ending pleasures of a blissful paradise, from which their less deserving enemies would, fortunately, be forever excluded.

It should be carefully borne in mind, however, that the race to which the later ancestry of many of us belonged was a composite one—a race in which the blood of the rude Caledonian was mingled with that of the sturdy Saxon and the turbulent Norman. Early in the seventh century, the Northumbrians, under King Edwin, pushed their conquests on Scottish soil to the estuary of the Forth, where they erected the fortress which gave its name to the present metropolis of North Britain; but in consequence of their disastrous defeat at Dun-Nechtan, sixty-eight years later, the dominion of the invaders shrank again within the waters of the Tweed, never to be re-asserted beyond its northern bank. Nevertheless, the lost territory continued to be occupied by its Anglo-Saxon population, which was subsequently augmented from time to time by slight accessions from Northumberland and its adjacent counties in the north of England, whose inhabitants, from somewhat similar circumstances, had acquired many of the moral traits and social customs of their more northern neighbors. In addition to this, the tide of immigration which followed the marriage of Malcolm Canmore with the Saxon Princess Margaret, and continued with increasing activity through the succeeding reigns of their sons, Edgar, Alexander, and David, not only changed the civil and ecclesiastical institutions of Scotland, but carried with it, among thousands of lesser note, the founders of many of those illustrious houses which have figured so conspicuously in its subsequent annals.

It must not be supposed, however, that the hereditary peculiarities of the original Celt disappeared with his traditionary customs, upon the introduction of Anglo-Norman jurisprudence, with its accompanying civilization, from the South. On the contrary, until the twelfth century, the only language spoken north of the two friths was the ancient Gaelic, while throughout the Lothians and the districts further south, it was heard as frequently as the Anglo-Saxon; and as a large majority of the immigrants were mere military adventurers employed in the service of the Scottish kings, they no doubt intermarried with the daughters of the land, as the soldiers of Cromwell afterward did in Ireland. Thus the blood of the Sassenach, in process of time, became largely transfused with that of their Celtic predecessors, transmitting the leading characteristics of each of the confluent races, mutually modified by each other, as an inheritance to the common posterity of both.

Consequently, he who chooses to thread the intricate mazes of their history back to the period when that transfusion became general, will invariably find in the mixed race of Middle and Southern Scotland, side by side with the rugged common sense, plainness of speech, frugality, and thrift of the Anglo-Saxon, and the aggressive self-assertion of the imperious Norman, the predominant traits of their Caledonian ancestry centuries before; the same impetuous courage, often amounting to an utter recklessness of personal peril; the same self-appreciation, impelling them to resent the slightest aggression upon their private concerns; the same relentless disposition, frequently exhibiting itself in acts of remorseless cruelty or implacable revenge; the same impatience of all restraint inconsistent with their own sense of right, drawing them into repeated and bloody rebellion; the same romantic reverence for the family tie, influencing, to a greater or less degree, all their relations to church or state; the same stubborn adhesion to a religion, whether under prelatic or Presbyterian auspices, recognizing the immediate interposition of an omnipotent providence in all their temporal concerns, and frequently inspired more by a dread of his vengeance than an appreciation of his mercies, and the same unquestioning confidence in the guidance of their spiritual leaders, especially when bound to them by the ties of kindred.

The thoughtful student will observe, moreover, that in the great revolt against the parent church, in the sixteenth century, the overthrow of its supremacy among such a people could lead to but one result, so far as their ecclesiastical relations were concerned, and that was the ultimate establishment of precisely such a system of church polity as took place upon the triumph of the Reformation in Scotland. How much the lust of power and the jealousies of ambition may have had to do in bringing about that result, it is needless now to inquire. Without pausing, therefore, to consider the intricate and controverted details of that long and angry contest between the crown, assisted by the magnates of the established church on the one side, and the nobility, aided by the spirit of clanship which pervaded their multitudes of retainers, and the active influence of numbers of the native clergy, who felt the same potent spell of family names and associations, on the other, which culminated in the downfall of the papal hierarchy in Scotland, it is sufficient to say that, when the moment for the final catastrophe arrived, the man for the hour had also come; one who, with a single blow of his stalwart arm, hurled the venerable but tottering fabric from its base, and proceeded at once to rear upon its ruins a superstructure better suited to the genius of his race.

That man, I scarcely need say, was Knox—the living, breathing incarnation of the highest virtues of his people, though not wholly exempt from many of their no less striking vices. Familiar with all their peculiar characteristics, passionately devoted to their interests and their honor, the impersonation of a lofty and intrepid zeal, tempered by a deliberate and self-reliant judgment, with a commanding intellect, profoundly versed in all the learning of the age and thoroughly in sympathy with its quickening progress, inspired by an ardent love of religious freedom, and burning with a bitter scorn for all forms of self-assumed authority, he seemed almost to have been specially designed for the great work of ecclesiastical reconstruction of which he was, by common consent, the acknowledged architect.

Detesting prelacy and papacy alike, he conceived a scheme somewhat after the design of Calvin, with whose views he was deeply imbued, which, though not fully executed in his lifetime, resulted in the development of a system of church government based upon the fundamental principles of representative democracy—a system in which no minister or other ecclesiastical functionary could be foisted upon a congregation without its own consent, nor its humblest member be deprived of any right within the cognizance of the church, without the privilege of appealing to the highest tribunal known to its jurisdiction, a tribunal composed, like the lowest court in the system, of representatives chosen by the free suffrages of the people constituting the congregations respectively. In short, a popular government in ecclesiastical affairs, in which the will of the majority, regularly expressed through its legally constituted agencies, was the supreme controlling power.

I will not pretend to say that the people, under this form of church government, were more pious or orderly in their daily walk, or that their ministers were any more correct in their religious teaching, or more faithful in their sacred calling, than they had been under the system which they had just demolished; but it can be safely asserted that its effects upon the destinies of the English speaking people, if not ultimately upon those of the general mass of mankind, are beyond the possibility of adequate conception.

We may admit, if you please, that its laity for generations were left to grovel in the lowest depths of ignorance, superstition and vice, while its clergy were narrow-minded, grasping, tyrannical, insolent, intolerant and cruel. We may concede all that its most malignant enemy has said in denunciation of the Presbyterian Church of Scotland for more than a century after its establishment, and even agree that the colors in which the repulsive picture has been drawn should have been ten-fold darker. Yet its influence in promoting the spirit of democracy, which lingered in the Scottish heart from the rudest ages of its savage independence, will entitle it to the highest meed of gratitude and admiration as long as human liberty has a votary among men. We not only find in it the germ of our own free institutions and the original type of our own magnificent form of civil government, but the sacred flame from which the beacon fires of freedom have been kindled every-where. It spurned with bitter contempt the impious pretensions of princes, and taught the true dignity of man. Its very existence was a perpetual rebuke to every claim of hereditary power, and a constant illustration of the great truth that men are capable of governing themselves. The choice of its official agencies by the free suffrage of the congregation was a practical assertion of the vital principle underlying all republican institutions, that "governments derive their just powers from the consent of the governed," while its presbyteries and assemblies demonstrated the fact that the will of popular majorities can be conveniently and safely exercised through their own chosen representatives.

But if mankind is thus deeply indebted to the mere passive example of the Scottish church, how much more is due to the intrepid zeal and tireless vigilance of its clergymen in the darkest period of its history. To show this, I have but to use the words of a distinguished English writer, who delighted to excoriate their faults with the burning lash of indignant denunciation: "Much they did to excite our strongest aversion; but one thing they achieved which should make us honor their memory and repute them the benefactors of their species. At a most hazardous moment they kept alive the spirit of national liberty. What the nobles and the crown had put in peril, that did the clergy save. By their care the dying spark was kindled into a blaze. When the light grew dim and flickered on the altar, their hands trimmed the lamp and fed the sacred flame. This is their real glory, and on this they may well repose. They were the guardians of Scotch freedom, and they stood to their posts. Where danger was they were foremost. By their sermons, by their conduct, both public and private, by the proceedings of their assemblies, by their bold and frequent attacks upon persons, without regard to their rank, nay, even by the very insolence with which they treated their superiors, they stirred up the minds of men, woke them from their lethargy, formed them to habits of discussion, and excited that inquisitive and democratic spirit which is the only effectual guaranty the people can possess against the tyranny of those who are set over them. This was the work of the Scotch clergy, and all hail to them who did it. It was they who taught their countrymen to scrutinize with a fearless eye the policy of their rulers. It was they who pointed the finger of scorn at kings and nobles, and laid bare the hollowness of their pretensions. They ridiculed their claims and jeered at their mysteries. They tore the veil and exposed the tricks of the scene which lay behind. The great ones of the earth they covered with contempt, and those who were above them they cast down. Herein they did a deed which should compensate for all their offenses, even were their offenses ten times as great. By discountenancing that pernicious and degrading respect which men are apt to pay to those whom accident, and not merit, has raised above them, they facilitated the growth of a proud and sturdy independence, which was sure to do good service at a time of need."

The seeds thus sown from the pulpits and assemblies of the Scotch church in the latter part of the sixteenth century not only produced an ample harvest from the rugged but congenial soil upon which they fell, but were cherished in the bosoms of the Scottish people, who carried them to other lands, where they brought forth abundant fruits, to the dismay and ultimate overthrow of those who threatened their liberties.

Soon after his accession to the English crown, King James I., true to the instincts of the most perfidious family that ever disgraced the throne of a civilized people, having secured the flight and outlawry of the earls of Tyrone and Tyrconnel upon a cunningly devised pretext of some treasonable conspiracy between them, seized upon their vast estates, comprising nearly eight hundred thousand acres in the fertile province of Ulster, in the north of Ireland, upon which he commenced the plantation of a Scotch and English colony in the year 1609.

The fertility of the soil, the favorable terms upon which it was proposed to be let to immigrants, and the advantages offered to them by a variety of other circumstances, soon lured a number of his countrymen to this promising plantation, whither they were followed from time to time by others of their kindred until they became eventually the predominant element throughout the province. Thus were the descendants of the ancient Scots brought back to the identical scenes from which their savage ancestry had emigrated nearly two thousand years before; and thus originated the name Scotch-Irish.

But notwithstanding the suffix to their national patronymic, the irreconcilable difference in religion between them and the native inhabitants, together with other prejudices naturally resulting from their peculiar relations to each other, presented such an obstacle in the way of a coalition of the two races that the colonists and their descendants for generations, if, indeed, they have not to the present time, remained thoroughly Scotch in all their leading characteristics. They carried with them to their new homes not only the personal traits peculiar to their race, but its political and religious prejudices as well as its ecclesiastical polity. They built their churches, organized their presbyteries, established their schools, and pursued their respective callings with a thrifty industry which soon transformed the province of Ulster from the wildest and most disorderly to the best cultivated and most prosperous portion of Ireland.

It must not be supposed, however, that they were permitted to enjoy any very protracted period of repose during the century and a half immediately following their advent into Ulster. Whether the enforced flight of Tyrone and Tyrconnel, and the subsequent confiscation of their estates were justifiable or not, such circumstances were naturally calculated to incite the deepest indignation of their neighbors, retainers, kindred, and friends, even granting them to have been less passionate and turbulent than we have reason to believe they were at that period of Irish civilization. We, ourselves, with all our moral culture and Christian refinement, could but feel an insuperable repugnance to a colony of strangers, differing from us in politics and religion, thrust by the government into our midst against our wills, and placed in possession of the property of our leading citizens, forced to flee from their homes to save their lives, upon a charge which we believe to be not only unjust, but unfounded. It is not surprising, therefore, that the animosity of the native inhabitants toward their new neighbors should manifest itself in repeated and bloody deeds of violence.

But little more than five years had elapsed, indeed, before a conspiracy was detected, which is said to have had for its object the seizure of the British fortresses and the extirpation of the foreign settlers in the province. And in less than three decades later, the jealousies and enmities growing out of the plantation of the colony showed themselves in one of the most sanguinary tragedies that ever stained the annals of a civilized land, in which the Scots in Ulster were treated with the most diabolical cruelty, which, in turn, was retaliated by a fearful and ferocious revenge.

They fared but little worse, if any, at the hands of their hostile neighbors, however, than at those of the government, under whose patronage they had settled in their new homes. Presbyterian and Papist alike were disfranchised by its infamous test oaths, which neither could conscientiously take, and both were punished with the same relentless rigor for non-conformity. Their houses of worship were repeatedly closed, their congregations dispersed, their members persecuted, and the people, irrespective of age or sex, tendered an oath repugnant alike to their judgments and their consciences. Yet the young and more intrepid leaders of the Scottish church assembled their flocks at noon-day in the open fields, and in secluded chambers in the small hours of the night, in vast crowds, and in little groups, every-where denouncing the tyranny under which they languished, and exciting their hearers to a more enthusiastic pitch of sectarian zeal. It is true, there were periods in which, by special indulgence or through official indifference, they were permitted to worship in their own chosen way; yet it is easy to see how even an occasional interference with that cherished privilege increased their attachment to their church, while it fed their hereditary hatred to the English crown, and made them hail with supreme satisfaction the downfall of the detestable dynasty of the Stuarts.

Among the scenes which closed the ignoble career of the last of that disreputable house, there was one which not only exhibited the leading traits of the Scotch-Irish character in the strongest possible light, but which will challenge the admiration of mankind as long as our language shall be spoken, or the memory of heroic deeds cherished among the children of men. On the second day after his arrival in the city of Dublin, with a body of foreign mercenaries at his heels, the cowardly fugitive from the British throne signalized his return to the territory of his lost dominion by issuing a proclamation to his former subjects of the Catholic faith, gratefully acknowledging their vigilance and fidelity, and enjoining such of them as had not already taken up arms in his service, to hold them in readiness until it should be found necessary to use them to his advantage, and by conferring the ducal rank upon Tyrconnel, who had disarmed the Protestants throughout a large portion of Ireland, and assembled an army of thirty thousand foot and eight thousand horse for the assistance of his fallen master.

These, with other circumstances, gave rise to wild and exciting rumors, which rapidly spread throughout the province of Ulster, to the effect that it was the intention of the desperate Stuart to extirpate the Protestant religion, and re-establish the authority of the Roman church by fire and sword. The effect, especially among the Scottish population, may be easily imagined. Their ministers were every-where heard exhorting the people, in words of rude but burning eloquence, to arise in defense of their faith and their firesides; while their women adjured them, by all the sacred associations of the family tie, to defend themselves and their homes with the last drop of their blood.

The grim courage and determined self-reliance of their race were thoroughly aroused, their religious enthusiasm excited, and their undying animosity to papal power inflamed to the highest pitch of frenzy. Betrayed by their governor, abandoned by the commanders of the small force which had been sent by the government for their protection, with no military experience themselves, and but a limited supply of the munitions of war, they improvised an army of seven thousand men, with one of their preachers, assisted by a couple of faithful and courageous officers of the king's service, at its head, and hastily entrenched themselves behind the fortifications of Londonderry, where, for one hundred and five days, they withstood a siege in which they exhibited a sublimity of courage and fortitude without a parallel in human history since the fall of Jerusalem before the conquering arms of Titus Vespasian.

After more than three months of continuous battle, aggravated by the horrors of disease and famine, during which their heroic women, often with weapons in their hands, stood side by side with their brave defenders in every scene of danger and distress, the memorable contest around the walls of Londonderry was brought to a close with eight thousand of its besiegers slain and more than half its devoted garrison in their graves. But George Walker, the faithful pastor of Donaghmore, whose pious eloquence inspired the spiritual fervor of his brethren from the pulpit, and whose genius and courage directed their perilous duties on the ramparts and in the sortie, survived the siege, and, bidding adieu to the shattered fragment of his command, now worn by disease and wasted by famine, followed the fortunes of William of Orange to the bloody banks of the Boyne, where he fell, side by side with the Duke of Schomberg and Caillemote, the heroic Huguenot.

But the Scottish Presbyterians, whose deeds in the heroic defense of Londonderry resemble more the fabled exploits of Homeric fiction than the transactions of modern warfare, fared but little better at the hands of the new government than the Irish Catholics who besieged it. So far from having any of the restrictions upon their freedom of religion removed, they were left almost as completely under the ban of those fatuous and despotic enactments in derogation of religious liberty, which so long disgraced the jurisprudence of Great Britain, as their neighbors of the Roman faith, who had been so recently in rebellion against the crown. They still remained under the denunciation of the penal laws against non-conformity, without even a legal toleration, until 1720, while they were excluded from all offices of honor, profit, or trust under the government, by the rigorous requirements of the oath of supremacy, and the still more obnoxious provisions of the Test Act, until 1780.

In addition to these irritating circumstances, they were subjected to a variety of vexatious burdens, which influenced large numbers of them to quit the province of Ulster, and seek more peaceful and propitious homes in the colonies of America, whither they brought with them an undying hatred to the British crown, and a burning desire for some suitable opportunity for its gratification. That opportunity was soon presented, and if any of them failed to avail himself of it with promptness and pleasure, it was not from any lack of inclination, but because he was prevented by circumstances beyond his control.

They came often in groups of families, neighbors, perhaps, in the homes they had left in Ulster, and located themselves, generally, in the colonies of Pennsylvania, Virginia, and the Carolinas, where, as their fathers had done in Ireland, they organized their congregations, set up their neighborhood schools, and by a sedulous attention to their own affairs, set an example of industry, economy and morality, the influence of which is still visible in the intelligence, thrift, refinement and orderly deportment which distinguish the communities in which they settled.

The part played by this remarkable race in preparing the popular mind of their adopted country for independence, as well as in the bloody contest which terminated in that glorious result, it would be difficult, if not impossible, to overestimate. Whether the Mecklenburg declaration was really the work of Ephraim Brevard and his associates, or only the clever after thought of some obscure person whose name history has failed to record, it embodied the cherished sentiments of every genuine Scotch-Irishman in America. The tide of immigration which brought them to our shores set in near the beginning of the century, reached its flood near the period when Washington and many of his illustrious compatriots were born, and continued without retiring ebb until the final break between the colonies and the mother country. Wherever they went, they repeated, with feelings of bitter hate, the story of their wrongs, and taught by precept and by example, in season and out of season, the sublime doctrine of civil and religious freedom which had been burned into their very souls by generations of cruelty and oppressions. Wherever they went they transfused the community around them with their own deathless spirit of democracy; and when the tocsin sounded for the mighty struggle, they sprang to the front and offered their blood as a joyous oblation to the God of battles upon the altars of their faith. They craved none of the Dead Sea fruit of a selfish ambition; they sought none of the barren laurels of an empty fame. They were plain, earnest, determined men, who wanted results—results which would secure to their children and their children's children, the priceless patrimony of freedom—and for that they rushed to the fiery front of battle, reckless as to who might lead them so he led to victory or to death.

Would you know their names? In every walk of private usefulness and public honor; in every avenue of active enterprise and popular progress; in every department of literature, and in every branch of science; in every theater of honorable ambition; in the pulpit and at the bar; on the field and in the cabinet, on the bench and in the halls of legislation; in the chambers of our highest courts, and in the presidential chair, they and their sons have written them in imperishable characters upon the brightest pages of our country's history. Go read them there.

The children of the race are now scattered throughout all this broad continent, mingling like drops of water in the mighty ocean, with a vast and wondrous people gathered from many lands; but wherever they may be, they and their descendants will cherish with affectionate veneration the honor of their ancient sires, and keep the sacred fires of family love brightly burning on their domestic altars as long as a drop of the old Scotch-Irish blood shall trickle through their veins; and should the grasping hand of consolidated wealth, the wild fury of communism, or the insolence of foreign power ever menace the fair fabric of constitutional liberty erected by their fathers, they will rush to its defense, with the same intrepid devotion with which their rude ancestors followed the slogan of the clan.

WHAT THE SCOTCH-IRISH HAVE DONE FOR EDUCATION.

BY G. MACLOSKIE, D.SC., LL D., PROFESSOR OF BIOLOGY IN PRINCETON COLLEGE.

The close alliance of Scotland and Ireland dates from the time of St. Patrick, who died in A. D. 465. He appears to have been educated in the southern part of Scotland, and he preached the Gospel and established religious houses in Ireland. His monasteries were not the homes of lazy monks, but seats of learning and centers of missionary effort. They resembled the schools of the prophets of the Old Testament, and were repeated in the last century in the log colleges of America. The early Irish monks, many of them married men, were zealous students and copyists of Scripture, and enthusiastic itinerant preachers. An old tradition says that one of them, St. Brendin, discovered the new world, and, after returning to Ireland to report his discovery, he set sail a second time (in the year 545), to preach the Gospel to the natives of the newly discovered land. He was never heard of again, but his name is immortalized by a bay on the west of Ireland, from which he is said to have sailed. Another tradition associates colonists from the north of Ireland with Scandinavians as the first settlers of Iceland, which became a home of learning.

Two men from Ulster, both bearing the name of Columba, became missionaries of learning and religion, one in the Highlands of Scotland, the other in continental Europe. One of them Columba, or Columbkille, from County Donegal, in west Ulster, established the religious house at Iona, an island west of Scotland, and himself and his disciples carried the Gospel over Scotland and into the north of England. Hence arose the Culdees, or worshipers of God, who cherished the Gospel in the homes of Scotland even in the dark ages; and their descendants quickly responded to John Knox when, at a later age, like Columbkille resurrected, he preached Christ to his beloved Scotland. Lindisfarne, in the north of England, was a fruit of the work of the Culdees; and it has been lately found that the Lindisfarne Illuminated Gospel, kept in the British Museum, and long supposed to be a gem of Anglo-Saxon learning, is an Irish work, probably penned by some English student in one of the celebrated Irish schools.

The other Columba came from a school in County Down, on the

eastern coast of Ulster, and went as a missionary to Eastern France and Switzerland, where he is better known by the name of Columbanus. His biography has been recently discovered in the civic archives of Schaffhausen, in Switzerland, written in the pure ancient Celtic language, and has given an impetus to the study of that language. One of the cantons of Switzerland commemorates by its name (St. Gallen, *Irish county*) these old Irish missionaries, members of the genuine Clan-na-Gael. Boniface, the apostle of Germany (A. D. 738), belonged to them; and he and other Scotch-Irish missionaries established religious houses, among them the monastery of Erfurt, where Luther, at a later date, found the Reformation in a Latin Testament. Thus, by easy steps, we go from St. Patrick to Iona and the Culdees and Knox in Scotland, and to Switzerland, with its Zwingle and Geneva, and to Germany and Luther. Germany, which now leads the world in scholarship, was content to receive its first schools from humble Scotch-Irish itinerants.

The quality of the teaching of those times may be estimated from the Confession of St. Patrick, from the love generally shown for the Scriptures, and from the Commentary on Scripture of Sedulius, abbot of Kildare, in Ireland, ninth century. Pure Gospel is found in these writings, without any hint of a pope, and Sedulius praises Paul for his censure of Peter, and gives an evangelical interpretation of the Lord's Supper. A traveling Irish-Scot, named Ferghil (or Virgil) taught that the world is globular, and that the further side is probably inhabited. He was summoned before the pope for such teaching, but escaped the fate of heretics. Johannes Scotus Erigena (which name may be interpreted as Scotch-Irish John) gave the celebrated repartee to Charles the Bald, who asked him across the table, "John, what is the difference between a Scot and a sot?" and was promptly answered, "Nothing whatever, please your majesty, except the table."

Another tradition awards to St. Comgall's school, at Bangor, in County Down, the *alma mater* of Columbanus, the additional honor of supplying Alfred the Great with the first batch of professors for Oxford University, in England, as, at a later date, Scotland gave its first professors to Dublin University, in Ireland, and as many of our American colleges have been started by Scotch-Irish ministers.

The twelfth century brought in the age of darkness to Ireland. In 1110, the Irish Synod of Rathbreasil sold their religious independence to an Italian pontiff, and, within the same century, the Italian pontiff bargained away its civil independence to a dissolute English monarch, in return for a promise of payment of Peter's pence. Thus a double servitude, both spiritual and temporal, was imposed on the country, the ecclesiastical and civil potentates sometimes quarreling, sometimes courting each other, but always oppressing the people. In 1315, Edward Bruce, the brother of Scotland's hero, endeavored to free Ireland from the English; but the church excommunicated him, and he lost his life in the struggle. During the dark ages, schools disappeared from Ireland, and the only men who perpetuated its reputation for learning were such as spent their days abroad at the courts of European monarchs. Ireland then became a good country to leave. So low had it sunk, that the Reformation, which stirred other nations, was scarcely felt there. Even the Bible had become forgotten; yet, when the Roman Catholic Archbishop of York presented two fine copies of the Scriptures to the two cathedrals of Dublin, the people welcomed the gifts and eagerly studied the books.

The Reformation in Scotland was the outcome chiefly of university scholarship. Men with the training and spirit of Columbkille—such men as Patrick Hamilton, George Wishart, John Knox, and Andrew Melville—revived the times of the Culdees, and Scotland, the poorest of the nations, soon took a leading position for scholarship and piety.

Early in the seventeenth century, the north of Ireland was vacated by turbulent chiefs, and Scotchmen were invited to enter and lend a helping hand in its civilization. That was an age of religious persecution, even among Protestants. It was the time at which pious Non-conformists were driven from England, first to Holland, and afterward, in the Mayflower, to America, in quest of liberty to pray to God. At first, the king of England encouraged Scots to migrate to Ireland with a prospect of religious liberty. This "plantation of Ulster" was the counterpart, in some measure, of the emigration of the Pilgrim Fathers; but the Scotch took nearly a century in moving from Scotland by way of Ireland to America, and they had to pass through a hot fire in the transit, and to come out, not as Scots, but as Scotch-Irish, with new experiences and new characteristics.

Though the "plantation of Ulster" by Scotch immigrants was numerically a small affair, only a million of acres being open to colonization, and not half of these falling to the newcomers, yet a complete change of habits and mode of cultivation ensued, and the entire province felt the benefit of the change. The men who came from Scotland were many of them the "floaters," of bad principles and a coarse type, and they intermingled with semi-savage natives. There came over, however, along with them, the religious and educational methods of Scotland. John Knox had established a system of schools, so that every minister had a hand in teaching during some part of his career, and every boy, however poor, had before him the opportunity of gaining education up to his ability. The church and the school went together, as both of the people and for the people. James Melville (nephew of Andrew) informs us that, at one of these schools, in Montrose, Scotland, he was instructed by a Christian minister, who was "a guid, kind, learned man," in the three important subjects of a boy's education, (1) book learning, (2) religion, (3) athletics. He learned Latin and French; also, archery, swimming, fencing, and jumping; and his piety grew with the discipline of the school. In Scotland, this educational system culminated in the great universities, that of Edinburgh being itself a child of the Reformation.

The religious history of Ulster begins with the ministrations of a few immigrant Scottish ministers, some of them men of noble blood, who had to flee from persecution, and who were for a time permitted to occupy the churches in Ulster. In 1636, a great religious awakening took place, which spread among all classes, Roman Catholics as well as Protestants, and transformed the province. There was hope of times of blessing coming to all Ireland, when, as usual, the English government stepped in to interrupt the work by persecuting the ministers and people for non-conformity. What is known in history as the Black Oath was enforced in Ulster, people being fined and imprisoned for failing to swear obedience to the king in all things, and ministers being silenced or banished. Thereafter followed a long series of religious oppressions in Ireland; and these persecutions subsequently followed the Scotch-Irish to America.

The colonization of Ulster from Scotland brought over schools fashioned after the Scottish model, but without the civil encouragement which had been secured by Knox for his people. The Irish schools were private schools, often of an humble character. Those which have persisted even till our memory were conducted by picturesque, poor, but often enthusiastic teachers, who were remunerated by sods of peat, dishes of potatoes, fresh eggs and butter, and occasionally by a fat goose at one of the great festivals. The scholars would go barefoot, with arms out at the elbows, carrying the peat under one arm, and a copy of an old arithmetic or Ovid's Metamorphosis under the other. No Irish colleges welcomed these boys, as the only Irish university, though at first it was started under Scottish teachers, was soon closed against their characteristic faith. The Scotch-Irish lads, after their school training was completed, had to go on foot to the seaside, whence they embarked on a packet for Scotland, and again went afoot in groups to Glasgow or Edinburgh University, whence they were sent back, in the course of a few years, with the university diploma. On returning, they were trained in theology under the supervision of the presbytery. Francis Makemie, the father of American Presbyterianism, gives us an account of his own education in the latter half of the seventeenth century. At a school in County Donegal, he experienced, as he says, "a work of grace and conversion in my heart at fifteen years of age, by and from the pains of a godly schoolmaster, who used no small diligence in gaining tender souls to God's service and fear." His theological training was faithfully superintended by the presbytery, though it was not permitted to hold public meetings, some of its members having been imprisoned and fined for holding a session of presbytery. Soon afterward, Non-conformists were forbidden to teach school. Moreover, the Scottish colonists of Ulster came to experience extortions by landlords, and to be denied the rights of freemen in the country for which they had done so much. In Ireland, as in America, a three-fold struggle for liberty had to be carried on: (1) for liberty to be educated; (2) for religious liberty; (3) for civil liberty.

We will not follow the struggle as it went on in Ulster. Suffice it to say, that the men who saved England by closing the gates of Derry, were robbed of the honor of their services, were afterward declared unfit to hold office in the city which they had defended, or anywhere under the British crown; and laws were passed to destroy their woolen trade, to make their marriages null and their children bastards, and to deprive them of Christian burial; nor were they relieved of their disabilities until the rebellion of the American colonies taught England to deal gently with the oppressed at home. Step by step, Ulster has fought its way to political equality, to protection for its tenant farmers, to religious freedom, and to high educational rank. Belfast, at present, holds the third place in Great Britain as a seaport, being surpassed in the tonnage of its shipping only by London and Liverpool. Ulster is remarkably free from crime, and has few police, as compared with the rest of Ireland, or even England. And men who have gone from Ulster, with the education and principles of the Scotch-Irish, occupy the highest positions as teachers or statesmen in England, India, China, Australia, and America.

The advent of the Scotch-Irish to America dates from the time when oppressions became unbearable at home; especially from the time of James II. It was about 1683 that Francis Makemie arrived, the first Scotch-Irish clergyman whose history is known to us. He was put in jail in New York city for the crime of preaching the gospel in a private house; and he defended the cause of religious liberty with heroic courage and legal ability, being helped by a Scottish lawyer from Philadelphia (who was silenced for his courage), and being ultimately acquitted by a brave New York jury. Thus was begun the great struggle for religious liberty in America.

Some of the immigrants established colonies in New England, as in Massachusetts, New Hampshire and Maine. In 1718 a large company arrived in five ships at Boston, introducing four characteristic Scotch-Irish institutions: (1) potatoes, (2) a spinning-wheel, (3) a school to teach even the Bostonians how to spin, (4) a Presbyterian minister ready at once to form them into an organized church. This last was Rev. John Moorehead, for long time the representative of the cause in Boston. Other churches were established, as at Andover, Londonderry, N. H., and in Maine.

The influx of this class into Pennsylvania soon changed the character of the middle colonies. The governor of Pennsylvania, during fifty years (1699 to 1749), was a Scotch-Irish Quaker, James Logan, a native of county Armagh, Ireland, an able judge, a patron of learning, a friend of the Indians, but not fond of his own countrymen when they were not Quakers. He feared that ere long they would turn matters their own way. "It looks as if Ireland were to send all her inhabitants hither," was his complaint in 1725; "if they will continue to come, they will make themselves proprietors of the province;" and he condemned the bad taste of people who were forcing themselves where their presence was not desired. We may estimate the rate of the invasion from the rise of the population of Pennsylvania from 20,000 in 1701, to 250,000 in 1749. Shortly before the revolutionary war, a new outbreak of oppression in Ireland sent a larger stream, chiefly of farmers and manufacturers. Most of these men were Presbyterians, of a sturdy spirit; they sailed in search of liberty, and they were the earliest and most persevering of our people in our struggle for civil liberty. John Stark, who had fought for England against the French, rushed, when the great struggle came, to fight for America against British tyranny, his pious Irish wife, by her letters, encouraging him in what she said was God's cause. Richard Montgomery, who fell at Quebec, was Scotch-Irish, as was the other Montgomery, who presided over the first meeting of the Scotch-Irish in Cumberland Valley, where resolutions were passed for independence, and money was raised, and a regiment of soldiers soon despatched to aid Washington at Boston. This regiment was under the command of Colonel Chambers, a Scotch-Irish elder. Thomas McKean, another of them, was one of the fourteen of the race who signed the Declaration of Independence, and was governor of Pennsylvania during the great struggle. A Scotch-Irishman wrote, another publicly read, a third first printed the Declaration of Independence. Joseph Reed, son of an Irish father, himself a graduate of Princeton college, was the trusted secretary of Washington, though he died young. It was he that replied to king George's officers: "I am not worth bribing, but such as I am, Britain is not rich enough to buy me." Charles Thomson, from Maghera, Ireland, was then secretary of Congress, "the man of truth;" as the proverb ran, "as true as if Charles Thomson's name were to it." Henry Knox, the Scotch-Irish bookseller of Boston, was Washington's efficient chief of ordnance, from Ticonderoga to Yorktown. The Scotch-Irish of Philadelphia and of Boston, came forward in times of financial embarrassment, to help the popular cause by their contributions. Scotch-Irish pastors were foremost in their patriotism. Rev. John Murray, of Maine, and David Caldwell, of North Carolina, were honored by the British offering rewards for the capture of either of them. Dr. George Duffield, an excellent cross between the Scotch-Irish and the Huguenot; said from the pulpit that he was sorry to see so many able-bodied men at church, when their country needed their services at Valley Forge. In those days it was an offense calling for discipline before the New England and Pennsylvania presbyteries, if a minister did any thing that might excite suspicion of disloyalty to his country's cause.

The military services of the race, at first against the French and Indians, and afterward on behalf of independence against the British, were merely an incident in their history. Their greatest achievements were in peace, with the axe, the plow, and the loom, clearing the forest, subduing the land, and developing mechanical arts and trade. Above all other public institutions, they loved the church and the school. With them religion and education were inseparable; no religion without the training of the intelligence; no education divorced from piety. The school was always planted near the church, the schoolmaster was often the pastor, or a candidate for the ministry, or one of the pillars of the church. An attempt was made, early in the eighteenth century, to exclude non-conformists from the office of teaching; nobody was to teach in New York (at least of the English-speaking people), unless provided with a certificate from the bishop of London. But in Pennsylvania and southward, greater liberty was allowed, at least as to common schools. The present condition of the middle states bears testimony to the use made of this liberty. Whilst New England was colonized by the cream of old England's puritanism, and Pennsylvania only a century later by the outcasts of the poor province of Ulster, yet the progress of the Keystone State may compare with the vaunted achievements of the Plymouth colony.

The man to whom, above all others, our country is indebted for his influence on its education, is the Rev. William Tennent, founder of the log college at Neshaminy, in Bucks county, Pennsylvania. He was a native of county Armagh, Ireland, at first an Episcopalian, probably a graduate of Trinity college, Dublin. His wife, Catherine Kennedy, was the worthy daughter of an Irish Presbyterian minister, who had suffered persecution for his faith. They came to America with their young family, in 1716, and ten years later he was ordained and settled as pastor at Neshaminy. There he started a school which aimed to be a college, in order to prepare young men for the Christian ministry. It seems to have been a hybrid between the hedge schools of Ulster and Dublin university, with poor equipment as to finances or buildings, called in derision a "log college," but claiming to impart sound classical, philosophical, and theological education. This institution was established in order to provide a home supply of ministers, and the men who issued from it were the most zealous and successful that have been given to our country. It was opposed by worthy clergymen, who demanded that all candidates for the ministry should produce a degree from one of the older universities, that is, either from Yale or Harvard, in New England, or from Scotland. But the New England colleges were hostile to evangelical religion. Yale had expelled David Brainerd, really, as was believed, because he attended prayer-meeting, and formally complained because after its censure, this best of missionaries was ordained by a presbytery. It was pronounced in its hostility to revivals of religion. Harvard placed itself on record, by a manifesto signed by its president and professors, against George Whitefield, the gravamen of his sin being that he preached without paper. And Governor Belcher, himself a graduate of Harvard, wrote that Arminianism, Arianism, and Socinianism were being propagated in the New England colleges. Thus the hope of securing a supply of godly ministers from New England was futile. Nor was there any better prospect from abroad. Some good men did come over, as Francis Makemie and William Tennent. But in answer to the entreaties of our presbyteries that the British churches should send them out pastors, most of those who came were "crooked sticks." One was sent back after being convicted of plagiarism, and a complaint was made to the synod of Ulster, for imposing on the Americans by sending bad men. Others were narrow and quarrelsome; not a few were intemperate. The best of the immigrants was a man who had fled from a charge before an Irish presbytery of forging his credentials, who was afterward deposed from the ministry on the same charge by the presbytery of Philadelphia, who went to Maine, where he was irregularly restored to the ministry by a congregation, and who filled a long and devoted ministry, under this charge, which he never dared to meet.

In such circumstances it was suicidal to depend on a foreign supply of ministers, and in fact the Presbyterian churches of New England, by continuing in a dependent condition, prepared the way for their extermination. Nor could the Presbyterians hope for a college of their own; on the contrary, they were informed that no college charter would be granted to dissenters; and it was not till the success of the log colleges was assured, that a charter was given, in an irregular way, to the more moderate section of the denomination, for Princeton college.

The attempt to train young men for the ministry in the Log College, and their ordination without the degree of a chartered university, though sometimes condemned by historians, seems to us to have been the Declaration of Independence by the church for the right to train its own ministry. The charge recently made, that Tennent and his friends took a low view of education for ministers, may be met by the facts that they gave the best education they could command, that so soon as Princeton college was established, they rallied to its support and its further development, and that the alumni of the log colleges were deemed good enough in scholarship to be appointed professors or presidents of the high-class colleges which were at length established. The Log College preachers have also been condemned for venturing to preach within the precincts of ministers who opposed revival methods, but their conduct in this respect would be justified with us, on the ground that ministers may not interpose to prevent the preaching of salvation to sinners, even though the sinners are of their own flocks.

Like the monasteries of St. Patrick, Tennent's Log College became a home of learning and a center of missionary movements. Besides William Tennent, senior, and Mrs. Tennent, it was blessed by worthy disciples, including four sons of its founder. One of these, Gilbert Tennent, may be named along with George Whitefield and (at a later date) Bishop Asbury, as the three men who were, above all others, used of God for the development of spiritual religion in the New World. Besides these, there were Samuel Finlay, Samuel and John Blair, John Robinson, John Rowland, and Charles Beatty. The last named was an Irish peddler, who offered his wares in elegant Latin at the Log College, was invited in, educated, and became a faithful preacher. He was the ancestor of devoted men, the last of whom, Charles Beatty, of Steubenville, O., died a few years ago, after a long service as missionary, educator, and benefactor of the Western Theological Seminary, and of Washington and Jefferson College.

The example of the Tennents was followed by other Scotch-Irish pastors in Pennsylvania, Delaware, and southward. Thus a number of high-class schools were established, bringing education to the doors of the people, independently of government. The office of teacher was not highly esteemed in England (it was apologized for, on behalf of John Eliot, that he was in early life a teacher), but it was always appreciated among the Scotch-Irish; and the teachers often gave their services without pay, so that the poorest boy might be educated up to his capacity. As examples of these institutions, may be named one at Fagg's Manor (New London, Chester county, Pennsylvania), established in 1790 by Samuel Blair, one of Tennent's pupils; subsequently, under Francis Allison, who was encouraged in his work by the Synod. Allison afterward removed to Philadelphia, where he was preacher and teacher, and at length professor, when the University was started. Nottingham Academy, in Maryland, was established by Dr. Samuel Finlay, in 1744, who was descended from John Finlay, one of the early martyrs burnt at the stake in Scotland, and was himself, like nearly all the other founders of these schools, a native of Ireland. This academy of Nottingham produced some of our greatest men, as Governor Martin, of North Carolina, Dr. Benjamin Rush, Colonel Bayard, and preachers Waddell, McWhorter, etc. Pequea School, in Lancaster county, Pennsylvania, was established by Robert Smith, one of Tennent's disciples, himself Irish, and blessed with an Irish wife (who was sister of Robert Blair). His son, Samuel Stanhope Smith, was another great educationist, president of Hampden Sydney, and afterward of Princeton College; remarkable for his services in developing the higher studies in college. His brother, John Blair Smith, was successively president of Hampden Sydney and of Schenectady College. A school was established at Newville, in the Cumberland valley, Pennsylvania, by John Blair, brother of Robert; another at West Canococheague, by John King. Rev. David Caldwell, in North Carolina, had at once an academy, college, and theological seminary, and was also a red-hot patriot. John McMillan went out to the wilds of West Pennsylvania, where he established a church and a log college. Thaddeus Dod followed his example at Red Stone, in South-western Pennsylvania, and John Smith started another school. These western institutions afterward developed into Washington and Jefferson College.

The humble academies gave a completion to our education before we were blessed with colleges, and they prepared the way for chartered institutions, so soon as these could be obtained. Immediately on the establishment of Princeton College, the Tennents gave up their school at Neshaminy, and bestowed all their great influence toward the advancement of the new institution. We find that, in 1748, the roll of trustees of Princeton College included, with others, Gilbert Tennent, William Tennent (the younger, his father having died), Richard Treat, Samuel Blair, all these being pupils of the Log College and earnest preachers; and we find Whitefield, Lady Huntington, and others collecting money for Princeton as a seat of learning and piety. In 1756, the year in which Wesley's friends were banished from Oxford for holding prayer-meetings, Whitefield was invited to preach in Princeton, and he informs us of a revival in which many of the students were converted. Other colleges were soon founded after the same pattern. In this way was evolved our American type of college, as seen especially in our middle and western states, homes of scholarship and religion, independent of state control, yet producing patriotic citizens as well as ardent students and Christian heroes, bringing education near to the people, and raising the poor to a par with the rich in respect of scholarship. We cordially respect the achievements of the great New England colleges, but we plead that, under special disabilities, the Scotch-Irish of the middle states have fought their way to the same results, with the important addition that, with equal zeal for learning, a warmer religious tone has been manifested in its pursuit. Our colleges have received the significant encomium of James Bryce in his "American Commonwealth." He remarks that, in America, we desire to have our business men furnished with college education, and adds that this is a result of the dispersion of colleges, of their accessibility, and the cheapness of education; that nearly all the eminent men of the last forty years, including several Presidents of the United States, have taught school in some part of their earlier years; and that our American universities are at this moment making the swiftest progress and have the brightest promise for the future. This praise comes from a Scotch-Irishman, the first Presbyterian, we believe, who was admitted to the honors of Oxford without selling his conscience, who afterward became a professor in that university, and is now coming to the front as one of England's greatest statesmen.

Such colleges are now rapidly extending over our own land. Even to the golden gate of California, they have been established by Scotch-Irish founders. They are often objects of benevolence with the pious, and themselves nurseries of piety. They are overflowing into other lands: Roberts College, at Constantinople, is giving trouble to Russian as well as Turkish despotism; Beyrout College is becoming the light of Western Asia; and in Pekin, Canton, and Tokio, similar lights appear. The Imperial University of Pekin is now under control of Dr. Martin, one of our American missionaries, with the aid of an international faculty of educators, so that the whole educational system of the empire is being changed. Sir Robert Hart, controller of the customs system of China, is Scotch-Irish, son of a mill-worker in Belfast, and educated under Dr. McCosh; and John McLeavy Brown, his coadjutor, is the same. We hope, ere long, to see another of these colleges in Brazil.

We can not venture into the *personnel* of Scotch-Irish educators and inventors of recent times, as in theology the Alexanders and Hodges; in science, Fulton of the steam-engine, McCormick of the threshing machine, Joseph Henry of the telegraph and electro-magnet. In biology, the chief place in Cambridge, England, and in Johns Hopkins, of America; in political science, the chief place in Princeton College, and in the University of Pennsylvania—are held by the race, as are a host of positions of varying importance over the whole country, such as the superintendents of public schools and many of our most successful workers in the higher schools. The present generation of the race remember their traditions as devotees of learning; lovers of the country that shelters them, and true to their God; and they find in these traditions a stimulus to their enthusiasm. There is a continuity in the record of their history, as there is a community between the kinsmen who are now serving as educators over all the continent. And hereby are we taught not to seek for ourselves phenomenal accumulations of wealth, which can not raise us to a higher plane, but to cultivate the attainments which have already proved a blessing to our race, and which have made them a wholesome factor in human society.

SCOTCH-IRISH CHARACTERISTICS.

BY REV. JOHN HALL, D.D., OF NEW YORK.

My Fellow Citizens, Ladies and Gentlemen: -I can not give expression to the pleasure that I feel in being permitted to come and speak to so many of you, and in the circumstances in which we are gathered together.

I shall explain to you, in a word or two, the purpose that is before my mind. Many months ago, I received a communication from your friends who organized this society, asking me to come and take part in its proceedings. It appeared to me extremely improbable at the time that I could accept the invitation; and I took the liberty of naming an alternate, in the person of Dr. MacIntosh, of Philadelphia. Accordingly, it was arranged that he should come, and, properly speaking, my address will be delivered by Dr. MacIntosh, at such time as the committee may select.

It is said of a countryman of mine who settled in America, that he liked it so well that he resolved to make it his native land. You smile audibly at this statement, but, in point of fact, it is the very thing that Dr. MacIntosh did. He came over to Pennsylvania to be born, then went back to Great Britain to be educated, and finally came back to America, and has done nothing but honor to it ever since. (Applause.)

I do not propose, ladies and gentlemen, to go into the field of history that has been traversed already, and that will be traversed again, with so great ability. It is the story of a marked race. We all know how voluminous the authors of Germany are. One of them proposed to write a history of the world, and he set about the task. He completed three full volumes before he reached the creation. (Laughter.) I do not want to set out on that line, but rather to talk to you, in the simplest and most informal manner, about my observations among the people in the land from which the Scotch-Irish came. I belong to their race. I am of the sixth generation that moved over from Scotland into Ireland. They continued to live upon the same land, and I have the happiness of being the eldest son of the family, and of having the land upon which my ancestors dwelt for the six generations; and if ever you hear any thing spoken in the way of calling out sympathy for the tenants of Ireland, I hope you will extend a part of your sympathy to me, for I belong to that category. It is two and twenty years since I left Ireland and became a resident of these United States. Speaking of this date reminds me of a circumstance that may interest some of you. One of our most prominent ministers, Rev. Dr. Beatty, made a visit to Belfast years ago, and a reception was tendered him and his associates by the town. When he was called upon to speak, as I am doing now, he came upon the platform and said: "It gives me great pleasure to be back here among my people. I left Ulster one hundred and thirty years ago." They opened their eyes widely, for they could not take in the thought that he was one hundred and thirty years old; but he explained that that was the time when his forefathers left the land and came to reside in America. It has been twenty-two years since I left that land, and, though I can say that I have in me the spirit of a true American citizen, I have not lost a particle of the love and affection that I cherish, and will ever cherish, for the people of my own native Ulster. (Applause.)

When I was in Cincinnati, in 1867, being sent over as a delegate to this country to the meeting of the general assembly, I went into a church. A gentleman was sitting by me in the audience, and was volunteering information to me about things that were going on around. My eye rested upon a man in the audience, and I said: "Is his name McKee?" My friend said: "Yes, he is McKee, of Louisville; a famous preacher there, I believe." A day or two afterward, I was introduced to the same gentleman; his face was so like that of the McKees in Ulster that I identified him at once. A few days after our introduction, he told me he came from Ulster, and that he heard there were several persons of his name in the ministry over there. I say to you, as I looked over the faces of the people here yesterday, I could hardly keep the tears from my eyes, as they rested upon so many heads and faces and figures like those with which I had been familiar in Ulster. The changes of a physical kind are far less than one would at first suppose; and I wish for nothing better than that you may keep pure the moral characteristics and the habits of private life that made the Scotch-Irish what, by the grace of God, they have been made.

I will say a few words as to the characteristics of the people as I lived among them. In the first place, I think it is true to say, that they are remarkably industrious as a people, and they succeeded in securing a degree of comfort in their homes, and respectability in dress and appearance, that would hardly be expected from their limited means. I remember that four or five or six acres of land was enough for a family. They raised crops upon it for the support of the family, and by means of weaving at other times, the men and the women were accustomed to supplement the produce of the little farm, and secure a certain degree of independence and respectability. Those industrious traits are propagated still, and I hope they will continue to be. Just as soon as machinery came into use, the people of the north of Ireland availed themselves of it. They adapted themselves to the new conditions and circumstances, and its effect is visible at the present time. The one manufacturing region in Ireland you will find in Ulster. The only thing that has succeeded in money making in the way of manufacturing in the three other provinces are two forms of enterprise known as distilling and brewing; but in Ulster it is the other way. Many people in Ulster feel apprehensive in regard to contemplated legislation, for they say that, if a high rate of taxation should be put upon the provinces, the amount which would fall upon Ulster would be out of proportion to that upon the other provinces, and would tend to embarrass its industries.

We should do the best that we can to propagate these habits of hard working and industry among the people with whom we come in contact. I will mention an incident that occurred in Ulster during the terrible famine in 1844–5–6. Owing to the complete failure of the potato crop in Connaught, the suffering there was very intense. Many contributions from America and elsewhere were sent in. Christian ladies resolved to make the people in Ireland self-sustaining. They corresponded with the people mostly in Ulster, and asked that teachers be sent out to give instruction in sewed muslin work. The result was, that female teachers, mostly the daughters of farmers in Ulster, capable and educated, were sent into Connaught, where the people were starving; and the result was the introduction, not only of a high moral training, but a teaching of industry, and habits of self-support and self-reliance, which is still visible in their condition to this day.

The second thing I have to notice, in connection with these Ulster people, is a certain unwillingness on their part to be the recipients of charity. There were various forms of charity scattered over the country, governmental and ecclesiastical. The Scotch-Irish, as a class, were usually the last to avail themselves of these opportunities. It is a governmental regulation in the old world that in the poorhouses there should be chaplains of the respective denominations. Presbyterian ministers used to smile over the fact that it was difficult to get their people into the poor-house. They had a small constituency in there. For nine years, I was chaplain of the Presbyterian order to the female convict establishment in Dublin, which represented all the female convicts of the country. My salary was not particularly extravagant, but I used to feel compunction in taking it. We had in the establishment seven hundred female convicts. Usually, there would be about sixty-five that were Protestants of any kind, and fifteen of these were as many as usually fell to my lot, although the Protestant people represented a fourth of the population of the country. This unwillingness to be dependent upon charity is characteristic of the people. I am sorry to say, that there are some of my fellow-countrymen who do not inherit this self-respect. I remember a man that, some time ago, made application to me for aid on the ground that he was a Presbyterian "like I was," and therefore thought it best to apply to me. There was a certain brogue in his voice that put me a little in doubt. "Well," I said, "I know nearly every man that is in the congregation I serve, and I don't remember seeing you there." He convicted himself when he said, "Well, I am always there at vespers." The American way of describing it is, that he gave himself away without knowing it.

Let us cultivate in America this proud spirit of self-reliance. Where is there a land with the resources that this country has? I was taken out yesterday eight or nine miles to the old historic church, and as I gazed at the fertile land, the beautiful fields, the growing crops, the magnificent trees, the treasures of the southland, I could not but think what responsibility rests upon the people of these regions; how much God has given them, for which they should magnify, glorify, and honor him!

The third thing I would like to mention in connection with these Scotch-Irish people, is that they are very strict and conscientious in the matter of their religious observances. My memory goes back to the scenes that made the greatest impression upon me, I mean the communion seasons in the country congregations. There was a solemn assemblage of the people on Wednesday or Thursday, when the people were expected to be in church. There was another service on Saturday, the ministers generally getting some of their brethren to assist them in the exercises. The services of the communion Sabbath would last three, four, and five hours, and yet there did not seem to be any weariness on the part of the people.

I remember how, before the elders gave the cup, the people sang:

"I'll of salvation take the cup,
And on God's name will call;
I'll pay my vows now to the Lord
Before His people all."

They would take a seat at the table, then communion services would follow, and thanksgiving would be raised for the blessings they enjoyed, and then the visiting minister would take charge. The impression made by those services I will carry to my dying day, and I could wish nothing better for the Scotch-Irish race than that, reasonably dependent upon new conditions, we should retain the same loyal attachment to God's truth, the same high appreciation of Christian privileges, and the same spirit of consecration to him whom we call the God of our salvation, and before whom we rejoice as the God of our fathers. I remember the first time I was taken to Sunday-school. Two girls, relations of mine, told me that they would call for me. I can remember the picture that was then presented to me. They had on their Sunday dresses, of course, nice, clean, with a pocket handkerchief wrapped reverently around a little Bible, a flower stuck in the end of the Bible. The girls carried this in their hands in a decent, quiet way, and they brought me thus to school. At that time we had no international lesson system, and no modern methods of teaching. We boys, after school, would compare notes and say: "How many chapters did you read? We have read thirteen." The reply would be, "Oh, we did better than that; we read fourteen." The work consisted mainly in the children being grouped together and reading verse after verse. The teacher confined his instruction mainly to correcting errors in pronunciation, and keeping the boys in good order. An immense change has taken place to-day, and you would not find in Christendom better organized Sunday-schools and better teachers than there are in Ulster at the present time. Let us continue the same methods over this land, without partisanship, but in the true spirit of patriotism. You and I will agree in the declaration that if we would have the righteousness that exalteth a nation, and keep away the sin that disgraces a people, we must get the word of the Lord into the hearts of the people, we must educate the conscience and keep it educated, and then men will fear God, and work righteousness.

One other thing characteristic of the people as I knew them: that is, the great interest they felt in education. This is a fruitful theme, but I will not dwell long upon it. I will only mention that for generations, in the province of Ulster, an educated ministry was always sought and obtained; but that these men might be educated had given the greatest trouble and difficulty. No college would admit them. Trinity college was founded upon a broad basis, and the two first fellows were Presbyterians and Scotchmen. But this was taken away, and the boys had then to go to Scotland. They walked fifty or sixty miles with a package on their shoulders. They stopped at the farm-houses, and they never were refused hospitality. They would land at Glasgow and walk to Edinburgh, and accept hospitality from the people. Dr. Henry Cook, one of the greatest men that Ireland ever produced, made his way thus to a Scottish university. The process of conflict, of self-denial, of constrained ingenuity that these young men were compelled to go through in order to obtain an education, made them in a high degree strong men, capable men, business men, effective men in doing the work that was given them as leaders of the people, and instructors in the interests of good. Some of the best instructors that the people call Scotch-Irish were found in the persons of ministers. A minister would set up a classical school to which boys would come to get an education that was necessary to fit them for entering college. Many came who did not want to learn the classics. All paid school fees regularly, and maintained their independence. In this connection I think of the Rev. Mr. Blakely, minister in Monohan, where there are hundreds of men, and not a few upon this continent to-day, who will tell you that they owe every thing in life to the teaching of that faithful minister, who did the duties of his charge at the same time he was giving this instruction. Another specimen was Dr. McKee, a kinsman of the man to whom I have alluded.

It is my misfortune that I am tall. I am a high churchman by nature. I was tall as a boy, but Mr. McKee was taller, six feet, seven, and perfectly straight. I remember to-day with pride that he laid his hand upon my head and gave me a pleasant word. I was a student then, but I never forgot it. He had a fine school and a large congregation. He was a farmer, and managed his farm with skill and ability. He had a good horse, and like Mr. Bonner here, he was very proud of horses, but he never touched any thing like betting or gambling on races. He was driving through his parish one afternoon on one of his extremely good horses. It was a day like this, with a strong sun. There was a poor man working in a field by the roadside, with his coat off, and his shirt badly torn. The consequence was that the sun had reddened that portion of his skin which was exposed, as if it would blister it. McKee looked at the man and pitied him. He dismounted, and having long legs, stepped over the fence. "My friend, come here," and McKee took off his waistcoat and shirt, and made the man put on the shirt, and then buttoning up the coat, said, "Nobody will miss my shirt before I get home," and he left it there. He was the only Presbyterian minister in Ireland that was invited to go and to speak in a Roman Catholic Church. The people regarded him as an honest, God-fearing man, and they said: "Whatever he says we must do." He passed away, but left a son behind who was my successor in the large church in Dublin. He was minister in the north of Ireland before being brought to Dublin. I heard a circumstance concerning him that I will repeat now. "You ought to have a better salary," said some of his deacons to him. "Why?" said he. "Well, you have to go to more expense than we," they said. "You have to wear better clothing, and keep up better style." "Clothing," said he, and he turned around and laid his hand upon the head of one of his elders who was near, and said: "He is a better man than I; why should I have a better coat than he?" That was the style of the man; unselfish, noble, heroic, living for the truth; and when his health broke down, and he had to go to Australia with the hope of improving it. It was proposed by and by, in the course of time, that there should be established a national system of education. All united secular education was fought by the Catholics. The Presbyterians first took their stand in the support of that system. The time was when my poor countrymen who came here from the other provinces of Ireland could neither read nor write, and came as navvies, porters, and railroad hands. The corresponding class coming to this country to-day does not come to be porters and railroad workers, but present themselves at the dry-goods stores and other such occupations, because they have an education that can sustain them. There have been established in Ireland colleges—three Queen's colleges and two other institutions under the control of the General Assembly, and the best educational facilities are enjoyed by the people; and it is with great satisfaction that I notice from time to time in the contests in the three kingdoms, that the male and female students from these Irish institutions take their places among the foremost. Ulster is keeping its ground in the forefront in the education of the country.

I am unwilling to take up too much of your time, but will say a single word in relation to things denominational there at this time. A very intelligent man said to me a short while ago: "I am glad to see you, and to shake hands with you. When an Irishman becomes a Presbyterian, he is sure to be a good one." That gentleman had in his mind the idea that all Irishmen in their native land were other than Protestant. That is a mistake. I might say in rough numbers that one-fourth of the people of Ireland are Protestant, and nearly one-half of these retain the Scotch Presbyterian type. The other half is the Protestant Episcopal church, which is strongest in Ulster, but is to some extent spread over the kingdom. I accordingly say to the gentlemen who are round about me, that when you are trying to form an estimate of proposed legislation for Ireland, of which we read so much, take into consideration the historic claims of this portion of Ireland, and its peculiar position; for, unless we do so, we can not rightly judge of the situation. The Irish General Assembly does not contain many rich people. They are found mostly in Belfast and the manufacturing centers, but although these people were poor they founded colonial missions; preachers were sent to Canada and Australia, and these reflected gratitude to the feeble Presbyterian church of Ireland by establishing kindred institutions in those two dominions. The General Assembly now has missions in India, and in China, and in Spain. It has six hundred congregations as many ministers, and I might say that to-day there can not be found in Christendom a more determined body of ministers. And I am also glad to speak a word on behalf of the Protestant Episcopal church, which has working members and ministers. The disestablishment which took place, it was supposed by many, would destroy that institution, the state and church being so intimately connected. But the crisis was passed, and the members of the church found a responsibility resting upon them which they did not feel before, and though there have been a few local troubles, the Protestant Episcopal church in Ireland is stronger and better than before the disestablishment. This is one more illustration of the way in which the United States is setting the example to the nations and the countries of the world, of breaking down prejudice and making friends.

This meeting is the beginning of a series, the commencement of an organization that I think may do great good over this land. Let us know one another, and have sympathy with one another. Let it be intelligent sympathy. Let us try to understand the historical incidents of the country, and of the people to which we belong. Let us know how God led them. I can but think that the eye of America is seeing more distinctly than it once did, the way in which its life was shaped. There were Huguenots who suffered temptations and learned the trials of freedom. The Puritan passed through the same experience. He knew the blessing of free conscience, free worship, free legislation; and there are Scotch-Irish well fitted to be their companions, their comrades, their fellow soldiers, and fellow workers in the building up of a great nation, where God on the one hand shall have his rights, and his creatures on the other hand shall have their rights that he intended them to enjoy, and with which He blessed the community. Let us know one another, care for one another, love one another; let us help one another, and feel that it is a dignity that God has put upon us when he permits us to co-operate with these, our brethren, without sectionalism, partisanship or political feeling, in developing our great nation. On higher grounds let us come together and co-operate in building up and perpetuating the power of this great and glorious country: and then we, the children of the Scotch-Irish, will be moving upon the lines along which our fathers have gone in the generations that preceded us.

THE SCOTCH-IRISH OF THE SOUTH.

BY HON. WM. WIRT HENRY, LL.D., OF VIRGINIA.

Mr. President, Members of the Congress, Ladies and Gentlemen:—In obeying the call to take part in this celebration, I recognize the compliment paid the state from which I come, a state so rich in historic memories, and whose history has been so interwoven with that of the people in whose honor we have met, that her greatness may be said to have been the outgrowth of their sterling qualities, rather than of any other portion of her population.

In the name of Virginia, the mother of states and of statesmen, I salute you, and bid you God-speed in gathering up and preserving the records and traditions of the noble race which has ever been foremost in the march of Christian civilization.

The history of the human race in its progress along the path of civilization is filled with the migrations of the more vigorous races or nations, who have left their native lands to seize and occupy the countries possessed by inferior or degenerate populations. Sometimes, these migrations have been of nations, as was that of the Israelites, but generally they have been simply colonies, which have preserved for a longer or shorter time their connection with or dependence upon the mother countries. Among the nations of antiquity, the Greeks and Romans were most distinguished for their spirit of colonization, and to this was due, in great measure, the wonderful influence they severally exerted. But of all the race movements, that which has most affected the history of the world has been the colonization and subsequent occupation of North America by the English-speaking people, and, among these, none can claim just precedence over the Scotch-Irish, whom we are met this day to honor.

The vain efforts of the civil power to exterminate early Christianity by fire and sword were followed by its embrace, under the Emperor Constantine, in the fourth century. The adulterous union which ensued was more disastrous to the pure religion of Christ than persecution. The one purified, but the other corrupted it. From it followed a debasement of both church and state, and a long reign of civil and religious tyranny. The face of the divine author of civil and religious liberty seemed veiled, and the dark ages of the world followed, in which human rights seemed hopelessly enchained by priest and king. But liberty, like truth—

> "Though crushed to earth, will rise again,
> The eternal years of God are hers."

Finally, after a thousand years of darkness, the light of the approaching day began to empurple the horizon. The fifteenth century witnessed the preparation for the coming reformation in the invention of movable type, the revival of letters, and the discovery of America, destined to be the great field for the development of civil and religious liberty, and the asylum of the oppressed.

The sixteenth century was resplendent with the light of reformed Christianity, but, as at the first, it derived much of its brilliancy from the sparks struck by the rough hand of persecution.

The claim of Spain to America was based upon its discovery by Columbus, and the grant of Pope Alexander VI. These so-called muniments of title were fortified by explorations and settlements. From these last Spain derived immense riches, and became the most powerful nation of Europe. But her wealth was devoted to the destruction of the reformed faith, which, kindled in Germany by Luther, was spreading rapidly over the continent. But God, who restrains the wrath of man and makes the remainder thereof to praise him, brought good out of the evil designed.

The refusal of the pope to divorce the Spanish wife of Henry VIII. of England, caused that royal Blue Beard to separate his kingdom from the domination of the Catholic see, and to encourage its tendency to embrace the principles of the Reformation. The effort of the papacy to crush out the Reformation in France and the Netherlands led to the implantation in America of the Protestant English race.

Among the English who volunteered, in 1569, for the defense of the Protestant religion on the continent, was a youth of seventeen, who left Oxford and his studies to learn the art of war under Admiral Coligny and William the Silent. While thus engaged, he conceived a mortal hatred to Spain, and perceiving that her strength lay in her American possessions, he conceived the idea of wresting the New World from her by English colonization. This youth became the celebrated soldier, statesman, courtier, poet, historian, and philosopher, Sir Walter Raleigh. When, by his courage, he had won military renown, and by his address had won the favor of his great sovereign, Elizabeth, and wealth came with honor, he devoted it to the realization of his great design. His colony at Roanoke Island, planted in

1584, perished, indeed, because he was forced to neglect it to aid in the defense of England against the great Spanish Armada, designed to crush out Protestantism in that kingdom. But the inspiration of his genius did not die. The pusillanimous James, who succeeded his heroic mistress on the throne, cast him into the Tower, after the mockery of a trial for treason, and finally beheaded him, at the behest of the Spanish king. But if Catholic Spain compassed his death, it was not till he had struck that power a mortal blow, at Cadiz, on 21st June, 1596, in the destruction of her fleet and the capture of the city, a blow which marks the beginning of her decadence as a great power. Nor was he put to death till he had seen the beginning of the fulfillment of his prediction, that he should " live to see America an English nation." In his prison walls, he heard of, if he could not see, the departure of the little fleet which carried the English colony to Jamestown, in 1607; and before his execution, in 1618, Virginia had become a vigorous colony under the London Company, which had succeeded to his charter rights.

The planting of that colony marks a most important era in the history of the world. It was the beginning of the system of English colonization, which has belted the earth, and has made the inhabitants of the little British Isles the greatest power in the world. From that feeble germ, preserved from destruction by an Indian maiden, has been developed an English nation which controls the continent of North America, and, within three hundred years, has become one among the foremost nations of the earth. Had not Pocahontas thrown herself between the heroic Smith and the uplifted club raised for his execution, the feeble colony would have lost its protecting genius, and would, doubtless, have perished. Had it perished, the Latin nations, with imperialism in church and state, would, doubtless, have possessed the continent they already so largely occupied. What would have been the result we may see by looking upon Mexico, with her degenerate people and unstable government, permanent in nothing but in oppression and misrule.

But in the councils of heaven it had been determined that the tree of liberty should be planted in America, and should so flourish in its genial soil that it should fill the land and cast its benign influences over all the earth. For this great trust, but one people was fitted— the liberty-loving, the liberty-preserving Anglo-Saxon race. They came with English Protestantism, and English constitutional law, developed under Magna Charta by free Parliaments. In the keeping of that handful of men who landed at Jamestown in 1607, was the hope of America for free institutions.

But, as has been the history of liberty in all ages, its preservation here has cost a continuous struggle. Not only on American soil, but on European fields, the possession of America was the bone of contention between Catholic and Protestant powers for a century and a half. Finally, in 1763, Protestant England was left in possession of the continent east of the Mississippi, except the Floridas bordering the Gulf of Mexico. The hand of Providence had thus prepared the way for the great republic, soon to succeed the British power in all of its territory south of the lakes. In this preparation, as we look back at it now in the light of history, nothing is more striking than the training of the peoples for their great work of establishing free institutions in America. In the school of tyranny, they learned to value liberty.

The history of the English, the Dutch, and the French settlers, who united to found the United States, is of the deepest interest, exhibiting, as it does, the dealings of God in preparing a suitable population for this great republic. But on this occasion, our thoughts are turned to but one of the peoples to whom the world is indebted for the America of to-day, with all of its grand achievements in the past and its power for incalculable good in the future.

The kingdom of Scotland, first known as "Scotia Minor," was settled by the ancient race of Celts, who came over from Ireland, then known as "Scotia Major." But, in the course of time, this rude people were almost entirely supplanted by, when not commingled with, the sturdy race from the south of the Tweed, the admixture of the Norman and Saxon, with a slight infusion of Danish blood. Says Macaulay: "The population of Scotland, with the exception of the Celtic tribes, which were thinly scattered over the Hebrides and over the northern parts of the mountainous shires, was of the same blood with the population of England, and spoke a tongue which did not differ from the purest English more than the dialects of Somersetshire and Lancashire differ from each other."

The air and food north of the Tweed, and the Celtic infusion, as years rolled around, gave the distinguishing characteristics of the Scotch people, and intensified in them the noble traits of the English—stern integrity, high sense of duty, hatred of tyranny, and devotion to God.

Presbyterianism, after a long and bloody struggle with Romanism, was at last established on its soil, in the sixteenth century, under the leadership of that great man " who never feared the face of clay," the brave John Knox, who laid the foundations of a free and well-ordered church so broad and deep that Scotland has ever since remained Presbyterian to the core. When asked by Queen Mary, "Think you that subjects, having power, may resist their princes?" his memorable reply was, "If princes exceed their bounds, madam, no doubt they may be resisted even by power." This Froude styles "the creed of republics in its first hard form." It contained the germ of American liberty. His mantle fell on a worthy successor, Andrew Melville, who, in his noble rebuke to King James, proclaimed that principle of religious freedom which has ever been characteristic of the Scotch church, and which developed into the complete divorce of church and state in America.

Said he: "There are two kings and two kingdoms in Scotland. There is King James, the head of this commonwealth, and there is Christ Jesus, the king of the church, whose subject James the Sixth is, and of whose kingdom he is not a king, nor a lord, nor a head, but a member. We will yield to your place, and give you all due obedience. But again I say, you are not the head of the church."

Under the influence of general education and a pure Christianity, the Scotch character developed to the greatest excellency yet attained by civilization. Nothing has ever surpassed the peasant life described by Burns in "The Cotter's Saturday Night," or the Scottish lords and ladies pictured by the pen of Sir Walter Scott.

The effort of Catholic Spain, in the sixteenth century, to wrest the Emerald Isle from Great Britain, stimulated a series of rebellions, which were finally quelled toward the close of the reign of Elizabeth. Upon her successor was laid the task of pacifying the island. In September, 1607, four months after the settlement at Jamestown, the earls of Tyrone and Tyrconnel, the great leaders in the Catholic rebellions, sailed from the beautiful Lough Swilly, on the northwest coast of Ireland, followed by thousands of their old companions in arms, and sought a new home on the continent. The day of their departure dates a new era in Irish history. They left large tracts of land in north Ireland unoccupied and forfeited to the crown, and these were parceled out among a body of Scotch and English, brought over for the purpose. The far greater number of these plantations were from the lower part of Scotland, and became known as "Scotch-Irish." Thus a new population was given to the north of Ireland, which has changed its history. The province of Ulster, with fewer natural advantages than either Munster, Leinster, or Connaught, became the most prosperous, industrious, and law-abiding of all Ireland. Indeed, the difference between Scotland and Spain is not greater than between Ulster and her sister counties, even to this day.

But the Protestant population thus transplanted to the north of

Ireland was destined to suffer many and bloody persecutions, culminating in the world-renowned siege of Londonderry, in the reign of James II., the unparalleled defense of which saved Protestantism in the island, and enabled William of Orange to secure his throne. Tempered by these, the iron in the Scotch character became finest steel. During the reign of William they had rest, but the accession of Anne, "the good Queen Anne," as she is often called, was the occasion of the renewal of the persecution of the Presbyterians. In 1704, the test-oath was imposed, by which every one in public employment was required to profess English prelacy. It was intended to suppress Popery, but was used by the Episcopal bishops to check Presbyterianism. To this was added burdensome restraints on their commerce, and extortionate rents from their landlords, resulting in what is known as the Antrim evictions. There had been occasional emigrations from the north of Ireland from the plantation of the Scotch, and one of the ministers sent over in 1683, Francis Makemie, had organized on the eastern shore of Maryland and in the adjoining counties of Virginia the first Presbyterian churches in America. But in the early part of the eighteenth century the great movement began which transported so large a portion of the Scotch-Irish into the American colonies, and, through their influence, shaped in a great measure the destinies of America. Says the historian Froude: "In the two years which followed the Antrim evictions, thirty thousand Protestants left Ulster for a land where there was no legal robbery, and where those who sowed the seed could reap the harvest." Alarmed by the depletion of the Protestant population, the Toleration Act was passed, and by it, and further promises of relief, the tide of emigration was checked for a brief period. In 1728, however, it began anew, and from 1729 to 1750, it was estimated that "about twelve thousand came annually from Ulster to America." So many had settled in Pennsylvania before 1729 that James Logan, the Quaker president of that colony, expressed his fear that they would become proprietors of the province.

These emigrants brought with them and retained in their new homes distinctive characteristics. These may be summed up as follows:

1. They were Presbyterians in their religion and church government.

2. They were loyal to the conceded authority of the king; but they considered him bound, as well as themselves, by the engagements of "the Solemn League and Covenant," entered into in 1643 by the Westminster Assembly and Parliament on the one side and

the Scottish nation on the other, and adopted by the Presbyterians of Ireland in 1644, pledging the support of the reformation and of the liberties of the kingdoms.

3. They claimed the right to choose their own ministers, untrammeled by the civil powers.

4. They practiced strict discipline in morals, and gave full instruction to their youth in common schools and academies, and in teaching them the Bible, and that wonderful summary of its doctrine contained in the Westminster Assembly's Catechism.

5. They combined, in a remarkable degree, acuteness of intellect, firmness of purpose, and conscientious devotion to duty.

It has been well said of them by one who had watched their development in spite of opposition: "Man might as well attempt to lay his interdict upon the coming forth of vegetation, when the powers of nature are warmed and refreshed by genial influences from above, as to arrest the progress of such a people in knowledge and improvement."

This bold stream of emigrants struck the American continent mainly on the eastern border of Pennylvania, and was, in great measure, turned southward through Maryland, Virginia, North Carolina, and South Carolina, reaching and crossing the Savannah river. It was met at various points by counter streams of the same race, which had entered the continent through the seaports of the Carolinas and Georgia. Turning westward, the combined flood overflowed the mountains and covered the rich valley of the Mississippi beyond. As the Puritans or Round-heads of the south, but freed from fanaticism, they gave tone to its people and direction to its history.

It is of these that it is my privilege to speak to-day.

Leaving Pennsylvania, southward, the first colony into which this race entered was Maryland. Their settlements were principally in the narrow slip which constitutes the western portion, but we find them in every part of the colony. It was due to them that Maryland was among the foremost of the colonies in the Indian wars and in the Revolution. Of this blood was her great Revolutionary leader, Charles Carroll, and that model soldier, John Eager Howard. He seized the critical moment with his brave Maryland line at the battle of Cowpens, and turned the fortunes of the day, and was equally deserving of success, but less fortunate, at Guilford and Eutaw. Of him General Greene wrote, introducing him to a friend: "This will be handed to you by Colonel Howard, as good an officer as the world affords. He has great ability and the best disposition to promote the service. My own obligations to him are great—the public's still more so. He deserves a statue of gold no less than the Roman and Grecian heroes."

It was to this population, and to the Puritans driven from Virginia to Maryland, that Protestantism is indebted for the rescue of the colony from the Romish faith; and in all that has made the state so conspicuous on the page of American history, we find traces of the Scotch-Irish.

Proceeding southward, we next enter the great colony of Virginia, and here we can more clearly discover the effect of this people upon her destiny.

Traces of the Scotch-Irish were found in Virginia east of the Blue Ridge in the latter part of the seventeenth century, and early in the eighteenth they were found in Albemarle, Nelson, Campbell, Prince Edward, and Charlotte counties, and along the great valley west of the Blue Ridge. But it was after the year 1738 that they entered that valley in great numbers, and, with the exception of some German settlements near its lower end, completely possessed it from the Pennsylvania to the North Carolina line. In that year the Synod of Philadelphia (upon the application of John Caldwell, a Scotch-Irish elder, afterward settled at Cub creek, in Charlotte county, Va., and the grandfather of the great statesman, John Caldwell Calhoun), sent a commissioner to the governor of Virginia with a proposal to people the valley with Presbyterians, who should hold the western frontier against the Indians and thus protect the colony, upon one condition only, "that they be allowed the liberty of their consciences and of worshiping God in a way agreeable to the principles of their education." To this Governor Gooch, himself a Scotchman, returned a gracious answer and a promise of the protection afforded by the Act of Toleration.

With this agreement the territory west of the Blue Ridge was soon filled with a Scotch-Irish population, who were glad to defend the cavaliers of the colony from the implacable savage as the price of civil and religious liberty. Living in continual danger from the treacherous foe, their faithful rifles were their constant companions, and were seen even in the school-houses and the churches which invariably marked their settlements. In the pulpit the trusty rifle was as convenient to the preacher as the Bible. With such a training, no wonder that this noble race soon demonstrated their right to control the destinies of their colony, in peace as well as in war. As the country filled up, new counties were set off, and the delegates from these and from the Piedmont counties of kindred blood, together known as back or upper counties, began to control the House of Burgesses. In the wars which preceded the Revolution the soldiers of Virginia were mainly drawn from this section. They suffered defeat with Washington at the Meadows, and with Braddock at Fort Duquesne, and, by their firmness, saved the remnant of that rash general's army. They won the signal victory at Point Pleasant, in 1774, which struck terror into the Indian tribes across the Ohio, and was the prelude to the War of Independence, for which the officers engaged in that battle at once offered their swords.

In 1765, when England, having driven the French from North America, began her oppressive measures against her own colonies, and, regardless of their chartered rights and the English constitution, imposed a stamp tax upon them through a Parliament in which they had no representation, it was the youthful son of a Scotchman who introduced the resolutions into the Virginia House of Burgesses denying the validity of the act, which aroused the continent and "set in motion the ball of the Revolution." And it was Scotch-Irish votes that secured their passage, against the combined efforts of the old leaders of the House. In the long struggle which followed, in which, step by step, Virginia led her sister colonies along the path to independence, it was the same bold leader, with his Scotch-Irish cohorts, that directed her steps. Says Mr. Jefferson, speaking of Mr. Henry to Daniel Webster: "He was far before us all in maintaining the spirit of the Revolution. His influence was most extensive with the members from the upper counties, and his boldness and their votes overawed and controlled the more cool or the more timid aristocratic gentlemen of the lower part of the state. After all, it must be allowed that he was our leader in the measures of the Revolution in Virginia."

At the first call of Congress for soldiers to defend the town of Boston, Daniel Morgan, of Scotch-Irish blood, at once raised a company of riflemen among his people in the lower valley of Virginia, and, by a forced march of six hundred miles, reached the beleaguered town in three weeks. His company was but the advance of a steady supply of soldiers from the same hardy race, which, whether in the continental line or the militia ranks, made glorious the name of Virginia in the seven years' struggle which ensued. To the soldiers of this blood, it was given to turn the tide of war at more than one critical period in the desperate struggle of our fathers for freedom. It is proper, on this occasion, to recall some of these instances. Morgan, after distinguishing himself in the ill-fated expedition against Canada, was taken prisoner before Quebec. Upon his exchange, he returned to the valley of Virginia, and raised a corps of riflemen from among its Scotch-Irish people. Joining Washington, he was sent by him to aid Gates in meeting the British invasion from Canada under Burgoyne. The battle of Saratoga, 7th October, 1777, which followed, is included, with reason, by Creasy, in his volume entitled "The Fifteen Decisive Battles of the World," each one of which changed the current of human history. Before that great victory, neither in England nor on the continent was it believed that the American patriots would be able to maintain the struggle upon which they had entered. France, the hereditary enemy of England, was anxious to assist the revolted colonies, but only in case that they showed themselves capable of continuing the conflict, which they had not yet done. The British campaign for 1777 was well laid. It consisted of a movement from Canada under Burgoyne, to be met by a strong force from New York under Clinton, and the combined army to isolate and conquer New England. The American army, under Gates, was between Burgoyne and Clinton, and must needs engage and overcome Burgoyne before the arrival of Clinton, or be itself crushed between the two approaching armies.

On the memorable 7th October, the forces of Gates and Burgoyne met, the right wing of the British, and the flower of the army, being led by the brave Scotchman, General Simon Frazer, the idol of the army. On the American left, was the equally brave Scotch-Irishman, Colonel Morgan, with his regiment of sharpshooters, every one of whom was a marksman. In the desperate battle which followed, Morgan noticed that a British officer, mounted on an iron-gray charger, was most active in the fight, and that wherever he rode he turned the tide of battle. It was the gallant Frazer. Morgan called to Timothy Murphy, one of the best shots in his regiment, and pointing to the British officer on the iron-gray horse, he said, "Bring him down." At the crack of the faithful rifle, the British officer reeled in his saddle and fell. The forces he was leading at once became confused, and soon fell back. The crisis was passed, and the battle, upon which hung the fate of America, was won. In a few days, Burgoyne was forced to surrender his whole army. When introduced to Morgan, he grasped his hand and said: "Sir, you command the finest regiment in the world." The news of the victory produced an entire change in European policy. France at once acknowledged the independence of the American states, and entered into a treaty of alliance with them. War between her and England followed, and soon Spain and Holland joined in the conflict. With their aid, the American patriots were enabled to maintain the struggle four years longer, till finally England gave up the contest.

But during that four years, another critical period arrived, in which the stalwart Scotch-Irish soldiery, by one memorable battle, changed the face of the war.

Despairing of conquering the northern states with Washington to defend them, the British determined to attack from the sea, of which they were the masters, the southern states, and to subdue them in detail, striking first at Georgia, the weakest of them all. This work was committed to the celebrated Earl Cornwallis, and no one was more capable of executing the plan. He soon overran Georgia and South Carolina, having destroyed two American armies sent to check him—the first under General Howe, and the second under General Gates. He at once pushed northward, before another army could be organized to meet him, intending to overrun North Carolina and Virginia in rapid succession. Indeed, General Leslie was already in Virginia, ready to join him on his arrival, and, in the meantime, was to keep that state, if possible, from sending aid to her southern sisters.

In his movement northward, Cornwallis divided his army, and sent a portion of it, under Colonel Patrick Ferguson, an accomplished Scotch officer, along the route which bordered the mountains of Carolina. His force threatened the Scotch-Irish settlements west of the mountains of North Carolina and in the south-west portion of Virginia. These rapidly organized a volunteer force, under Colonels Sevier, Shelby, McDowell, and Campbell, which rendezvoused at the Watauga settlement, in what is now East Tennessee. These were afterward joined by some of their race from the Carolinas, under Colonels Williams and Cleaveland. The veteran Colonel William Campbell, from Virginia, was chosen as commander, and crossing the mountains rapidly, they threw themselves in the path of Ferguson. The battle of King's Mountain followed, on the 7th October, 1880, in which the entire British force was killed or captured. Cornwallis was forced to come to a halt, fall back, and wait for reinforcements, which were drawn from the British force in Virginia. Before he recovered from the blow, General Greene, who had been sent by Washington to organize and lead another army against the invaders, was able to accomplish the task, and afterward, by his masterly movements, to so cripple the British general that he was forced to abandon his conquests and betake himself by another route to Virginia, there to be captured by the combined American and French armies. Every subsequent event which led in logical succession to the surrender of the British army at Yorktown and the close of the Revolution, may be traced to that memorable battle at King's Mountain, won by an army composed almost entirely of Scotch-Irish volunteers, who had not waited for the call of their government, but, upon the rumored approach of danger, had sprung to arms and hastened to meet it. In the subsequent battles of Cowpens and Guilford, we find the same Scotch-Irish element following up the work so gloriously begun at King's Mountain.

But not alone in these and other battles of the Revolution did the Scotch-Irish of Virginia lay their country under never-ending obligations. To them is due the magnificent domain over which the original thirteen states have stretched in their expansion westward.

By the treaty of Paris, in 1763, the western boundary of the American colonies was fixed at the Mississippi river. England afterward extended the Canadian government over the territory west of the Ohio and south of the lakes, and established a chain of forts reaching from the lakes to the Mississippi, above the mouth of the Ohio. This territory was embraced in the charter of Virginia, and she distinctly claimed it in 1776, on assuming state sovereignty. But it was held by British troops, who at the same time continually instigated the Indians to murderous raids on the white settlements south and east of the Ohio. Early in 1778, Governor Henry commissioned Colonel George Rogers Clark to lead a secret expedition against these north-western forts, with a view of occupying, with Virginia troops, the territory she claimed. Clark collected his men from the Scotch-Irish inhabitants west of the Blue Ridge, in what was then Augusta county, and from the district of Kentucky, then beginning to be peopled by the same race. In a campaign which John Randolph has aptly compared to that of Hannibal in Italy, he possessed himself of the British posts south of the lakes, capturing Hamilton, the British governor, and securing to Virginia the entire northwest.

This campaign, unsurpassed in daring, and unequaled in results by any recorded in history, was conducted with less than two hundred Virginia militia. The noble commonwealth, which had taken the first steps looking to Union, finding that some of the states were reluctant to sign the confederation while Virginia held so large a territory, with unequaled generosity and patriotism ceded her entire conquest to the United States, and thus secured the Union. When England and Spain in succession attempted to deprive the American states of this magnificent domain during the negotiations for peace, the American commissioners, under direction of Congress, relied on the conquest of Clark and subsequent occupation of Virginia.

The rule of *uti possidetis* prevailed, and independence was acknowledged by Great Britain, with the Mississippi as our western border. Our extension to the Pacific has been only the logical result. Had not that Scotch-Irish band of heroes wrested from the British

Lion his western prey, the Alleghanies or the Ohio would have been our western border, and the original thirteen states skirting the Atlantic would, in all probability, have been our territorial limits to-day.

No one knew better than Washington the sterling qualities of this race, and he paid it the highest compliment ever paid to any people when, in the darkest moment of the Revolution, he said, that if all others failed him, he would plant his standard on the Blue Ridge of Virginia, rally around him the people of the valley, and make his last stand for the liberties of America.

Nor has the virtue in the blood lost its power of making heroes to this day. It was from this people that the immortal Stonewall Jackson sprang, and from them he drew the troops that followed him, and excited for themselves and for their great commander the admiration of the world.

But, however glorious in war, this race in Virginia have won triumphs in the peaceful halls of legislation no less beneficial to humanity than any won on battle-fields. It was Scotch-Irish blood that moved the pen that wrote the Declaration of Independence, the first draft of the United States Constitution, and the divorce between church and state. The influence of these upon the history of the race is incalculable. The last has been justly described as the contribution of America to the science of government. Though claimed by the founder of Christianity and his early followers, religious liberty was never accorded to the Christian Church. The state claimed the right to control the religious beliefs of her citizens, and the claim was not relinquished when the Christian Church formed its unholy alliance with the state. The Reformers of the fifteenth century did not undertake to deny this power of the state over the church, but in their creeds appealed to the state to enforce the penalties pronounced by church courts. In Virginia we have seen there was a church establishment, and toleration was all that the Scotch-Irish could obtain in repayment for their protection of the western border.

In 1774, we find their Presbytery petitioning the House of Burgesses for as much freedom in religious matters as the British constitution afforded in secular matters. When two years afterward, the Virginia convention, after taking up independence for herself, and ordering it to be moved in Congress for America, engaged in forming, as a basis of government, a declaration of the rights of man, the greatest state paper ever written, the same voice that stirred the continent to resist the Stamp Act, moved to insert as one of the inalienable rights of man his right to worship his God according to the dictates of his conscience. Adopted into the Virginia Bill of Rights, it has been copied into every constitution in America. At the very next session of the Assembly, the same Presbytery, controlled by Scotch-Irish voices, sent a memorial written by a Scotch-Irish pen, held by Caleb Wallace, enlarging upon the great principle embodied in the Bill of Rights, and showing its guarantee of perfect religious liberty. It was following in their wake that Jefferson afterward wrote his celebrated act for the establishment of religious liberty, which has effected the divorce of church and state, not only in Virginia, but throughout the Union, and whose principles seem destined to unfetter the Christian conscience throughout the world. Thus there was completed by the Scotch-Irish of Virginia, in 1776, the reformation commenced by Luther two hundred and fifty years before.

To this people Virginia is indebted also for her earliest educational institutions of high grade, except the royal college of William and Mary; and one of their number, Thomas Jefferson, was the founder of the State University.

In the year 1736, Henry McCullock, from the province of Ulster, obtained a grant of 64,000 acres in the present county of Duplin, North Carolina, and introduced upon it between three and four thousand of his Scotch-Irish countrymen from the north of Ireland. About the same time the Scotch began to occupy the lower Cape Fear, and after the defeat of the Pretender, at Culloden, in 1746, great numbers of Scotch Highlanders, who had adhered to his fortunes, emigrated to North Carolina, taking up their residence in the counties of Bladen, Cumberland, Robeson, Moore, Richmond, Harnett, Chatham, and Ansom, and giving the Scotch the ascendancy in the upper Cape Fear region. In the meantime, the current of emigration to America from Ulster had become a bold stream, entering the continent mainly at Philadelphia and flowing westward. Braddock's defeat rendering border life dangerous, many of the new-comers turned southward, moving parallel to the Blue Ridge through Virginia and North Carolina until they met the other stream of their countrymen which was moving upward from Charleston along the banks of the Santee, Wateree, Broad, Pacolet, Ennoree, and Saluda, and this emigration to North Carolina continued for forty years, till checked by the Revolution.

It is not known with certainty when the Scotch-Irish were first introduced into the country between the Dan and the Catawba, but they were found in the counties of Granville, Orange, Rowan, and Mecklenburg previous to 1750. So great was the proportion of this race in North Carolina before the Revolution that they may be said to have given direction to her history. With their advent begins the educational history of the state, and during the eighteenth century that history is inseparably connected with the Presbyterian Church. One name stands out pre-eminent in this history. It is that of the Scotch-Irish minister, David Caldwell, whose classical school, established in 1767 near Greensborough, was the Eton of the south. But besides classical schools they established academies and colleges. Queen's College, located in the town of Charlotte, in Mecklenburg county, was chartered in 1770, but its charter was repealed by George III., of whom it was said that "no compliments to his queen could render Whigs in politics and Presbyterians in religion acceptable to him." It continued, however, to flourish under the royal frown, and was incorporated in 1777 as "Liberty Hall." But the Revolution closed its doors, and Cornwallis first desecrated it by quartering his troops within it, and afterward burned the buildings. Davidson College, in the northern part of Mecklenburg county, established by the Presbyterians long after the war, may be considered the successor of this venerable institution, which was sacrificed upon the altar of patriotism.

It was to the Scotch-Irish delegates that is due the credit of inserting in the first constitution of the state the provision for a state university, which has proved such a blessing to the state and to the South.

In North Carolina, as in Virginia, this race was earliest in claiming the rights of freemen against British oppression. Indeed, four years before the battle of Lexington, Scotch-Irish blood was shed in North Carolina by a royal governor, simply because the people dared ask redress for tyrannous abuses. Governor Tryon, instigated by one of the worst of men, David Fanning, first caused the complainants to be indicted by a packed grand jury, and then marched against them with an army, and, treating them as outlaws, shot down and hung some thirty of them. It is known in history as the War of the Regulators. Says Bancroft concerning it: "The blood of rebels against oppression was first shed among the settlers on the branches of the Cape Fear river." Says Alexander, speaking of this engagement on the Alamance, 16th May, 1771: "These Regulators were not adventurers, but the sturdy, patriotic members of three Presbyterian congregations, all of them having as their pastors graduates of Princeton. Mr. Caldwell was one of them, and, on the morning of the battle, was on the ground, going from one side to the other, endeavoring to prevent the catastrophe."

As a result of this merciless attack upon a patriotic people, they left their homes, crossed the mountains to the west, and laid the foundation on the Watauga of the State of Tennessee.

While the Scotch, who had emigrated to North Carolina after the battle of Culloden, considered themselves bound by their oath of allegiance to side with the king in the American Revolution, and were generally Tories, the Scotch-Irish of that colony were among the foremost of the patriots. In no locality was their zeal more conspicuous than in the counties of Mecklenburg and Rowan. Tarleton, in his memoirs, bears testimony to the fact that those counties were the most rebellious in America, and Cornwallis designated Mecklenburg county as " the hornet's nest of the Revolution."

When the people of this county heard of the battle of Lexington, they did not wait for others to move with them, but at once assumed the powers of government.

It is due to her Scotch-Irish people, also, that North Carolina is entitled to the honor of being the first colony that authorized her delegates in Congress to vote for independence.

Dr. David Ramsey, the historian of South Carolina, after giving the various sources of the population of that colony from its first settlement, and according full prominence to the Huguenots, adds: " Besides foreign Protestants, several persons from England and Scotland resorted to Carolina after the peace of 1763. But of all other countries, none has furnished the province with so many inhabitants as Ireland. Scarce a ship sailed from any of its ports for Charleston that was not crowded with men, women, and children." . . . "About this time, above a thousand families from the northward (Pennsylvania and Virginia), with their effects, in the space of one year, resorted to South Carolina, driving their cattle, hogs, and horses overland before them. Lands were allotted them in its western woods, which soon became the most populous parts of the province."

These were Scotch-Irish, and it is to them he refers later when he says: " The Scotch and the Dutch were the most useful emigrants. They both brought with them, and generally retained in an eminent degree, the virtues of industry and economy, so peculiarly necessary in a new country. To the former, South Carolina is indebted for much of its early literature. A great proportion of its physicians, clergymen, lawyers, and schoolmasters were from North Britain."

These settlers in the western part of the colony were long without the protection of law administered through judicial tribunals, and, of necessity, were forced to band themselves together to punish crime, of which the most frequent and irritating was horse-stealing. Against them, the royal governor, Montague, sent a man named Scouil, in

1764, with an army, and with great difficulty a civil war was averted. Fortunately, the establishment of courts, in 1769, pacified the country. The division thus created was not obliterated, but reappeared in 1775, on the breaking out of the Revolution, when the Regulators, as they were called, became Whigs, and the Scouilites, as the other party had been called, became Tories. Before and during the Revolution, the Scotch-Irish in Western South Carolina, as in North Carolina, Virginia, and Pennsylvania, were the defenders of the border against the hostile Indian tribes beyond.

But this did not relieve them of the duty of fighting the British coming from the Atlantic seaboard.

In the terrible fate that overtook South Carolina during that struggle, when Cornwallis rode rough-shod over the devoted state, it was to her noblest son, Governor John Rutledge, a Scotch-Irishman, that the destinies of the state were committed. Unable to meet the haughty invader in the open field, the little bands of patriots who survived the trying ordeal, gathered in the east around the standard of Marion, and in the north and west around the standards of Sumter and Pickens. These devoted men kept alive the flame of liberty in the swamps of South Carolina, while the British tyrant was stamping it out wherever its flicker could be discovered. When the brutal oppressor believed it was entirely extinguished, it burst forth in electric flashes, striking and withering the proud invader.

Through the veins of these incomparable leaders and their brave troops Scotch-Irish blood coursed, and gave nerve to the arms which struck for liberty.

Of the famous Andrew Pickens we have a pen-picture by his brilliant companion in arms, Light-horse Harry Lee, which is so typical of a Scotch-Irishman, that it may be well reproduced here.

"He was a sincere believer in the Christian religion, and a devout observer of the Presbyterian form of worship. His frame was sinewy and active; his habits were simple, temperate, and industrious. His characteristics were taciturnity and truth, prudence and decision, modesty and courage, disinterestedness and public spirit."

In South Carolina, as elsewhere, this people provided schools and churches for their communities, and have been foremost in advancing the interests of the state.

Georgia was the youngest of the old thirteen colonies, but, like those north of her, she was indebted to this race for some of her best population. As early as 1735 a colony from the Highlands of Scotland were conducted to the mouth of the Savannah river, and thence southward to New Inverness, on the Alatamaha river. When told on the way that the Spaniards would shoot them from their fort near by their new home, they replied, "Why, then, we will beat them out of their fort, and shall have houses ready built to live in." This valiant spirit never flagged in the subsequent war with Spain and the Revolution, and it is hard to estimate the services to Georgia rendered by the McKays and McIntoshes who came from this settlement.

Before the Revolution, however, emigration from the Carolinas set in toward North Georgia, bringing many Scotch-Irish families. Governor Gilmer, in 1855, describes the community they formed, with all the privations and simple enjoyments of their life, and his description is applicable to all their new settlements. Among other things, he says: "The pretty girls were dressed in striped and checked cotton cloth, spun and woven with their own hands, and their sweethearts in sumach and walnut dyed stuff, made by their mothers. Courting was done when riding to meeting on Sunday, and walking to the spring when there. Newly married couples went to see the old folks on Saturday, and carried home on Sunday evening what they could spare. There was no *ennui* among the women for want of something to do. If there had been leisure to read, there were but few books for the indulgence. Hollow trees supplied cradles for babies. The fine voices which are now heard in the pulpit and at the bar from the first native Georgians began their practice by crying when infants for want of good nursing."

These settlers were of the kindred of Andrew Jackson and Thomas H. Benton.

Besides these, the Scotch-Irish who had followed the Alleghanies had not ceased their southward movements until, crossing the Savannah river, they had entered the northern portion of Georgia.

Later, and after the Revolution, some of the Virginians who had served in Georgia, notably General George Mathews, induced a colony from Albemarle and the valley of Virginia to move to the north of Georgia, and they settled along the Broad river. Among these were, of course, a strong infusion of Scotch-Irish blood.

The subsequent prosperity of Georgia is attributed in large measure to these people and their descendants by Governor Gilmer. From them, he tells us, the blood was scattered throughout the southern and southwestern states.

A race which so completely filled the western side of the old colonies was naturally that which would soonest occupy the country still further westward, extending to the Mississippi.

This came to pass. As the Scotch-Irish increased, they pressed upon the Indians, driving them westward until, early in the nineteenth century, but few of the native tribes were left east of the great river. Only a short notice of these new states in the southern valley of the Mississippi need be given.

Kentucky was settled by the Scotch-Irish of Virginia and North Carolina. Thomas Walker, of Virginia, first explored it in 1747; John Finley, of North Carolina, followed in 1767; and afterward, in 1769, he, with Daniel Boone, John Stewart, and three others, all from the same colony, penetrated to the Kentucky river. By the year 1773, the whites began to take up lands, and afterward there was a steady stream of emigrants, almost entirely from the valley and southwest Virginia, and, of course, of Scotch-Irish blood. A roll of the Presbytery in 1802 shows a list of forty-three names, nearly every one of which is Scotch-Irish, and the families that first constituted the county of Kentucky can nearly every one be found in a history of the Virginia valley. Often the transplanting gave additional vigor to the scions, and the Clarks, the Browns, the Breckenridges, the Campbells, the Bullitts, the Wallaces, the Robertsons, the Prestons, the Todds, the Rices, the McKees, and others, rose to greater eminence in Kentucky than had ever been attained in Virginia.

The Indian name, Can-tuck-kee, meaning "the dark and bloody ground," was given to it by the savages, because it was the hunting-ground on which the northern and southern tribes met in constant conflict. The whites found it well deserved the name, as the Indians ceased to fight each other in their common hostility to the settlers, against whom they waged continuous war. The prediction of the Cherokee chief to Boone at the treaty at Watauga, ceding the territory to Henderson and his associates, was fully verified. "Brother," said he, "we have given you a fine land, but I believe you will have much trouble in settling it." Any other race would probably have abandoned the effort, or rather never undertaken it. No border annals teem with more thrilling incidents or heroic exploits than those of the Kentucky hunters, whose very name at length struck terror into the heart of the stoutest savage. The people developed in the midst of constant danger into a bold, independent, and magnanimous community.

So thoroughly was Kentucky settled by this race that it may be called a Scotch-Irish state.

The state of Tennessee was the daughter of North Carolina, and was first settled by the Scotch-Irish driven over the mountains by the cruel war of the Regulators, as we have seen. Upon no field has this remarkable race shown to greater advantage than upon the soil of

Tennessee, but as they have been assigned to the special care of one more competent than myself for the task, I will not trench upon his domain.

Mississippi and Alabama, which were cleared of the dominion of the warlike Creeks early in the century by Andrew Jackson and his band of Tennesseans and Georgians, were filled up by settlers from the adjacent states, and these were necessarily largely Scotch-Irish in their descent. And so after the Louisiana purchase in 1803, Louisiana, Missouri, and Arkansas were successively brought into the Union, with a population drawn in great measure from the nearest Scotch-Irish communities. Florida also, when acquired from the Spaniards, received her quota of this people. But among all these new states a strong infusion is found of Virginia blood, drawn in large measure from Scotch-Irish veins.

The last and the largest of the southern states which entered the Union was Texas, and we are indebted to a Scotch-Irishman from the Virginia valley for this principality.

Samuel Houston, a native of Rockbridge county, Virginia, saved Texas from Mexican dominion by his celebrated victory over Santa Anna at the battle of San Jacinto, 21st April, 1836. He became the first president of the independent State of Texas on 22d October following, and, during his term, took the first step toward its annexation to the United States, which was accomplished in 1845. In the meantime, a large and constantly increasing population from the southern states was pouring into its borders, which, of course, was largely Scotch-Irish in its origin.

In the wars which succeeded the Revolution, the United States have been greatly indebted to the Scotch-Irish of the South for their renown in arms.

It was with troops of this blood that the Scotch-Irish General Andrew Jackson, in 1814, broke the power of the Creek Indians in Alabama, drove the British from Florida, and defeated Wellington's soldiers, under his brother-in-law, Sir Edward Packenham, at New Orleans. In the war with Mexico, no fighting was surpassed by that of southern volunteers, under the leadership of the Scotch-Irishman, Zachary Taylor.

In the war between the states, time would fail me to even mention the Scotch-Irish heroes who followed the Confederate flag.

I have thus hastily glanced at the diffusion of the Scotch-Irish over the southern states, and, in doing so, it has become apparent that a history of this race would be a history of the southern states.

Certainly, as to the South, they are bone of its bone and flesh of its flesh.

The task would be almost endless to simply call the names of this people in the South who have distinguished themselves in the annals of their country. Yet some rise before me, whose names demand utterance in any mention of their people—names which the world will not willingly let die.

Among the statesmen they have given to the world are Jefferson, Madison, Calhoun, Benton.

Among the orators. Henry, Rutledge, Preston, McDuffie, Yancy.

Among the poets, the peerless Poe.

Among the jurists, Marshall, Campbell, Robertson.

Among the divines, Waddell, the Alexanders, Breckinridge, Robinson, Plummer, Hoge, Hawks, Fuller, McKendree.

Among the physicians, McDowell, Sims, McGuire.

Among the inventors, McCormick.

Among the soldiers, Lee, the Jacksons, the Johnstons, Stuart.

Among the sailors, Paul Jones, Buchanan.

Presidents from the South, seven—Jefferson, Madison, Monroe, Jackson, Taylor, Polk, Johnson.

Great as this race has been in victorious war and prosperity, it has been greater in defeat and adversity. Struck down at Appomattox, the South lay helpless at the feet of the conqueror, pale from loss of her best blood, impoverished by the hand of the despoiler, and held in the embrace of an inferior race. Her prostrate form seemed to be in the grasp of death. It was then I heard the clear voice of one of her greatest orators repeating over her the impassioned words of Romeo over the body of Juliet—

> " Death that hath sucked the honey of thy breath,
> Hath had no power yet upon thy beauty.
> Thou art not conquered; beauty's ensign yet
> Is crimson in thy lips and in thy cheeks,
> And death's pale flag is not advanced there."

It was as the voice of prophecy recalling her to consciousness. The indomitable Scotch-Irish blood still coursed in her veins. She arose, not like Juliet, to suicidal despair, but to renewed hope and a new life, with fresh strength drawn from the embrace of mother earth. With head erect and her eyes fixed on God, she commenced a new career. A quarter of a century has not passed, and we see her to-day, her pallor replaced by the crimson tide of life, and her every motion instinct with the genius of progress. Generous nature whispers her secrets, decks her with richest treasures, and points her the way to prosperity. With unswerving faith in the God of her fathers, and unfaltering steps, she presses onward and upward, her right hand lifting to the kiss of heaven her spotless banner, displaying the emblazoned legend, *Sic itur ad astra.*

SCOTCH-IRISH OF TENNESSEE.

BY REV. D. C. KELLEY, D.D.

In this honorable presence, it is well to express, in the beginning of what I shall attempt to say, my regret that the task assigned me had not fallen into far more competent hands.

I had little dreamed, when I began the inadequate study I have had time and opportunity to make, of the richness of the mine into which I was to strike my pick. My childhood had been amused, my wonder aroused, and my ambition for a virtuous life kindled around the fireside where tales of a Scotch-Irish ancestry were the theme of the winter evening talk. When the true magnitude of the work before me began to appear, I should have quickly withdrawn my promise to speak for the Scotch-Irish of Tennessee, had it not been for a sense of obligation to those teachers of my childhood. The traditions of childhood mingling with ancestral blood bade me do what the race has ever done—"my simple duty as best I could." As my best apology, however, for standing here, allow me to make good my right by blood. Perhaps few of the race have claims of earlier date. My paternal blood speaks for itself, going back to the early Irish chiefs, to which is added the Thompson blood of North Ireland. My maternal claims are as follows:

Before the work of royal plantations in Ireland had begun, as early as 1584, "a thousand Scotch Highlanders, called Redshanks, of the septs and families of the Campbells, Macdonnells, and Magalanes, led by Surleboy, a Scottish chieftain, invaded Ulster. These invaders in time intermarried with the Irish, and became the most formidable enemies of England in her designs of settlement. It was ostensibly to root out this Scottish colony that Elizabeth sent Essex to Ireland; but his failure only fixed them more firmly in their place."

But a more singular settlement than this of the Scotch Redshanks was one effected by private speculation, namely, that of the Montgomeries in the Ardes of Down.* The head of this new and important settlement in the Ardes was Hugh Montgomery, the sixth laird (esquire) of Braidstane, in Scotland; his father had married the daughter of Montgomery, laird of Haislhead, an ancient family descended of the earls of Egliutown. The first laird of the name, Robert Montgomery, was second son of Alexander Montgomery, earl of Eglintown.

---

* Montgomery Papers.

Hugh, the leader of the Montgomeries into Ireland, was thus a well descended adventurer, and in addition to his good birth he possessed spirit and talent. The circumstances which led to his settlement in Down are these: In 1603, an affray took place in Belfast, between a party of soldiers and some servants of Conn O'Neill, who had been sent with runlets to bring wine from that town to their master, " then in great debauch at Castlereagh with his brothers, friends, and followers." The servants came back with more blood than wine, having got into a *melee* with some soldiers, who captured the servants and sent home the messengers with a severe handling. They confessed to Conn that they were more numerous than the soldiers, on which, " in rage, he swore by his father, and by all his noble ancestors' souls, that none of them should ever serve him or his family if they went not back forthwith and did not revenge the affront done to him and themselves by those few Baddagh Sassenach." The result was a violent affray, and some of the soldiers were killed. An office of inquest was held upon Conn and his followers, and a number of them were found guilty of levying war on the queen. O'Neill was sent to prison to Carrickfergus, and Elizabeth in the meantime dying, the Laird Montgomery, who knew these matters well, with thrift speed which became his country, made his humble application to the new Scotch monarch for half Conn's estates, leaving the remainder to Conn himself. But the modest proposal was not accepted, and he hit upon a happier expedient, which was to obtain a grant from Conn O'Neill himself of half his lands on the condition of effecting his escape and giving him a shelter. The grant was obtained. Some change was subsequently made in these letters, by the intervention of a courtier of the name of Sir James Fullerton, one of " the busiest bodies in all the world in other men's matters which may profit themselves," who having an eye for a friend, Mr. James Hamilton, and anxious to obtain for him a share of Conn's lands, represented, in a courtier's way, that the two moieties granted were too large for two men, forgetting or omitting the small circumstance that they were their own by right, and prevailed on the king to make a fresh division. " But the king, sending first for Sir Hugh, told him (respecting the reasons aforesaid) for what loss he might receive in not getting the full half of Conn's estate, by that defalcation, he would compensate him out of the Abbey lands and impropriations, which in a few months he was to grant in fee, they being already granted in lease for twenty-one years, and that he would also abstract, out of Conn's half, the whole great Ardes for his and Mr. James Hamilton's behoof, and throw it into their two shares; that the sea-coasts might be possessed by Scottish men, who would be traders proper for his majesty's future advantage, the residue to be laid off about Castlereagh (which Conn had desired), being too great a favor for such an Irishman."

Whether the Campbells, Montgomerys, and Hamiltons were known to each other in Ireland, tradition does not tell. We find from these Campbells Duncan Campbell, whose son, John Campbell, came from Donegal, Ireland, and settled in Donegal township, Lancaster county, Pensylvania. His descendants passed down the valley of the Shenandoah to South-western Virginia, where we find among the branches on an old family tree, revived and added to from time to time, General William Campbell, of King's Mountain fame, and his grandson, Wm. C. Preston; the brothers, Colonel Arthur and Captain John Campbell, of Virginia (the latter of whom was the father of Governor David Campbell, of Virginia); Judge David, of the State of Franklin, afterward the State of Tennessee, with their cousin and brother-in-law, Colonel David, of Campbell's station, East Tennessee; his son, General John Campbell, of the War of 1812; grandson, Governor William B. Campbell, of Tennessee. Another branch bears upon it the name of the gallant Confederate, General Alex. W. Campbell, of West Tennessee. Scotch-Irish on both sides.

From these before-mentioned Montgomerys, we find in North Carolina, at Saulsbury, in the Revolutionary War, Hugh Montgomery, who equipped a regiment of patriots for the Continental army—a man with the shrewd business characteristics of his ancestors. From him we trace the children, Hugh and Jane; Hugh, the father of Major Lemuel P. Montgomery, a brilliant young lawyer of Nashville, who fell leading a dashing charge at the battle of Horseshoe, and for whom the fair city of Montgomery, Ala., is called; and Hugh, a lawyer of Chattanooga, for whom the beautiful avenue in that city is named. Jane became the wife of Samuel Cowan, the first merchant of Knoxville; later, was married to Colonel David Campbell, before mentioned, a private in the battle of King's Mountain, the founder of Campbell's Station, near Knoxville. Of this union of the Scotch-Irish Campbells and Montgomerys, your annalist of to-day is, in the second generation, the only living representative. Three of his children have in their veins the added blood of the Hamiltons, Hays, and Cunnynghams. And yet two other Scotch-Irish additions, the history of which is here given as an illustration of the methods by which this blood has been so widely spread in our country:

John Bowen, a wealthy planter of Lancaster county, Pennsylvania, as was the custom of the times, at harvest, gathered the lads and lassies of the surrounding country to his harvesting. One of these, Lilly McIlhenny, by her grace and ·beauty, so attracted the old bachelor's heart that he bowed at the shrine of matrimony. From this marriage came Captain William Bowen, the Indian fighter, and the more celebrated Reese Bowen, who was killed at King's Mountain. Captain William was one of the early settlers of Sumner county; the father of John H. Bowen, lawyer, and idol of his county of Sumner, and of whom the venerable Judge Thomas Barry says, he was the best and most loved man he ever knew. Such was his reputation for probity, that the juries gave him credence when he differed with the court on a point of law; he was elected to Congress before he was of the age to take his seat. His sister married David Campbell, a son of Colonel David Campbell, and brother of General John Campbell, of the war of 1812. This David Campbell and Catherine Bowen were the father and mother of Governor William B. Campbell, of our good State of Tennessee. Speaking, therefore, for our home, your annalist and his wife, daughter of W. B. Campbell, represent, of the Scotch-Irish blood, the united strains of the Kelleys, the Thompsons, the Montgomerys, the Hamiltons, the McIlhennys, the Cunninghams, Hays, and Adams.

My only claim to be heard is the blood that tingles in my veins, and the love and veneration in which I hold the race which first spoke for independence on American soil, which poured out the first blood for liberty from "taxation without representation," and which, in the language of Bancroft (Ransey, p. 102), when defeated in the first battle of the Revolution (Alamance), "like the mammoth, they shook the bolt from their brow and crossed the mountains." Of this mammoth, Tennessee is the child—I speak for this goodly child on her own soil in the fairest domain of America—in old Maury, par excellence the home of the race, which, having spoke first for American independence, made good her words with the *first* blow to tyranny. The race which gave to liberty not only the first blood, but if we are to accept the authority of the author of the "Rear Guard of the Revolution," twice at the most critical juncture of the Revolutionary struggle,

CUT THE COILS

of the anaconda, which, with its head on the lakes and its extremities in Southern Georgia, combined in one gigantic plan, embracing British power and pelf combined with Indian hate and lust of gain, threatened to crush by a single concerted movement the hopes of the young America. Nursed in the heart of this race, the mammoth of liberty has proven thenceforward not only too strong to be held in restraint by the coils of the anaconda of tyranny in America, but has become the apostle of freedom to all the world.

The contribution the Scotch-Irish of Tennessee have to bring to this honorable gathering would be a meaningless fragment without a few words showing the origin of the race, and tracing the source of their marked characteristics.

WHY HAVE THE SCOTCH-IRISH CONTRIBUTED MORE TO CONSTITUTIONAL LIBERTY THAN ANY OTHER PEOPLE?

In the little sketch of the immigration, as early as 1584, of the Scotch Campbells, McDonnells, Montgomerys, and Hamiltons into Ireland, given in our introduction, we have the settlement of a hardy, industrious, sturdy, and liberty-loving population, in the midst of a brave, reveling, quick-witted, emotional, and law-hating race. The two begin to act and react, the one upon the other. Henry the Eighth's contest with the religion of his realm brings a new element to the compound. More Scots come over, to escape wars and persecution at home. Henry VIII. sets up religious persecution, and begins the long-continued and oft-repeated attempt to transfer the possession of Irish lands to the hands of Englishmen. When Elizabeth had come to the throne of England, she continued the work begun by her father. By conquest or by contract, she gave to her favorites, Raleigh and Essex, and other English adventurers, vast estates in Ireland, to be peopled by English.

Following upon her imperfect work, came the more extensive plan of Lord Bacon, under James the First, by which hundreds of thousands of acres of Irish lands were parceled out by allotments to "English and Scots, requiring the Irish to remove from the precincts allotted to them."

During the reign of Charles I., no scruples were felt by the king in awarding to adventurers who had been of service to him estates in Ireland as a reward, nor did the adventurers hesitate as to the morality of the methods used to possess themselves of their estates. But the great settlement of Ireland by English and Scots came about under the government of Cromwell. I have taken from first hands.*

"From the days of the first invasion, the king and council of England intended to make English landed proprietors in Ireland the rulers of Ireland, as William the Conqueror had made the French of Normandy landlords and rulers of the English. Though the government of England were interrupted in this course by the wars of Edward I. for the subjection of the Scotch, by the wars of Edward III.

---

* "Cromwellian Settlement of Ireland," by Prendergast—a book in the hands of Colonel Thomas Boyers, of Gallatin—the shortest epitome that can be made intelligible of the motives and methods of these settlements.

and his successors for the crown of France, and finally by the civil wars of England, called the 'Wars of the Roses,' the design was never abandoned. And when Henry VIII., disencumbered of any foreign war or domestic treason, had time to destroy the house of Kildare, he projected the clearing of Ireland to the Shannon and colonizing it with English. But the new conquest of Ireland only really began in the reigns of his three children, Edward VI., Queen Mary, and Queen Elizabeth, when the conquest of the lands of the Irish for the purpose of new colonizing or planting them with English was resumed, after an interval of more than three hundred years. During this interval, the English Pale, or that part of Ireland subject to the regular jurisdiction of the king of England and his laws, had been gradually contracting—partly by the English of Ireland throwing off the feudal system, and partly by re-conquests effected by the Irish, until in the reign of Edward VI., the Pale was nearly limited by the line of the Liffey and the Boyne. Beyond the Pale the English and the Irish dwelt intermixed. And in all the plans for restoring the regular administration of the king's laws in Ireland it was proposed that these English should be brought back to their ancient military discipline, and should conquer from the Irish the lands in their possession, in order that they might be given to English under grants on feudal conditions by the king.

" But the English of Ireland clearly foresaw that the effect of the complete conquest of the Irish would be to give the government of Ireland to the English of England. Their armed retainers, called Gallowglasses and Kerne, would be put down, as there would no longer remain the pretense of defending the land from the king's Irish enemies. With the regular administration of English law would come back wardships, marriages, reliefs, escheats, and forfeitures, which they were only too happy to have thrown off in the days of Edward II.; and the final result would be to bring over new colonists from England who would be rivals to supplant them in the favor of the government and in all the offices of the state. The English of Ireland, consequently, were secretly indisposed to effect the reconquest, and it was not until they were subdued that the second conquest began.

" The first blow to the English of Irish birth was the limiting the power of the Parliament. In the reign of Henry VII., Sir Edward Poynings forced from the Irish Parliament a statute whereby the Privy Council of England were made virtually a part of the Parliament of Ireland; from thenceforth it could originate no statutes, and could pass only such as had been first approved by the Privy Council of England. The Parliament had, in fact, long become devoted to the earls of Kildare, who had thereby become too powerful for the kings of England. The next and final blow to the power of the English of Ireland was the fall of the House of Kildare, when Silken Thomas, Earl of Kildare, and his five uncles, were executed at Tyburn for treason, at the end of Henry VIII.'s reign. The head of the ancient English of Ireland had now fallen; their parliament had been already deprived of its power; the main obstacles to the design of England were removed, and in the following reigns the reconquest of Ireland by plantation began.

"At first it was the native Irish that were stripped, as the O'Moores, the O'Connors, and the O'Neils. The earl of Desmond's great territories, extending over Limerick and Kerry, Cork and Waterford, were next confiscated and planted. Finally, in James I.'s reign, the native Irish, not only of Ulster, but of Leitrim and whereever else they continued possessed of the original territories, were dispossessed of portions of their lands, varying from one-third to three-fourths, to form plantations of new English. During the reign of Queen Elizabeth, the old English of Ireland, though they agreed in point of religion with the native Irish, always adhered to the English in any rebellion of the Irish, as in a national quarrel. In James I.'s reign, as all the planters were of the new religion, the old English found themselves supplanted by them in all the offices of the state, as the Irish found themselves supplanted by them in their native homes.

"It is needless here to recapitulate the long continued injuries and insults by which the ancient English of Ireland were forced into the same ranks with the Irish in defense of the king's cause in 1641. Chief among them were the attempts to seize their estates under the plea of defective title, in order to plant them with new English. It was thus Lord Stafford got Connaught and parts of Tipperary and Limerick into his power, with the intention of forming a new plantation at the expense of the DeBurgos and other old English. One of the old English in 1644 thus graphically expresses their feelings: 'Was it not the usual taunt of the late Lord Stafford and all his fawning sycophants, in their private conversations with those of the Pale, that they were the most refractory men of the whole kingdom, and that it was more necessary (that is, for their own crooked ends) that they should be planted and supplanted than any others,' and that 'where plantations might not reach, defective titles should extend.' He had known many an officer and gentleman, he adds, who had left a hand at Kinsale in fighting in defense of the Crown of England, when the Spaniards and the Earl of Tyrone were defeated by Lord Mountjoy, to be afterward deprived of his pension for having refused to take the oath of supremacy and allegiance in the Protestant form, though, as one of them answered, on being questioned before the state for matter of recusancy (as they termed it), 'it was not asked of me the day of Kinsale what religion I was of.'

"The Scotch and English, however, having rebelled against the king in 1639 (for the march of the Scottish rebels to the border in that year was on the invitation of the leaders of the popular party in England, though they themselves did not openly take the field till 1642), the Irish rose in his favor. They were finally subdued, in 1652, by Cromwell and the arms of the Commonwealth, and then took place a scene not witnessed in Europe since the conquest of Spain by the Vandals. Indeed, it is injustice to the Vandals to equal them with the English of 1652, for the Vandals came as strangers and conquerors in an age of force and barbarism, nor did they banish the people, though they seized and divided their lands by lot; but the English in 1652 were of the same nation as half of the chief families in Ireland, and had at that time the island under their sway for five hundred years.

"The captains and men of war of the Irish, amounting to 40,000 and upward, were banished into Spain, where they took service under that king; others of them, with a crowd of orphan boys and girls, were transported to serve the English planters in the West Indies; and the remnant of the nation, not banished or transported, were to be transplanted into Connaught, while the conquering army divided the ancient inheritances of the Irish amongst them by the lot."

This writer, in speaking of old English, includes under that term Scotch as well.

Space does not allow more detail. Our object has been to show you the original training which made of the Scotch-Irish the race we find them afterward.

ELEMENTS WHICH MAKE THE CHARACTER OF THE COMPOUND.

The Scotch-Irish in the earlier years of the settlement were often intermarried. We quote a paper which throws light on this point, and on much more:*

"The humble petition of the officers within the precincts of Dublin, Catherlough, Wexford, and Kilkenny, in the behalf of themselves, their souldiers, and other faithful English Protestants, to the lord deputy and council of Ireland."

They pray that the original order of the council of state in Eng-

---
* Cromwellian Settlement of Ireland.

land, confirmed by Parliament, September 27, 1653, requiring the removal of all the Irish nation into Connaught, except boys of fourteen and girls of twelve, might be enforced: "For we humbly conceive (say they), that the proclamation for transplanting only the proprietors, and such as have bin in arms, will neither answer the end of safety, nor what else is aimed at thereby. For the first purpose of the transplantation is to prevent those of natural principles (i. e., of natural affections), becoming, one with these Irish, as well in affinity as idolatry, as many thousands did, who came over in Queen Elizabeth's time, many of which have had a deep hand in all the late murthers and massacres. And shall we join in affinity (they ask) with the people of these abominations?

"Would not the Lord be angry with us till he consumes us, having said, 'The land which ye go to possess is an unclean land, because of the filthiness of the people that dwell therein. Ye shall not, therefore, give your sons to their daughters, nor take their daughters to your sons,' as it is in Ezra, ix, 11, 12, 14. 'Nay ye shall surely root them out before you, lest they cause you to forsake the Lord, your God.' Deut. vii, 2, 3, 4, 16, 18."

We have mention, in the documents giving details of the transplantation, of the names of many high born persons who had thus intermarried. Even Cromwell's old soldiers, full of pious cant and great fear of the abominations of idolatry in the lands where thousands of Irishmen had been slaughtered, and tens of thousands sent out of the land into Spain and the West Indies, found the charms of the Irish maidens, full of vigorous life, chastity, and redolent with healthful beauty, more than they could resist, and so made them wives of the daughters of the land.

We have thus the indomitable, prudent, calculating, metaphysical, God-fearing, tyrant-hating Scotch, brought by marriage into blood relationship with the brave, reckless, emotional, intuitive, God-loving, liberty-adoring Irish.

We shall see the results when we find these people the cautious builders of free constitutional government, and at the same time, the pioneers of American civilization.

ENVIRONMENT.

The Scotch settlers in Ireland, for the government of which the English and Irish were often at war, found themselves so greatly in the minority that they could only stand and see their own civil and religious rights the foot-balls of a government where they had *no representation*. Their religious and civil rights subject to the whims of kings, courtiers, lord lieutenants, bishops, either Romish or Protestant.

In one reign rewarded for services by wrongful gifts of Irish estates, in a subsequent, deprived of their possessions and their services forgotten that more hungry adventurers, or the exchequer of needy monarchs might be replenished. They had for three hundred years been compelled to know by actual daily experience the evils of *provincial* government by kingly favorites, the arrogance, hate, and cruelty of episcopal interference and control. Added to these they felt the narrow hatred and hypocritical cruelty of the Puritan soldiers who prayed to God for strength to visit untold horrors on the men, women and children whom they were robbing in their acts of transportation. Besides these ever recurring religious and political perplexities, they saw their industries at the mercy of the orders of the throne or the English parliament. In other words, government without representation had burnt its evils into their very souls, until in despair of any desirable future to be found in Ireland, and in resolute determination to win a future on the high plane of their own value of manhood and liberty, they deliberately chose to hazard the wilds of America. Their reasons for seeking America had little in common with the adventurers who had been induced by large promises to emigrate from England. They were in nowise allied to the people transplanted by force from England. They were the very people the English most desired to remain in Ireland. They had more in common with the Puritans than with their other persecutors, but even from these had marked distinctions. The strong points and virtues of the two were much the same. A sentence may show the line of distinction, they held in more contempt a restricted hospitality than they did May-poles, their laugh was as hearty, musical, and manly as the groan of the Puritans was affected, grating and inhuman. With this necessary allusion to the blood and environment which gave form, vigor and fitness to this race, we come to the period of their emigration to and settlement in America.

Before passing to the settlement of America, there are a few bright factors entering into the environment of our forefathers in Ireland that we pause on a moment with pleasure. Bishop Echlin, who was himself a native of Scotland in the ordination of Robert Blair, who came as a missionary from the Presbyterian church of Scotland to Ireland, attained a position of lofty Christian manhood little known to bishops of any era. Aided by the influence of Scotch Presbyterian learning and love of liberty, the University of Dublin was founded on very liberal principles. To Dr. James, afterward Archbishop Usher, a professor in this university, was assigned the task of drawing up a confession of faith for the Irish church. To him we are largely indebted for one of the most liberal and comprehensive confessions of faith ever drawn up in Christendom. Afterward, as archbishop, we find this great man standing firmly for liberty of conscience and the protection of the Scotch Presbyterian preachers, until overruled by orders from England. Again to Oliver Cromwell we turn for the exhibition of tolerance far in advance of the Puritan parliament.

These acts of toleration and protection were not without their due influence on the minds of our ancestors. They saw then what the world is slow to learn, *that the highest tolerance and the broadest freedom belong to the greatest men; not to one form of government; not to one form of doctrine.* The men grand enough to outgrow their environment, and defend freedom of thought for those who differ from them, have as yet been too few to pass by their names or forget their influence, in even the most meager historical sketch of the age to which they belong. These were grand beacon-lights, which shone on the struggling days of our forefathers.

Usher towered above the Church of England. Cromwell breached the iron walls of Puritanism. All honor to men who thus grow to proportions which may gladden our hope and confidence in the possibilities of the race.

EMIGRATION.

"The Protestant settlers in Ireland at the beginning of the seventeenth century were of the same metal with those who afterward sailed in the Mayflower—Presbyterians, Puritans, Independents—in search of a wider breathing-space than was allowed them at home. By an unhappy perversity they had fallen under the same stigma, and were exposed to the same inconveniences. The bishops had chafed them with persecutions. . . . The heroism with which the Scots held the northern province against the Kilkenny parliament and Owen Roe O'Neil, was an insufficient offset against the sin of nonconformity. . . . This was a stain for which no excellence could atone. The persecutions were renewed, but did not cool Presbyterian loyalty. When the native race made their last effort, under James II., to recover their lands, the Calvinists of Derry won immortal honor for themselves, and flung over the wretched annals of their adopted country a solitary gleam of true glory. Even this passed for nothing. They were still dissenters; still unconscious that they owed obedience to the hybrid successors of St. Patrick, the prelates of the Establishment; and no sooner was peace reestablished than spleen and bigotry were again at their old work. Vexed with suits in the ecclesiastical courts, forbidden to educate their children in their own faith, treated as dangerous to a state which but for them would have had no existence, and deprived of their civil rights, the most earnest of them at length abandoned the unthankful service. If they intended to live as free men, speaking no lies, and professing openly the creed of the Reformation, they must seek a country where the long arm of prelacy was still too short to reach them. During the first half of the eighteenth century, Down, Antrim, Tyrone, Armagh, and Derry, were emptied of Protestant inhabitants, who were of more value to Ireland than California gold mines." "In two years," says Froude, "which followed the Antrim evictions, thirty thousand Protestants left Ulster for a land where there was no legal robbery, and where those who sowed the seed could reap the harvest. . . . The south and west were caught by the same movement, and ships could not be found to carry the crowds who were eager to go."

A minister of Ulster, writing to a friend in Scotland, in 1718, laments the desolation occasioned in that region "by the removal of several of our brethren to the American plantations. Not less than six ministers have demitted their congregations, and great numbers of the people go with them." Ten years later, Archbishop Boulter wrote to the English Secretary of State respecting the extensive emigration to America: "The humor has spread like a contagious distemper; and the worst is, that it affects only Protestants, and reigns chiefly in the North." About the same time, we find James Logan, the President of the Proprietary Council of Pennsylvania, who had identified himself with the Quakers, and was prejudiced against the emigrants from Ireland, expressing "the common fear that, if they (the Scotch-Irish) continue to come, they will make themselves proprietors of the province." He further, in 1729, expresses "himself glad to find that the Parliament is about to take measures to prevent their too free emigration to this country. It looks as if Ireland is to send all her inhabitants hither; for last week *not less than six ships arrived, and every day two or three arrive also.*" Dr. Baird, in his History of Religion in America, states that, "from 1729 to 1750, about 12,000 annually came from Ulster to America."

These emigrants landed at the ports of Boston, Philadelphia, and Charleston. Comparatively few entered the country by way of New England. Those that did so, settled mainly in New Hampshire, while others found their way to Pennsylvania, and helped swell the tide which was pouring into this state by way of Philadelphia. These Irish settlers occupied the eastern and middle counties, bordering on the wilderness still occupied by the Indians. Such as landed at Charleston, located themselves on the fertile lands of North an

South Carolina and Georgia. The settlers in Pennsylvania afterward turned southward through the valley of Virginia, till, "meeting those extending northward from the Carolinas, the emigration passed westward to the country then called 'beyond the mountains,' now known as Kentucky and Tennessee." At a later period, Western Pennsylvania was occupied by the descendants of the settlers in the middle counties of the state, with Pittsburg as a center. From these points of radiation, the Scotch-Irish have extended to all parts of the country, and, being an intelligent, resolute, and energetic people, have left their name and mark in every state of the Union.

Their youth, at this early period, "were generally educated at home, and under parental instruction, and trained to obedience and subordination, as the unbending law of the family. The schools established by Presbyterian ministers, confirmed and extended the home education. The impress of such instrumentalities was not only manifested in the families of church members, but, by association and influence, extended beyond the pale of organized congregations, and their tendency was to reform and elevate public sentiment and morals, as well as the habits and manners of the people."

The mass of these emigrants were men of intelligence, resolution, energy, religious and moral character, having means that enabled them to supply themselves with suitable selections of land, on which they made permanent homes for their families, and from which they derived an ample support. By their own enterprise and industry they hewed out for themselves valuable farms from the primeval forest; and the toils, sacrifices, and perils, incident to their life in the New World, formed, in both men and women, the characters which were requisite to endure the hardships and dangers of their frontier situation. These traits of character were manifest also in their descendants. Brought up under such education and training, they have since been the "pioneers and founders of settlements in the North-western Territory, and the states formed out of it, and have been amongst the most prominent, useful, and distinguished citizens of the republic." "They were a God-fearing, liberty-loving, tyrant-hating, Sabbath-keeping, covenant-adhering race; trained by trials, made resolute by oppression, governed by conscience, and destined to achieve a mission and place in the history of the church and the race."

Of the early ministers, a very large proportion were from the Irish church. Francis Makemie (1682) was a member of Lagan Presbytery. George McNish (1705) was from Ulster. John Henry (1709) was ordained by the Presbytery of Dublin John Mackey was from Ireland. Samuel Young, of New Castle Presbytery, belonged originally to the Presbytery of Armagh. Robert Cross, Alexander Hutcheson, Thomas Craighead, Joseph Houston, Adam Boyd, John Wilson, and many other useful and honored ministers, were accessions to the ministry of the Presbyterian Church in this country previous to 1730. And from this period, the number who came was continually on the increase. Nor would it be difficult to prove to the satisfaction of all sincere inquirers after truth, that we are indebted to these same men "for the germs of our civil liberties and institutions, as really as for our own noble system of faith and order." As might be expected from their antecedents and providential training, they were ardent lovers, and strong defenders of civil liberty. They hated tyranny with almost "perfect hatred." They had received a discipline that could never be lost, and of all the memories of childhood, none could remain more fresh and impressive than those received from the lips of parents numbered among the heroic champions of freedom at Derry and Enniskillen. And the earliest Scotch-Irish emigrants to America were men who had been participants, or children of those who were participants, in the terrible drama which closed with the battle of the Boyne. Accordingly we find that these men were among the earliest champions of freedom, and the most earnest and persistent defenders of the rights of the people, as against the unjust actions of the British government. No less an authority than the historian Bancroft, states that, "the first public voice in America for dissolving all connection with Great Britain came not from the Puritans of New England, the Dutch of New York, nor the planters of Virginia, but from Scotch-Irish Presbyterians." Abbe Raynal, in his history contemporary with our Revolutionary struggle, though on the side of American independence, does not hesitate to say that the provocations by the British government to the American colonies were so much less than those to which the age was every-where accustomed that it was a matter of deep surprise how the Americans could have been brought to so heroic resistance on grounds so slight. He traces the fact that in the early years of the struggle the mass of our people were little interested in the result. The masses of Americans who had known nothing for generations of provincial government without representation were in no condition to see the dangers which threatened them.

The Scotch-Irish who landed in Boston and New York found colonists too readily submissive to foreign dictation, and preferred to seek Pennsylvania and Maryland, where the proprietary governors and the people governed were in immediate contact. There they pressed to the frontier, where they could organize local governments of their own choosing. Those who reached Virginia passed again to the frontier; they loved neither the aristocratic government nor the episcopal dictation of this colony. Those landing in the south passed north and west in search of similar freedom, so soon as they had met in sufficient proportions to realize their own power. They were led to find homes where they could exercise their attachment to the doctrine affirmed by one of their ministers, speaking for all, as early as 1650, when required by the Long Parliament to subscribe to the oath against a government of *king*, lords, and commons; in refusing, he said:

"Men are called to the magistracy by the suffrage of the people, whom they govern; and for men to assume unto themselves power, is mere tyranny and unjust usurpation." This he said on account of the self-constituted authority of this Parllament. This doctrine, new to civil government, which they had derived from religious convictions, traditions, and struggles, was first to receive the baptism of blood, May 10, 1771, at

ALAMANCE CREEK.

Having mentioned the battle of Alamance, and finding that in some of our histories the character and purposes of the Regulators engaged in this conflict have been greatly misunderstood, I offer the following extract from the life of David Caldwell, D.D., by Rev. E. W. Caruthers, of North Carolina.

"A people who have been religiously educated, as a majority of the Regulators had been, and who had been taught to regard the Bible as a revelation from heaven, are not apt to rise at once in open rebellion against the established government, or bid defiance to the regularly constituted authorities of the land. This is the work of time and reflection. There must be consultation and inquiry into facts for the purpose of satisfying their own consciences, and of justifying themselves before the world. There will be some regard to the voice of reason: some efforts will be made to obtain a redress of grievances without the hazard and sufferings attending a conflict with 'the powers that be.' And then they must have mutual encouragement and mutual pledges of fidelity and support. This is just what we find in the men whose principles and conduct are now under consideration, and it does not appear that hitherto they had as a body made any direct resistance to the operations of government. Fanning and others, who had in the same way become obnoxious to the people, were made the subjects of ridicule or of merriment by the wits and wags of the day, and, as usual in such cases, caricatures and pasquinades abounded. The meeting at Maddock's mills, as we have seen, resolved that they would pay no more illegal taxes, unless they were forced; that they would pay no more exorbitant fees to officers, except by compulsion, and that they would bear an open testimony against it; that they would hold frequent meetings for conference, which they would request their representatives to attend for the purpose of giving them information respecting what was done in the legislature, and of consulting together about the measures that ought to be adopted for the common welfare; that they would select more suitable men for the various offices in the gift of the people; that they would petition the assembly, governor, council, king and parliament, for redress of their grievances; that they would contribute to collections for defraying whatever expenses might be necessary in this undertaking; that whenever a difference of opinion might arise they would submit to the majority; and as a pledge of their fidelity in the performance of these things they bound themselves by an oath or affirmation." In all this we see nothing but the principles and spirit which covered the patriots of '76 with immortal honor; and only because they were better sustained, had more ample resources, and were more successful.

This battle was followed by the call of Colonel Thomas Polk, on the 19th day of May, 1775, for the convention, which gave an "unanimous aye" to the Mecklenburg Declaration of Independence, a declaration remarkable for its heroism, and at the same time its provision for continued government; there was no moment of anarchy between their Declaration of Independence from the British crown, and the erection of a government of their own ordination.

THOMAS POLK.

I have in my possession ample evidence of the Scotch-Irish blood of the Polks. The evidence of genealogy, and the details of service rendered by this distinguished family would occupy more space in this address than your time allows.

I shall, therefore, file these papers with the custodian of the historical papers of the society, and content myself with the mention of only a few prominent events in the lives of a few of the most distinguished members of the family. While dealing with Colonel Thomas Polk, we will complete what we have to say of his direct line, adding a few incidents not to be found in the regular histories. As has already been said, Thomas Polk, as colonel of the militia of the district, called the convention which passed unanimously the Mecklenburg Declaration of Independence. The document, which had been written before the meeting by his son-in-law, Ephraim Brevard, was read to the convention, submitted to a committee for revision, as revised, was re-read, unanimously adopted, and read by order of convention, at the court-house door to the assembled people by Colonel Polk. This had been immortality enough for one man or one family, but Colonel Polk was later a member of the colonial congress, and brigadier-general, was at the battle of Germantown, and in the colonial congress of North Carolina, which was the first to instruct for independence, April, 1776.

John Simpson, one of the witnesses of the Declaration of Independence, of May 20, in giving his testimony (before committee of North Carolina legislature), relates this anecdote: "An aged man near me, on being asked if he knew any thing of this affair (Declaration of 20th), replied: 'Och, aye; Tam Polk declared independence lang before any body else.'"

COLONEL WILLIAM POLK,*

Son of General Thomas Polk and Susan (née Spratt), was born, 1759. He left Queens College, Charlotte, when sixteen years of age (1775), and entered the army as lieutenant in Colonel Thompson's (Old Danger) regiment. He was detailed by Colonel Thompson with thirty men to watch the movements of tories in South Carolina. He was led into an ambuscade by his guide (one Sol. Deason) and was badly wounded in the shoulder, from which he did not recover in a year. "This was the first blood shed south of Lexington," so says General Andrew Jackson, in a sketch written in 1844, when James K. Polk was a candidate for the presidency, also an autobiography written by Colonel Polk, for Judge Murphy, of North Carolina.

General Jackson was a small boy at school with Colonel Polk, at Charlotte, North Carolina. They were life-long friends, and I think that Jackson, although not of military age, was a short time in service with Colonel Polk.

Colonel William Polk's Memoir.

He was with General Davis as volunteer captain at Beaver Creek (Wheeler, 190 page).

At Cowans Ford, July 20, 1780, by the side of General Davidson when he fell (Wheeler, 235).

With General Nash at Germantown, when he (Polk) was wounded in the cheek.

Captain in charge when liberty bell was removed from Philadelphia.

---

* MS. furnished by granddaughter.

He was the first representative from Davidson county (Tenn.) in North Carolina legislature.

Member of North Carolina assembly, 1787, 1790, 1791.

President of North Carolina state bank.

Was appointed by Washington supervisor of all the ports of North Carolina, which he retained until the office was abolished.

Was a member of the Cincinnati society.

At the surrender of Cornwallis at Yorktown.

At the "Cowpens," where his brother Thomas was killed.

Query: Did not Colonel Polk give the name of Nashville and Davidson to the city and county? Having been at the side of General Davidson when he fell, and with General Nash when he was killed, and being the first representative from Davidson, I think confirms the tradition that he named or caused them to be so named. Colonel Polk was offered the commission of brigadier-general by Madison, in the war of 1812 and '13, which he in a patriotic letter declined, and then tendered his service to the governor of North Carolina.

"It was certainly creditable to the Scotch-Irish of North Carolina, as they were the first to secede from the mother country, and so remained that the blood of one of their sons was the first shed (South) in the cause of Liberty," says Bancroft.

General Bishop Leondias Polk, whose life was given in the cause of the South, was a son of Colonel William Polk. General Lucius E. Polk is a grandson.

ANTOINETTE POLK.

A granddaughter of Colonel William Polk, Antoinette Polk, married Baron de Charette, nephew of Comte De Chambord, the Orleans claimant, until his death, of the French throne. She is a charming and noble woman, and is well remembered in Maury county for her courage and daring horsemanship, and also for a famous race.

Before Columbia, Tenn., was taken possession of by either army, General Wilder and his cavalry made a dash into the town to surprise and capture Confederate soldiers, who were scattered at Ashwood and country houses near the town.

Antionette Polk, then a girl of sixteen, was at her uncle's, Dr. William Polk's home, the site of the present U. S. arsenal. Hearing of the raid, she ran to the stable, saddled her fine blooded horse, and not taking time for gloves, started off to give the alarm to the soldiers along the pike, and at Ashwood. As she emerged from the woods she saw she was pursued by several cavalrymen. A countryman, seeing her danger, jumped from his cart, threw wide open the gate, and through she darted, followed by the cavalrymen, and then they raced six miles down the Mt. Pleasant pike. Though they picked up the long ostrich plumes and hat with which she whipped her horse, the lady, the soldiers said, vanished from their sight; but when she was taken fainting from her horse near Mt. Pleasant, she had accomplished her work, and not a soldier was taken prisoner at Ashwood.

The part taken by this distinguished family in the late war between the states is beyond the limits our time will allow.

Bishop (General) Leonidas Polk, and General Lucius Eugene Polk will appear in future history as the peers of the foremost men of their day. President James K. Polk belongs to another place in this address.

Let us return to our proper chronological point, the Declaration of Independence of Mecklenburg, May 20, 1775. The first voice publicly raised in America to dissolve all connections with Great Britain came from the Scotch-Irish Presbyterians. To those at Mecklenburg are to be added an assembly of the same people at Hanna's Town, Western Pennsylvania, May, 1776.

ALEXANDER CRAIGHEAD.

If Presbyterians were the first, and Scotch-Irish in the front line of advance in the march toward American independence, I would be untrue to history if I did not direct attention to the fact that Alexander Craighead was the single file at a good distance in front of the column. As early as 1743, we find Mr. Craighead in Pennsylvania, charged by Thomas Cookson, one of his majesty's justices for Lancaster county, before Presbytery, for the publication of a pamphlet " which tended to dissatisfaction with the civil government that we are now under." Later we find Mr. Craighead in Hanover, Va., and from thence we follow him to Mecklenburg, North Carolina, where we hear him thus spoken of by Rev. A. W. Miller in his centennial discourse, delivered at Charlotte, North Carolina, May 20, 1875.

" To the immortal Craighead, a Presbyterian minister of Ireland, who finally settled in Mecklenburg in 1755, ' the only minister between the Yadkin and the Catawba,' who found in North Carolina what Pennsylvania and Virginia denied him—sympathy with the patriotic views he had been publicly proclaiming since 1741—to this apostle of liberty, the people of Mecklenburg are indebted for that training which placed them in the forefront of American patriots and heroes. It was at this fountain that Dr. Ephraim Brevard and his honored associates drew their inspirations of liberty. So diligent and successful was the training of this devoted minister and patriot; so far in advance even of the Presbyterians of every other colony had he carried the people of this and adjacent counties, that on the very day, May 20, 1775, on which the General Synod of the Presbyterian Church, convened in Philadelphia, issued a pastoral letter to all its churches, counseling them, while defending their rights by force of arms, to stand fast in their allegiance to the British throne, on that lay the streets of Charlotte were resounding with the shouts of freemen, greeting the first declaration of American independence."

As we found an ancestor of Alexander Craighead (viz.) Rev. Robert, standing for liberty at a critical hour in the history of the church in Ulster, so we find later his son, Rev. Thomas B. Craighead, in Haysborough, six miles east of Nashville, the first President of Davidson Academy. The academy was erected into Davidson College, July 9, 1805, and Mr. Craighead became the first president. He, with John Hall, of Sumner, and Geo. McWhirter, of Wilson county, all Scotch-Irish, did more than any men of that day, west of the Cumberland mountains, to form on a high moral plane the manhood of the youth of the earlier part of the nineteenth century. Robust manhood, a high sense of honor, devotion to liberty, enthusiastic patriotism, with excellent mental training, gave to our state a bevy of great men in all that constitutes true greatness.

The first settler in Tennessee was perhaps Captain Wm. Bean, whose relation to the Scotch-Irish race is unknown. In 1770, came Scotch-Irish James Robertson, who should have by right the appellation of father of Tennessee. He was among the first settlers of Watauga. The troubled state of affairs in North Carolina soon begot a steady stream of hardy, daring settlers.

THE WATAUGA SETTLERS,

in convention assembled, formed a written constitution, and elected as commissioners thirteen citizens. They were: John Carter, Charles Robertson, James Robertson, Zach. Isbell, John Sevier, James Smith, Jacob Brown, William Bean, John Jones, George Russell, Jacob Womack, Robert Lucas, William Tatham Of these John Carter, Chas. Robertson, James Robertson, Zach. Isbell, and John Sevier, it is believed, were selected as the court—of which William Tatham was the clerk. It is to be regretted that the account of the lives of all these pioneers is so meager and unsatisfactory. The biography of each of them would be now valuable and interesting. All of the names mentioned, except Sevier, seem to be, from their agreement with the names of well known Scotch-Irish in North Carolina and the valley of Virginia, of the same race.

So far as I have been able to trace the facts, after some care bestowed upon the question, this is not only what Ramsey calls it, "the first written compact of civil government west of the Alleghanies," but the

FIRST WRITTEN CONSTITUTION

born of a convention of people on this continent. The old colonies brought with them the common law of England; they received charters from the English throne, added legislation under these charters; but of constitutions having their origin in the breast of the people, and born of a convention of the people, this is the first recorded in history. This act bears date 1772. The constitution of Virginia bears date, June 12, 1776; North Carolina, December 18, 1776; Maryland, August 14, 1776; New Jersey, July 2, 1776; Massachusetts, 1779.

These, so far as time has enabled me to ascertain, are the earliest state constitutions. I leave to the future historian the query as to whether Alexander Craighead or Patrick Henry deserves the first place as pioneers of American independence. Whether to James Robertson or Alexander Hamilton we are to give the name of constitution builder. In either case, the Scotch-Irish, with a trace of Huguenot blood, win the pre-eminence over all other races. Or if to Madison the greatest credit of the constitution belongs—his ancestors being unknown—we have the Scotch-Irish Donald Robertson, his first teacher.

It is a marvel how we have slept over these glorious achievements of our fathers, and have come to the last moment of possible rescue before we arouse ourselves to see that history shall do them justice. Had we begun this work, even thirty years ago, priceless facts had been saved from the oblivion to which they have gone. Massachusetts makes a rival constitutional claim, founded on the paper drawn up and signed by the Pilgrims before landing on Plymouth Rock. But this paper recognizes the loyalty of the signers to the king, and is destitute of the Scoth-Irish doctrine, long before announced, that right government must have its origin in the breast of the people. The author of the "Rear Guard of the Revolution," evidently on grounds of fancy, rather than proof, gives the chief credit of the constitutional movement at Watauga to John Sevier. I would pluck no laurel from the brow of Tennessee's first governor. He has many, and wears them worthily, but by every token of well attested history of the two men, this act is much more like the

SCOTCH-IRISH ROBERTSON

than the French Sevier; much more the act of the statesman than the soldier. Sevier was vivacious, frolicsome, brave; Robertson, sedate, subtle, wise, and brave, as well. The superior diplomatic powers of Robertson are seen in the early meeting with the Indians to settle the question of title.* Robertson was the spokesman. When all had been settled, on the last day of the gathering it had been arranged that a foot-race should take place between the younger braves and the young men of the settlement, on the open ground along the southern bank of the river. The race was in full progress, and among the younger men all was mirth, hilarity, and good-natured emulation, and even the older chieftains, catching the spirit of the occasion, had relaxed from their habitual gravity, and were cheering on the contestents, when suddenly a musket-shot echoed over the grounds, and one of the young braves, the near kinsman of a chieftain, fell in his tracks lifeless. The report came from the woods near the race-ground, and pursuit failed to discover the assassin, but there could be no question that

HE WAS A WHITE MAN.

It was as if the shot had been fired into a magazine of gunpowder. The Cherokees were there without arms, or there might have followed a bloody tragedy. As it was, they silently gathered their goods together, and, with threatening gestures and faces presaging a bloody vengeance, rapidly stole away into the forest.

It was subsequently discovered that the murderer was a young man named Crabtree, from the Wolf Hills (now Abingdon), Virginia, about fifty miles to the north-east. A brother of his had, not long before, been killed by the Shawnees, while engaged in exploring with Boone in Kentucky, and he had taken this inopportune time for his revenge. The Indians had left hastily, giving the whites no time for explanation or parley. Revenge—blood for blood—was the cardinal doctrine of their theology, and, if something were not done at once to avert it, war, bloody and exterminating, would soon be upon the settlers. What could be done to avert it? To flee the country would be to merely invite pursuit, and a hundred miles of wilderness lay between them and any safe asylum. To remain was just as hazardous, for how could this handful of one hundred men sustain a conflict with

THREE THOUSAND INFURIATED SAVAGES?

Hastily, the settlers gathered together in council, and then it was that Robertson volunteered, like Curtius, to ride into the breach—at the peril of his life, to visit and endeavor to pacify the enraged Cherokees. It was a hundred and fifty miles through an unbroken forest, with death lurking behind every tree that grew by the way; but

---

* Ramsey, and "Rear Guard of the Revolution."

what, he said, was one life periled to save five hundred? Thus Robertson reasoned with his neighbors and friends; and then, giving a parting kiss to his wife and child, he mounted his horse and rode off into the wilderness. History contains few acts so daring, so full of the highest courage, so truly altruistic. To charge with comrades on the field of battle in no sense reaches to the sublime height of an act like this. He succeeded in his mission, and four years of peace followed.

Robertson, as is well known, came early to the French Lick settlement on the Cumberland, now Nashville. Here he repeated the same act of founding constitutional government in which he had led at Watauga. Here he repeats his skillful diplomacy with Indian and Spanish agent alike. His manly bearing, his great strength of character, and profound knowledge of men, make him the trusted leader. After detailing many of his military expeditions and negotiations, Ramsey, the venerable historian, says: "The people of Tennessee have reason to

VENERATE THE MEMORY

of James Robertson, alike for his military and civil services, and the earnest and successful manner in which he conducted his negotiations for peace and commerce. His probity and weight of character secured to his remonstrances with Indian and Spanish agents respectful attention and consideration. His earnest and truthful manner was rarely disregarded by either."

While Robertson was thus building up constitutional government and laying broadly the foundation of western empire, Sevier allowed himself to become involved in the unfortunate feuds of the State of Franklin. Every-where he appears the glorious soldier, the magnanimous friend; but had Robertson been at Watauga instead of French Lick, Colonel Arthur Campbell, who was the real originator of the State of Franklin, could never have led him to the steps taken by Sevier. He, Robertson, would never have been led to the grave mistake of the attack on Tipton's house. Colonel Arthur Campbell was a restless spirit, full of theories; a man of much more educational culture than either Robertson or Sevier; did the writing that produced the State of Franklin; prepared the constitution first presented to the convention. Patrick Henry, then governor of Virginia, says, in a communication to the legislature: "The limits proposed for the new government of Frankland by Colonel Arthur Campbell, and the people of Virginia, who aimed at a separation from that state, were expressed in the form of a constitution, which Colonel Campbell drew up for public examination."

His county in Virginia did not follow his wishes and become connected with the new state. His brother-in-law, Colonel Wm. Campbell, of King's Mountain fame, opposed the movement, and was more influential with the people. Judge David Campbell, his brother, though not originally favoring the formation of a state, became afterward its ablest counselor and apologist, yet so retained, by his conservative course, the confidence of both parties, that he held the highest judicial positions under both states. I have no disposition to pursue the question growing out of the formation of the State of Franklin further than to make good a claim that the origin or maintenance of well-organized government in Watauga and in the French Lick settlement are to be attributed to the same great pioneer genius, James Robertson. I have seen the private papers of Colonel Arthur Campbell, which manifest a subtle genius, a fondness for elaborate writing. His letters, to the last, were very long, almost equal to a modern newspaper, and filled with political discussion. He was more than once on military expeditions with Sevier. In one of the most extended of the Sevier expeditions enumerated to the credit of Sevier in the "Rear Guard of the Revolution," he, and not Sevier commanded. I have seen his official report of the expedition in his own chirography.

I had at one time proposed to give the names of the early settlers of Tennessee, both east and middle, that could be identified as Scotch-Irish, but have been led to abandon that purpose for several reasons: First. We are a generation too late in attempting to gather many of the necessary facts the last generation might have given them; this generation can not; many families have not preserved the records back of the first settlers. I have found many descendants of our more prominent families ignorant of the fact that their ancestors were Scotch-Irish, when on examining the material at hand, I have been able to find ample proof of the fact; it would therefore be invidious to offer a list of names of families unless the list could be made comparatively complete. Second. On further study of the question, it is evident that an overwhelming majority of the early settlers of our state were Scotch-Irish, so that every Tennessean descending from our first hardy settlers is to be put down as of this people, if he can not prove his descent to be otherwise. The author of the "Rear Guard" thus speaks of the early settlers who came to Watauga after Robertson's peace with O-ka-na-sto-ta:

"They were nearly all from Virginia, and of Scotch-Irish descent, generally poor, and threading the old Indian war-path, or some narrow trace blazed by the hunters, with only a single pack-horse, which carried all their worldly possessions. But they had strong arms and stout hearts, and added at once to the wealth and security of the young community. They became, by the mere act of settlement, large land-owners, and their names are borne to-day by many of the leading families of the south-west. Forts, modeled after the one at Watauga, were built for the protection of the outlying settlers, and the colonists soon felt as secure as in their old homes in Virginia."

Later, Ramsey tells of further Scotch-Irish under Colonel David Campbell, forted near Knoxville, old soldiers of King's Mountain. To show that these were not the ignorant people the author of the Rear Guard seems to indicate, I here give the names of books taken from a single shelf in my library which have come down to me—books from homes of old Scotch-Irish:

Abbe Reynal's Histories, 1750 begun.
Hume's History.
Female Spectator, 1775.
Essays, Hugh Knox, Gettysburg, Pennsylvania, 1804.
Pollock's Course of Time.
Mosheim's Ecclesiastical History, 1766.
Dodridge's Works, 1792.
Life of Ireland, Winchester, Va., 1819.
Newton's Works, 1792.
Night Thoughts, 1770.
Hervey's Meditations.
Pope's Essays.
Newton on Prophecies, 1782.
Discourses on God's Sovereignty, 1772, by Elisha Coles.
William Cowper, 1792.
The Boston Collection of Hymns, 1808.
"A Plan for Female Education," by Erasmus Darwin, 1798.
On Solitude. Michael W. Hogan, Limerick, on one of the blank pages. Title page gone.
Sin in Believers, John Owen, D.D., Glasgow, 1758.
Josephus.

Taking the early histories of North Carolina, and the annals of the settlement of middle Tennessee, it is easy to see that the largest proportion of the settlers were from the Scotch-Irish counties of North Carolina and Virginia. Among the first we have from Ramsey: "A settlement of less than a dozen families was formed near Bledsoe's Lick (1778), isolated in the heart of the Chickasaw nation, with no other protection than their own courage, and a small stockade inclosure. In the early spring of 1779, a little colony of gallant adventurers, from the parent hive at Watauga, crossed the Cumberland Mountain, penetrated the intervening wilds, and pitched their tents near the French Lick, and planted a field of corn where the city of Nashville now stands. This field was at the spot where Joseph Park since resided, and near the lower ferry. These pioneers were Captain James Robertson, George Freeland, William Neely, Edward Swanson, James Hauly, Mark Robertson, Zachariah White, and William Overhall.

" While Robertson and his co-emigrants were thus reaching the Cumberland by the circuitous and dangerous trace through the wilderness of Kentucky, others of their countrymen were

UNDERGOING GREATER HARDSHIPS,

enduring greater sufferings, and experiencing greater privations upon another route, not less circuitous and far more perilous, in aiming at the same destination. Soon after the former had left the Holston settlements on their march by land, several boats loaded with emigrants and their property left Fort Patrick Henry, near Long Island, on a voyage down the Holston and Tennessee, and up the Ohio and Cumberland. The distance traversed in this inland voyage, the extreme danger from the navigation of the rapid and unknown rivers, and the hostile attacks from the savages upon their banks, mark the emigration under Colonel Donelson as one of the greatest achievements in the settlement of the west."

Without going into details, which would protract too much the time, I quote from Phelan's "Tennessee" his summary, leaving out such names as are known to be of other blood:

"The names of these adventurous navigators and bold pioneers of the Cumberland country are not, all of them, recollected; some of them follow: Mrs. Robertson, the wife of James Robertson, Col. Donelson, John Donelson, Jun., Robert Cartwright, Benjamin Porter, James Cain, Isaac Neely, John Cotton, Mr. Rounsever, Jonathan Jennings, William Crutchfield, Moses Renfroe, Joseph Renfroe, James Renfroe, Solomon Turpin, —— Johns, Sen., Francis Armstrong, Isaac Lanier, Daniel Dunham, John Boyd, John Montgomery, John Cockrill, and John Caffrey, with their respective families; also Mary Henry, a widow, and her family, Mary Purnell and her family, John Blackmore, and John Gibson. These, with the emigrants already mentioned as having arrived with Robertson by the way of the Kentucky trace, and the few that had remained at the bluff to take care of the growing crops, constituted the nucleus of the Cumberland community in 1780. Some of them plunged at once into the adjoining forests, and built a cabin with its necessary defenses. Col. Donelson, himself, with his connections, was of this number. He went up the Cumberland and settled upon Stone's river, a confluent of that stream, at a place on its south side. The situation was found to be too low, as the water, during a freshet, surrounded the fort, and it was, for that reason, removed to the north side."

The names Nashville and Davidson county are testimonials to the blood of the inhabitants, while Montgomery county adds another, and Sumner is dotted with licks and creeks which retain the names of these early Scotch-Irish settlers. The original Maury county is a cluster of Scotch-Irish with scarcely a drop of alien blood. The bravery of these people, coupled with their sturdy endurance of privation and savage warfare, is without any parallel in the early settlement of America. In the north-west the settler followed the soldier, often also the settler followed the roads; here the settler was the only soldier, and no roads were known until he created them under his own organized government.

At first, as we have seen, emigrants came by a circuitous route through Kentucky or along the dangerous navigation of the Tennessee; as soon as the settlers could organize they cut a road more than two hundred miles in length from Campbell's Station, in East Tennessee, to Nashville, and sent properly officered squads to protect the emigrants en route. The stories of the heroic actions and brave endurance of many of the women on these long journeys kindled in my boyhood a passionate admiration never to be forgotten. The part taken by Mrs. Buchanan in the fort just east of Nashville, molding bullets and carrying in her apron over an uncovered space to the men as they fired from the port-holes, has been often told. At Campbell's Station, on occasion of an attack, when the men reached the house from the field, they found the women had already barred the doors, loaded the rifles, and the commander of the fort found his wife, gun in hand, at the port-hole.

While two armies, one under General Harmar and another under General St. Clair, and, finally, a third, under that thunderbolt of war, General Anthony Wayne, had been sent forward by the general government for the protection of the north-western settlers, the Tennessee settlers were left to work out their own destiny, tempted by Spanish officers, importuned by French promises. "The Indians, incited by the British and Spaniards, constantly harried around the stations, the springs, and the fields, ambushed the paths from station to station, roamed the woods like sleuth-hounds to seize the adventurous hunter, stole their horses, killed their cattle, drove off the wild game to produce famine. So terrific at one time became the ordeal, that all the stations were abandoned except Eaton's and the Bluffs (Nashville). The stationers went in armed squads to the springs, and plowed while armed sentinels guarded the fields." Deaths by Indians were of almost weekly occurrence. Many of the settlers left in despair; but the Scotch-Irish blood in the veins of Robertson, Ewing, Rains, Buchanan, and Donaldson, after solemn counsel and compact, said, we will stay.* On the 22d of April, 1781, the Indians, by a well planned stratagem, attempted to take the Bluffs, which was considered the Gibraltar of the Cumberland. A decoy party drew the men away from the fort into an ambush. When they dismounted to give battle, their horses dashed off toward the fort, and they were pursued by some Indians, which left a gap in their lines, through which some whites were escaping to the fort. Just then another large body of Indians were seen from the fort emerging from another ambush, intercepting the whites and making for the fort. All seemed lost. We are ready to shut our eyes upon the horrid scene, and stop our ears against the wail of women and children as they are sinking under the tomahawk and scalping-knife. But no! the heroic women, headed by Mrs. James Robertson, seized the axes and idle guns, and planted themselves in the gate, resolved to *die* rather than give up the fort. Just in time, she ordered the sentry to turn loose a pack of dogs, selected for their size and courage to encounter bears and panthers, and that were frantic to join the fray. They dashed off, outyelling the savages, who recoiled before the fury of their onset, giving the men time to escape into the fort. It is said that Mrs. Robertson " patted every dog as he came into the fort."

Through it all, our first progenitors held true to their first compact *of equal rights, mutual protection, impartial justice, with the reserved power of removing the unfaithful from office,* and to the soil where they had elected to make their struggle for liberty and homes.

To give the temper of the Scotch-Irish women, I give the following:

A WHIG WEDDING IN DERBY DURING THE REVOLUTION.

In Dunlap's Pennsylvania Packet for June 17, 1778, then published at Lancaster during the occupation of Philadelphia by the British, we find the following reference to the marriage of Jane, daughter of the Rev. John Roan, to William Clingan, Jr.:

" Was married last Thursday (June 11, 1778), Mr. William Clingan, Jr., of Donegal, to Miss Jenny Roan, of Londonderry, both of this county of Lancaster; a sober, sensible, agreeable young

---

* Address of General Bright.

couple, and *very sincere Whigs*. This marriage promises much happiness as the state of things in this our sinful world will admit. This was truly a Whig wedding, as there were present many young gentlemen and ladies, and not one of the gentlemen but had been out when called on in the service of his country; and it was well known that the groom, in particular, had proved his heroism, as well as Whigism, in several battles and skirmishes. After the marriage was ended, a motion was made, and heartily agreed to by all present, that the young unmarried ladies should form themselves into an association by the name of the 'Whig Association of Unmarried Young Ladies of America,' in which they should pledge their honor that they would never give their hand in marriage to any gentleman until he had first proved himself a patriot, in readily turning out when called to defend his country from slavery, by a spirited and brave conduct, as they would not wish to be the mothers of a race of slaves and cowards."

All honor to the memories of those patriotic women of Dauphin in the war for independence! This was a Scotch-Irish county. Rev. John Roan was a Presbyterian, and the uncle who reared Archibald Roan, afterward governor of Tennessee. The latter was among the earlier settlers, and married the sister of Judge David and Colonel Arthur Campbell.

There are two men, Duncan Robertson and Montgomery Bell, who, on grounds of distinguished philanthropy and liberality, deserve to be mentioned in every sketch of the Scotch-Irish of our county of Davidson.

Monette, in his "Valley of the Mississippi," says: "Tennessee, not inaptly, has been called the mother of states. From the bosom of this state have issued more colonies for the peopling of the great valley of the Mississippi than from any one state in the American Union. Her emigrant citizens have formed a very important portion of the population of Alabama, of the northern half of Mississippi and Florida. They have also formed the principal portion of the early population of the states of Missouri, Arkansas, and Texas.

The first settlers of Tennessee not only through years of manly struggle and endurance combined the work of the pioneer settler with that of soldier, but early won as volunteers the rightful claim of protector of the regions beyond them south and west. We do not deem it proper to enter into the part taken by the Scotch-Irish of western Virginia and Tennessee, and North and South Carolina, in the critical battle of Kings Mountain—that has been left for others. I may be allowed to say the men who fought that battle were almost to a man of this heroic race. In their history they are three times called upon during the revolutionary struggle to repel the combined attempt of English and Indians to crush the struggling colonies—each time they cut the lines of the advancing foe, and so dismembered the parts of the plan of operation as to thwart its ends. This is the work so brilliantly described in the pages of the "Rear Guard of the Revolution." It is too well known to detain you with its recital.

As we find a band of Scotch-Irish grouped around William Campbell at Kings Mountain, so we find in the second period of Tennessee history,

ANDREW JACKSON,

Whose father came from Carrickfergus, Ireland, to North Carolina, becomes the central figure of all the military movements of the southwest. Alabama, Georgia, Mississippi, Florida and Louisiana alike, find in him and the Tennessee volunteers, who come at his call, their deliverers from Spanish, Indian, and British foes. The leaders who are the arms of his power are of his own race. Generals Coffe and Carrol, General Winchester, General William Hall and Colonel Henderson. In the fiercest hours of the struggle others of the race arrest the pen of history at the battle of Horseshoe. The Thirty-ninth regiment, under Colonel Williams, the brigade of East Tennesseans, under Colonel Bunch, marched rapidly up to the breastwork and delivered a volley through the port-holes. The Indians returned the fire with effect, and, muzzle to muzzle, the combatants for a short time contended. Major L. P. Montgomery, of the Thirty-ninth, was the first man to spring upon the breastwork, where, calling upon his men to follow, he received a ball in his head, and fell dead to the ground. At that critical moment, young ensign Houston mounted the breastwork. A barbed arrow pierced his thigh; but, nothing dismayed, this gallant youth, calling his comrades to follow, leaped down among the Indians, and soon cleared a space around him with his vigorous right arm. Joined in a moment by parties of his own regiment, and by large numbers of the East Tennesseans, the breastwork was soon cleared, the Indians retiring before them into the underbrush. The wounded ensign sat down within the fortification, and called a lieutenant of his company to draw the arrow from his thigh. Two vigorous pulls at the barbed weapon failed to extract it. In a fury of pain and impatience, Houston cried, "Try again, and if you fail this time, I will smite you to the earth." Exerting all his strength, the lieutenant drew forth the arrow, tearing the flesh fearfully, and causing an effusion of blood that compelled the wounded man to hurry over the breastwork to get the wound bandaged. While he was lying on the ground under the surgeon's hands, the general rode up, and recognizing his young acquaintance, ordered him not to cross the breastwork again. Houston begged him to recall the order, but the general repeated it peremptorily and rode on. In a few minutes the ensign had disobeyed the command, and was once more with his company, in the thick of that long hand-to-hand engagement, which consumed the hours of the afternoon. Toward the close of the afternoon it was observed that a considerable number of the Indians had found a refuge under the bluffs of the river, where a part of the breastwork, the formation of the ground, and the felled trees, gave them complete protection. Desirous to end this horrible carnage, Jackson sent a friendly Indian to announce to them that their lives should be spared if they would surrender. They were silent for a moment, as if in consultation, and then answered the summons by a volley, which sent the interpreter bleeding from the scene. The cannon were now brought up, and played upon the spot without effect. Jackson then called for volunteers to charge: but the Indians were so well posted, that, for a minute, no one responded to the call. Ensign Houston again emerges into view on this occasion. Ordering his platoon to follow, but not waiting to see if they would follow, he rushed to the overhanging bank, which sheltered the foe, and through openings of which they were firing. Over this mine of desperate savages he paused, and looked back for his men. At that moment he received two balls in his right shoulder; his arm fell powerless to his side; he staggered out of the fire, and lay totally disabled. His share in that day's work was done. After being elected governor of Tennessee, this man became the Washington of Texas.

A CHARACTERISTIC INCIDENT

of General Jackson, which I have not seen in print, was given me by Judge Thomas Barry, of Sumner county, who knew the general well. The judge himself is a fine specimen of the race. General Jackson, after his popularity had given him a large number of namesakes through the country, was invited to a public dinner in his honor at Hartsville, now in Trousdale county. After dinner, the fond parents claimed the privilege of a hand-shake for the namesakes. Judge Barry said that at a little distance he noted the fact that to each of the boys the general gave a silver coin, accompanied by a remark he could not hear. Selecting one of the larger boys, he asked him what the general had said to him. The boy replied, "He put his thumb-nail on the word liberty, and said, 'For this our country fought through seven years; never give it up but with your life.'" To him liberty had a meaning. Men who followed him adored it. There was a sacredness and awe in the tones in which they spoke of it, showing its profound impress upon the strong mold of their natures. Jackson not only delivered the south-west, but gave us much of what is distinctive in the principles, and all of what is marked in the methods of the Democratic party, affecting the life of the nation as no man after Washington and before Lincoln has done.

THE CONSTITUTION OF TENNESSEE,

in the formation of which he took a prominent part, was pronounced by Thomas Jefferson the "most republican of all the constitutions adopted by the states." Jackson's love of liberty and of the Union atone for much of his personal tyranny when in office. His force of will brooked no opposition; his intensity allowed no friendship beyond the bounds of agreement; his fiery temper was an exaggeration of true Scotch Irish devotion to principle and enthusiasm for right.

Besides the prominent soldiers who co-operated with Jackson, we have among his contemporaries of Scotch-Irish blood Hugh L. White, who in one of Jackson's greatest extremities left the judicial bench to lead a party of volunteers to the rescue. A man who was brave as Jackson, as deeply enamored of his country's freedom, but one who knew no arts to win popular applause beyond lofty adherence to principle, the man who as a candidate for the Presidency of the United States won the vote of his own state over Jackson's active opposition, one of the purest and ablest of American statesmen, second only as a statesman to one Tennessean—John Bell.

The father of John Bell, Samuel Bell, came from North Carolina to Tennessee. His wife was Margaret Edmonson, of a family largely represented in the battle of King's Mountain, and in all subsequent military expeditions from Tennessee—Scotch-Irish on both sides.

JOHN BELL

was a student with Craighead in his boyhood; elected to Congress over Felix Grundy, who was supported by the warm personal influence of General Jackson; a warm admirer of J. C. Calhoun, but of such thorough independence of character, that he was placed as chairman of the committee in the House before which it was supposed Mr. Calhoun's resolutions would come for consideration; elected speaker of the House over James K. Polk; supported Hugh L. White for President, and while White carried the state, Bell carried the Hermitage district over the whole force of the administration and the indomitable exertions of General Jackson; entered the Senate, where he stood for the Union through every change of administration; favored the right of petition on the part of the abolitionists when the whole South and many of the northern statesmen refused them the privilege; was secretary of war under Harrison; resigned when he could not agree with Tyler; declined the offer of re-election to the Senate, on the grounds that E. H. Foster deserved it at the hands of his party—rare man; was re-elected at the next vacancy; stood for the compromise of 1850; opposed the doctrine "to the victor belongs the spoils." One of the best, most independent of American statesmen, who through all his career loved the American Union more than he loved party or power.

Before leaving John Bell, duty to the race whose place in American civilization we are seeking to indicate, demands a reference to the remarkable attitude held by him and Stephen A. Douglas at the second most critical juncture in American history. We have seen our ancestral part in the earlier era; again, in the trying epoch of the nation, when the hour came to test the power of the Union to hold in one the states which had been gathered under the constitution, the race stands out with a prominence that I have seen accorded them in no annals of the times.

In the Presidential contest of 1860, Lincoln represented the extreme opinions of the North, Breckinridge the extreme opinions of the South. The Scotch-Irish Bell and Douglas stood for the Union under the constitution. They represented, the one, the conservatism of the old Whig party, the other, the conservative element in the Northern Democratic party. Whatever of honor there is in love of the Union, we claim that honor for the Scotch-Irish, as represented by these two sons in the hour of our country's greatest peril.

The chronological order of events demands that we turn back to the period of the last Indian war, with the Seminoles in Florida, when Tennessee again is found with her volunteers in the fore-front of the fight. General Robert Armstrong, Colonel Wm. Trousdale, and Captain Wm. B. Campbell, leading spirits of the hour, were all from Scotch-Irish ancestors. These we have traced; many, perhaps all others, were of the same blood, but the proof has not come to us, though asked for again and again.

We ought to mention that pure man, Mr. Sommerville, cashier of the bank at Nashville, by whose indomitable energy the money was raised that enabled General Carrol to reach New Orleans at the critical moment for the battle of New Orleans, where Jackson, with two Scotch-Irish general officers and an army of like blood, won deathless fame. The world has kept the name of the warrior, but allowed to he almost forgotten the name of the quiet patriot who "handled millions, but died poor."

JAMES K. POLK.

We have found the first President Tennessee gave to the United States of Scotch-Irish blood, so we find the second, James K. Polk. It is said by a historian that the most brilliant career of any man in the White House was that of James K. Polk. About his early career gather White, Bell, Cave Johnson, Catron, and the great Socratic lawyer, John Marshall, of Williamson county. They, with his first opponent for governor of the state, Newton Cannon, were of the same race. In this canvass the latest historian of Tennessee says: " Polk opened the campaign on his side by an address to the people of Tennessee perhaps the ablest political document which appeared in this state up to the time of the war."

His agency in adding the boundless West to the domain of the United States needs no eulogy at this late day. Without the Pacific coast, as we have it, the United States would have been one of the great nations of the world; with it, she inevitably must hold at no distant future an unrivaled pre-eminence. The time is now on us when the world must realize that in potency we can be classed with no other nationality.

In the Mexican war again we look for the Tennessee volunteers, and in addition to the names of Trousdale and Campbell, that of B. F. Cheatham, who had gone as captain in the First, when that regiment was disbanded at the close of the year for which it was enlisted, raised another regiment, of which he was made colonel. Cheatham had the blood of James Robertson in his veins. He proved in the war between the states a veritable thunderbolt of war; a man of the staunchest integrity. All the men from Tennessee prominent in the Mexican war were of Scotch-Irish blood, with, perhaps, the exception of General Gideon Pillow. I believe him to be of the same blood, from his relation to Colonel Wm. Pillow, of whom Ramsey says: "Among other emigrants from North Carolina to Cumberland was the father of William Pillow. He came through the wilderness with the guard commanded by Captain Elijah Robertson, and settled four miles south of Nashville, at Brown's station. The son, William Pillow, was in most of the expeditions carried on against the Indians, from the time of his arrival in the country to the close of the Indian war."

He was the hero and victor of Fort Donelson in the recent war. He has never been accorded his due for his brilliant fighting there. The Mexican war showed the volunteer spirit of Tennessee undimmed.

Ten men volunteered their services for one accepted. Phelan's history thus speaks of two of Tennessee's soldiers in this war:

GENERAL WILLIAM TROUSDALE,

whose popular *sobriquet* was the "War Horse of Sumner County," was born September 23, 1790, in Orange county, North Carolina, and was of Scotch-Irish descent. In 1796, his father removed with him to Davidson county, Tennessee. When a boy at school he had joined the expedition against the Creek Indians, and was at Tallahatchie and Talladega. During the Creek war, in pursuance of some duty, he swam the Tennessee river, near the Muscle Shoals, being on horseback, although unable to swim himself. He was also at Pensacola and New Orleans during the War of 1812. In 1835, he was in the state senate, and in 1836 major-general of the militia. He fought through the Seminole war of 1836. In 1837, he was an unsuccessful candidate for Congress. In 1840, he was a Van Buren elector. He fought through the Mexican war with great bravery, and was twice wounded at Chapultepec. He was made brigadier-general by brevet in the United States army for gallant and meritorious conduct in that engagement. Trousdale was a man of sound understanding and pure character, and intellectually not inferior to his competitor. He was elected by a majority of 1,390.

WM. B. CAMPBELL,

who opposed Trousdale in the next gubernatorial race, was descended from a line of distinguished Revolutionary heroes. He finished his education, which was solid and liberal, under his uncle, Governor David Campbell, of Virginia, under whose supervision he studied law. He returned to Tennessee, and in 1829 was elected attorney-general. In 1836, he resigned his seat as a member of the legislature, and as captain entered the Florida war, through which he fought with honor. In 1837, he defeated General Trousdale for Congress, and again in 1839. In 1841, he was elected without opposition. He fought gallantly through the Mexican war as colonel of the First Regiment, whose desperate bravery won for it the *sobriquet* of "The Bloody First." Campbell himself led the charge at Monterey, and his troops hoisted the first flag on the walls of the Mexican city. This was perhaps the most brilliant feat of arms accomplished during the war. The form of Campbell's command to charge, "Boys, follow me," became historic, and was also the favorite battle-cry of the Whigs during the campaign that elected him governor. In 1848, he was elected circuit judge by the legislature, and in 1851 he was nominated by acclamation for governor by the Whigs. Trousdale and Campbell were cast in the same mold. Both were men of pure character, of high purpose, of stern integrity, possessing sound practical sense, without brilliancy of parts or fluency of tongue, and both were conservative and courageous. "Two gamer cocks," says one writer, "were never pitted against each other in a canvass for governor."

"Virginia and Massachusetts are the only states which have furnished more names that stand higher on the national roll of honor than Tennessee. Not to mention Tennesseaus who, like Tipton, of Indiana; Houston, of Texas; Benton, of Missouri; Garland and Sevier and Hindman, of Arkansas; Claiborne, of Louisiana; Henry Watterson, of Kentucky; Sharkey and Yerger, of Mississippi; Gwin, of California; and Admiral Farragut, have attained influence and celebrity either local or national in other states, Tennessee has given the national government a number of

PRESIDENTS AND CABINET OFFICERS

entirely out of proportion to its wealth and population. George W. Campbell was secretary of the treasury under Madison. Andrew Jackson was President from 1829 to 1837. John H. Eaton was secretary of war under Jackson. Felix Grundy was attorney-general under Van Buren. John Bell was secretary of war under Harrison and Tyler. Cave Johnson was postmaster-general under Polk, and Polk himself was President from 1845 to 1849. Tennessee has furnished the House of Representatives two speakers, Bell and Polk, and the Senate one presiding officer, in the person of H. L. White, in 1832.

"In addition to this, Tennessee has had two unsuccessful candidates for the Vice-presidency, James K. Polk, in 1840, and A. J. Donelson, on the ticket with Fillmore, in 1856, and two unsuccessful candidates for the Presidency, H. L. White, in 1836, and John Bell, in 1860. John Catron was on the supreme bench of the United States from 1837 to 1865. Joseph Anderson was the first comptroller of the United States, from 1815 to 1836. William B. Lewis was the second auditor from 1829 to 1845. Daniel Graham was register of the treasury from 1847 to 1849, and A. A. Hall from 1849 to 1851 and 1853.

"In addition to this, Tennessee has furnished innumerable representatives to the diplomatic service abroad, two of them, George W. Campbell and Neil S. Brown, to the same court—Russia."

"The quaintest, the most striking, the most original figure in south-western history was David Crockett. Brownlow, the fighting parson, the caustic writer, the politician, was a Tennessean—governor and senator. The filibustering expeditions, just preceding the war, were full of romantic episodes. The leading figure in them was William Walker, the 'Grey-eyed Man of Destiny,' whose exploits in Nicarauga for a time attracted the gaze of Europe and America, and whose sad and tragic fate has been described in the glowing and sensuous verses of Joaquin Miller. The war between the states brought to the surface many men of strong character and pronounced individuality, but the most brilliant, the most original, the most attractive, the most dashing of all, was

N. B. FORREST,

a Tennessean. Joe C. Guild, the odd wag and the quaint humorist, whose memory still lives in the traditions of the story-teller and the anecdote-monger, was a Tennessean. Bailie Peyton, the peripatetic politician and brilliant orator, was a Tennessean. The period from 1836 to 1860 was an era of great men and great orators. The style of oratory was characteristic, and nearly always brilliant—full of fire and gorgeous flights of fancy and rhetorical adornment. Gus Henry was the eagle orator. James C. Jones was a figure of national prominence, and was frequently suggested as a candidate for speaker. M. P. Gentry was a leader in Congress, and an orator of the first magnitude. After his first speech in Congress, John Quincy Adams, who took pleasure in observing new members of Congress, declared that he was 'the greatest natural orator in Congress.' Landon C. Haynes, the Confederate senator, was also noted for the dazzling brilliancy of his rhetoric." The Irish-Scotch William Walker, here mentioned, was descended from the McClellans, a family whose genealogy is traced back through many of the early settlers of Virginia, Tennessee, and North Carolina to the north of Ireland, and thence to Scotland in the twelfth century, where they held noble position. To the same family belongs Prof. A. H. Buchanan, of Cumberland University. The record involves many of the best familes of Lincoln and Giles counties, and of North Alabama. It will be filed with the historical papers.

PRESBYTERIANS.

We turn from the secular to the religious, and in as compact manner as possible give the place of Scotch-Irish Presbyterians in Tennessee; as the family is largely represented in Tennessee, I begin with Dr. Witherspoon, a signer of the Declaration of Independence.*

Dr. Caldwell, of North Carolina, first president of the State University, has worthy descendants in Tennessee. The family honor has been maintained in the worthy representative in Congress from the Hermitage district, the Hon. Andrew Caldwell. Caruthers, of North Carolina, has a large progeny in Tennessee. One was Judge A. Caruthers, founder of the celebrated law school of Cumberland University, whose influence as lawyer and Christian has gone far toward peopling the south-west with Christian lawyers. His brother, Judge Robert L. Caruthers, of the Supreme Court, the most powerful force in giving success to the Cumberland Presbyterian Church. E. B. Currie, of North Carolina, whose descendants have held distinguished places in Tennessee history, especially in the postal service. Rev. Gideon Blackburn was a right arm of power to General Jackson through all the struggles of the early settlement of Tennessee. "It is worthy of remark that the first four prominent educators of Tennessee, Doak, Craighead, Carrick, and Balch, were all of Scotch-Irish descent, and members of the same Presbytery. The Bible and the school-book were borne together across the Alleghanies by men in whose veins flowed the blood which had withstood the oppression of three centuries."

That America should have owed its independence at the era when it occurred, to the Scotch-Irish settlers, and foremost among them to

THE PRESBYTERIAN PREACHERS,

that at the close of the revolutionary struggle, with the popularity and decided prestige which belonged to that ministry, with the education and purity of life which was theirs in so eminent a degree, with the priority of occupancy, that they should have been so quickly distanced in the struggle for the rescue from sin and vice of the hardy settlers and their children by the Methodist preachers, is a matter for profound study. The Presbyterians held, as pioneers of liberty, the foremost place in the popular mind and heart, and deserved the place they held. The Methodist preachers came out of the struggle almost without a single laurel of freedom on their brows, as preachers; as men, many of them were soldiers before they became preachers. The government of America had been fashioned in its fundamental principles after the pattern set them by the Presbyterian Church.

---

* Omitted, as he was fully represented by another speaker.

Before my recent studies, I had given to Thomas Jefferson and French political theories credit for a much larger share in our governmental principles and forms than I can ever do again. The great principle of no taxation without representation, we owe to the Scotch-Irish Presbyterians. For the insertion of the constitutional provision against the union of church and state, we are alike indebted to them. With all this debt of gratitude, we do well to ask why has a church whose government for nearly a hundred years gave no voice to the people on questions of taxation, and allowed little more individual freedom than Jesuitism itself, so surpassed in its growth the church of our fathers? Results so stupendous as these are not matters of chance. This is neither the time nor place to discuss the problem. I present it because it is incumbent on some future philosophic Christian historian of the race to solve it for the world's good.

Do we find a part of the solution the following?

Dr. McDonald, in his history of the Cumberland Presbyterian Church, just from the press, says:

"The Southern Presbyterian Church, which has been so wonderfully conservative, is seriously considering the propriety of changing its standard on this subject. A standing committee has been appointed to investigate the question. A long circular has been sent out by one of that committee, ably advocating the change. This circular shows that the ratio of increase in a hundred years between the Presbyterian and Methodist Churches is as 47 to 1051. It shows that 'aptness to teach,' which is a Bible qualification, is not proved by the possession of a college diploma, which *is not*. Indeed, there is no essential connection between the two."

SCOTCH-IRISH THREAD IN METHODISM.

We find the Scotch-Irish represented among the early Methodist preachers of Tennessee, by Thomas Logan Douglass, Hubbard Saunders, who married a daughter of General Russell, of revolutionary fame, whose wife, Madam Russell, was a sister of Patrick Henry, James Gwin, chaplain, adviser, and trusted friend of General Jackson, at some of the most critical periods in his stormy career, John McGhee, who, with his brother, a Presbyterian preacher, had a large part in the revival out of which sprung the Cumberland Presbyterian church. Among the early laymen we find as members of the first society organized at Nashville, General James Robertson and wife; a little later, Colonel Robert Weakley. Among the earliest converts in Sumner county, Lindsay, McNelly, Crane, the Carrs, Cages, and Douglass family. But a little later, Mrs. Bowen, who was another daughter of General Russell, and pronounced by general Jackson the most remarkable woman he ever knew—her place of prayer and devotional reading, the hollow of a sycamore tree, I have seen, the interior of which she had lined with devotional clippings, prose and poetry.

The bishop, who had most to do in planting Methodism in Tennessee, Bishop William McKendree, and the bishop who last died in the state, Bishop McTyeire, were, as I take it, both Scotch-Irish. Their names and places of birth indicate the fact, while their mental characteristics are markedly of the racial type. Both of them bold and urgent for the enfranchisement of the rank and file of the church before they were separated from the mass by their elevation to the episcopacy. Bishop McKendree, before he came under the personal influence of Asbury, sympathized greatly with O'Kelly in his cry for freedom of government, a cry which gave birth to Protestant Methodism.

H. N. M'TYEIRE,

Before his elevation, was the resolute, adroit, persistent, and finally victorious advocate for lay representation in the councils of the church. Yet when clothed with the episcopal office, they were both as prominent for their high exercise of episcopal prerogative as was Jackson himself in the presidential chair, or in the roll of military chieftain. Strenuous for liberty when under authority, stalwart for prerogative when gifted with authority. Of the men most marked in the history of Tennessee, as exerting the most influential and long-continued influence over the destinies of Methodism, we have John B. McFerrin and David R. McAnally. Dr. McFerrin, in his History of Methodism in Tennessee, speaking of Mr. Craighead, the earliest Presbyterian preacher, says, "Mr. Craighead was a man of learning, and long lived at his first residence in the state, and devoted most of his time to the education of the youth of the country. In this field he was very useful, and, as an educator, left a noble reputation. As a preacher he was formal, and somewhat eccentric, but he has left behind him the savor of a good name."

It can be little doubted that had Craighead been writing of McFerrin, he would have written "A strong man, gifted with power to sway the masses, but as a preacher, of marked eccentricity." Most of men who make the age feel them, and who leave behind them a distinct impress, are written down by the many as eccentric.

JOHN NEWLAND MAFFET,

From the North of Ireland, the wonderful orator who swept like a comet over the Union, followed by vast crowds, was for a time a resident of Nashville, and pastor of the leading Methodist church. Philip Neely, perhaps the most eloquent of Tennessee's many eloquent men, was Scotch-Irish. F. E. Pitts, who rivaled Whitfield in his power to move masses, was of Scotch-Irish blood. Jesse Cunningham, a preacher of East Tennessee, whose son, Rev. W. G. E. Cunningham, has won high position in Methodism, claims our notice, as well as Peter Cartwright and James Axley. Dr. McFerrin, in his Methodism in Tennessee, thus characterizes a band of Scotch-Irish preachers. "The pathos of Massie and Lee, the logic of McHenry and Burke, the polemical power of Page and Garrett, the zeal and piety of Walker and Lakin, the unction and poetry of Wilkerson and Gwin, the thundering and lightning of McGee and Granade, and the fine talents and noble bearing of McKendree and Blackman, drew the multitudes to Methodist meetings, and brought thousands of the best people of the land into the church. And these men of God went into the hovels of the poor and sought the halt and blind, the maimed and the distressed, preached to them Jesus and the resurrection, and won multitudes to the cross of Christ."

CUMBERLAND PRESBYTERIAN CHURCH, OR THE IRISH-SCOTCH CHURCH.

This church is the child of the Irish-Scotch of Kentucky and Tennessee. As the race itself is the synthesis of two races, the birth of the Cumberland Presbyterian Church is the analysis of the two races which reappear, the Scotch blood as Presbyterian, the Irish as Cumberland. The one true to its logic, the other striding along across all logical paths as enthusiasm may lead. Each is a source of honor to the other, and a second synthesis would be a blessing to our land, the chief religious curse of which is the multiplication of sects. The Cumberland Presbyterian Church has abounded in energy, which has produced large results.

A very characteristic statement of the standpoint of its origin is given in "McDonald's History," page 100.

"We have far more confidence in a system of theology growing out of a revival than in a system made by scholastics writing in the midst of their books and aiming at logical consistency."

Let us see the revival as it appears in history.*

The re-awaking Christian energy which ushered in the nineteenth century, and which introduced a new method of spiritual propagandism and enlightenment into American Christianity, was due to a man

---

* Phelan.

whose name has almost been forgotten by the great body of the people. This was James M'Gready, who was born in Pennsylvania, of Scotch-Irish parents. When young, he was removed to North Carolina, and was under the pastorate of John Caldwell. He was, as a boy, of a naturally grave and serious disposition, and was early destined for the ministry. He thought himself devout and a true Christian. But he accidentally overheard a remark made by one whom he respected, that he had not a spark of religion in his heart. He was aggrieved and surprised. He thought over what he had heard. Light began to dawn upon him. Returning to North Carolina, he commenced preaching in earnest. In 1790, he married, and took charge of a church in Orange county. He was accused of "running people distracted, diverting their attention from the necessary avocations of life, and creating unnecessary alarm in the minds of those who were decent and orderly in their lives." A letter written in blood ordered him to leave the country. His church was attacked. His pulpit was set on fire. In 1796, he removed to Kentucky. Here he took charge of three congregations in Logan county—Gasper river, Red river, and Muddy river. He infused new life into them. The people were aroused. His reputation spread. His influence grew. People came miles and miles to hear him. The walls of sectarianism were thrown down. He joined with Methodists in the work of reviving the love of Christ. William M'Gee, a Presbyterian, was located first at Shiloh, near Gallatin, Tennessee, then on Drake's creek, in Sumner county. His brother, John M'Gee, was a Methodist. In June, 1800, the two brothers assisted M'Gready at the Red river meeting-house, where the great revival fully developed itself. The crowd was enormous, and many were compelled to sleep in the open air under the trees. It was noticed that some had brought tents and food. This suggested the idea of a camp-meeting. The next month,

THE FIRST CAMP-MEETING

the world had ever seen was held at Gasper river church, in Logan county, Kentucky. The spirit spread wider and wider, farther and farther. A peculiar physical manifestation accompanied these revivals, popularly known as the "jerks." They were involuntary and irresistible. When under their influence, the sufferers would dance, or sing, or shout. Sometimes they would sway from side to side, or throw the head backward and forward, or leap, or spring. Generally, those under the influence would, at the end, fall upon the ground and remain rigid for hours, and sometimes whole multitudes would become dumb and fall prostrate. As the swoon passed away, the sufferer would weep piteously, moan, and sob. After a while, the gloom would lift, a smile of heavenly peace would radiate the countenance, and words of joy and rapture would break forth, and conversion always followed. Even the most skeptical, even the scoffers who visited these meetings for the purpose of showing their hardihood, would be taken in this way. As the inspiration spread, the

DEMAND FOR NEW PREACHERS

was greater than the church could supply. In this demand the Cumberland Church had its origin. David Rice, the leading member of the Transylvania Presbytery, visited the Cumberland country. Convinced that the revivals were doing great good, and appreciating the lack of preachers, he suggested that laymen possessing the proper qualifications for carrying on the work should be selected to apply for membership in the Presbytery. Alexander Anderson, Finis Ewing, and Samuel King applied, and were licensed to exhort.

Of Scotch-Irish we have marked these as prominent in the early days of this church: Robert Donnel, Thos. Calhoun, T. C. Anderson, J. M. McMurray. This church has come to number 150,000.

ALEXANDER CAMPBELL—THE SCOTCH-IRISH CHURCH.

So large a place has been gained by the followers of the Scotch-Irish Alexander Campbell in Tennessee, and he was himself so often here, that no sketch of the religions of the race would be complete without reference to him. A man who was bold enough to attempt to reform, and in most of what he taught reverse the theology of the ages, who fought his way single-handed and alone, who resorted to no appeals to the passions, who was the death of enthusiasm, and sought his conquests alone by the force of logic, arrests the pen of history while he claims rightful place. He stands uniquely apart from the religious reformers of the world as history has given them to us. His success, which has been as marked as his courage was dauntless, demands for him a foremost place among the celebrated men of the race. John C. Calhoun, perhaps, of all the race, is his peer in analytical powers, in persistence in unfaltering adherence to the results of logic without giving place to either passion or expediency. He belongs to the same Scotch-Irish family before referred to, was brought up in the Presbyterian Church, trained in the theology of the schools. He came on the scene of action just as the reverse tide began to set in after the great excitement and religious furor of the early part of this century. His movement has been improperly called a reformation; it was, in doctrine, methods, and purposes, a rebellion.

The creeds of Presbyterianism, the revivals of Methodists, Baptists, and Cumberland Presbyterians, were attacked with a persistency that knew no abatement. He had some grounds for his points of attack. Protestantism had gone much too far along the line of credal infallibility, while many of the churches of Kentucky and Tennessee had narrowed down evangelical methods to one, "the mourners' bench or anxious seat," the evidences of conversion had practically become the measure of the emotions. It has taken Alexander Campbell and his followers a half century to draw the old churches out of the pent-up Utica, into which reverence for misplaced creeds on the one hand, and exaggeration of emotion on the other, had drifted them. The evidences of the good accomplished by him along these lines in the life and action of the churches is becoming every day more apparent. When Christendom comes to

VALUE CREEDS AS MILE-STONES

to mark progress, instead of anchors to forbid further movement, the followers of Alexander Campbell may be able to meet us half way, and allow that creeds have a rightful place. Whether they do or not, the age owes to Alexander Campbell a debt larger, perhaps, than to any other one man of the pulpit of the century, Henry Ward Beecher excepted.

Beecher denounced the binding nature of creeds as fearlessly as did Alexander Campbell, but never was narrow enough in his intensity to be blinded to the fact that it was the abuse, not the use of creeds that had so dammed up Christian growth.

The Scotch-Irish stick-to-right exaltation of minor points into fundamental principles, the contentious character of the race, has no better example than in Alexander Campbell and his followers. His refusal of all creeds, his abandonment of all established forms of government, was carrying to its extreme logical results the central principles of Scotch-Irish Presbyterianism. Taking the Bible as interpreted by every individual as the only source of right belief and action, his Scotch-Irish blood at once goes forward along its hereditary tendencies to construe a book full of tropes, figures, and parables redolent of lofty imagery, by the literalism of the unimaginative Scotch metaphysics, resulting in the narrowest of possible structures on the broadest of foundations. Yet so just were many of his criticisms on the credal and emotional religions of his day, so welcome was his doctrine of equal rights in the kingdom of Christ to all members, so attractive has been the field for activity presented to laymen, that, measured by the number of his followers, he stands unrivaled in the history of the religious movements of the world.

A prophecy is on my lips, but I repress it. A single suggestion I make. Had it not been for the exaltation of a symbol into the place of a vital power by a faulty literalism, had it not been for the narrow refusal to utilize such helps of government as Christian enlightenment has approved, not as essentials, but as convenient scaffolding, their success would have been as the torrent compared with the wave-like growth of their history.

The following from Mr. Campbell shows his standpoint in contrast to that given by McDonald as characteristic of Cumberland Presbyterian church:

"What I am in religion, I am from examination, reflection, conviction, not from *ipse dixit*, tradition, or human authority; and, having halted and faltered and stumbled, I have explored every inch of the way hitherto. Though my father and I accord in sentiment, neither of us are dictators or imatators. Neither of us lead; neither of us follow." *

This, with the whole history of this church, so vividly recalls Parton's picture of Scotch-Irish character in his life of Jackson, that we call attention to it in closing.

"One trait in the character of these people demands the particular attention of the reader. It is their nature to *contend* for what they think is right with peculiar earnestness. Some of them, too, have a knack of extracting from every affair in which they may engage, and from every relation in life which they form, the very largest amount of contention which it can be made to yield. Hot water would seem to be the natural element of some of them, for they are always in it. It appears to be more difficult for a North of Irelander than for other men to allow an honest difference of opinion in an opponent; so that he is apt to regard the terms

OPPONENT AND ENEMY

as synonymous. Hence, in the political and sectarian contests of the present day, he occasionally exhibits a narrowness, if not ferocity of spirit, such as his forefathers manifested in the old wars of the clans and the borders, or in the later strifes between Catholic and Protestant." It is strange that so kind and generous a people should be so fierce in contention. "Their factions," says Sir Walter Scott, speaking of the

---

* Memoirs of Alexander Campbell, pp. 466, 467. [Letter to his uncle in Ireland.]

Irish generally, "have been so long envenomed, and they have such a narrow ground to do their battle in, that they are like people fighting with daggers in a hogshead." And these very people, apart from their strifes, are singularly tender in their feelings, liberal in gifts and hospitality, and most easy to be entreated. On great questions, too, which lift the mind above sectarian trivialities, they will, as a people, be invariably found on the anti-diabolic side: equally strenuous for liberty and for law, against "mobs and monarchs, lords and levelers," as one of their own stump orators expressed it. The name which Bulwer bestows upon one of his characters, *Stick-to-rights*, describes every genuine son of Ulster. Among the men of North of Ireland stock, whose names are familiar to the people of the United States, the following may serve to illustrate some of the foregoing remarks: John Stark, Robert Fulton, John C. Calhoun, Sam Houston, David Crockett, Hugh L. White, James K. Polk, Patrick Bronte, Horace Greely, Robert Bonner, A. T. Stewart, Andrew Jackson, Thomas Benton, James G. Blaine, Judge Jervis Black.

Judging by the ocean-like roll of his heart, I am inclined to add to these the name of Abraham Lincoln, and am much disposed to believe that the sturdy honesty of Grover Cleveland springs from the same source.

SCOTCH-IRISH ACHIEVEMENT.

BY COLONEL A. K. M'CLURE, OF PHILADELPHIA.

Ladies and Gentlemen:—You have had very excellent samples of the oratory of the Scotch-Irish, and I am not here to deliver an oration, but I will give you a recess from Scotch-Irish oratory, by devoting a short space of the evening to a confidential conversation about our distinguished race. The trouble with me is to know where to begin. If you are asked, Where have the Scotch-Irish been, and where are they now? the answer is, Where have they not been, and where are they not? If you are asked what they have done, the answer of every intelligent citizen must be, What have they not done? If you ask what distinguished places of trust and power they have filled, the logical answer is, What place is there, in civil, military, or religious authority, that they have not filled? To speak of such a race, is to speak of the history of the past achievements of our land; and, strange as it may seem, this people whose history is written in every annal of achievement in our land, is without a written history. There is not a single connected history of the Scotch-Irish in American literature, and there is not a history of any other people written in truth that does not tell of Scotch-Irish achievement. If you were to spend an evening in a New England library, you would find not only scores, but hundreds of volumes, telling of Puritan deeds; and if you were to study them, the natural inference would be that the only people that have existed and achieved any thing in this land were the Puritans. They have not only written every thing that they have done, but they have written more than they have done. The story that they generally omit is their wonderful achievement in the burning of witches. There is a complete history of the Quakers. You find it in connected form in almost every library of any city. There is a complete history of the Huguenots who settled in Carolina, and there is a connected history of every people of our land, save the one people whose deeds have made the history of this country the most lustrous of all. It is true, that those who write their history in deeds have least need of history in the records of our literature, but the time has come in this land when the Scotch-Irish owe it to themselves, and owe it especially to their children, who are now scattered from eastern to western sea, and from northern lake to southern gulf, that those who come after us shall learn not only that their ancestors have been foremost in achievement, but that their deeds have been made notable in history, as they were in the actions of men. Some of our more thoughtful historians or students of history will pretend to tell you when the Scotch-Irish race began. I haven't heard even our Scotch-Irishmen who have studied the question do the subject justice. No such race of men could be created in a generation; no such achievements could be born in a century. No such people as the Scotch-Irish could be completed even in century after century; and while you are told that the Scotch-Irish go back in their achievements to the days of John Knox, John Knox lived a thousand years after the formation of the Scotch-Irish character began. He was like the stream of your western desert, that comes from the mountains and makes the valleys beautiful, and green, and fragrant, and then is lost in the sands of the desert. Men will tell you that it disappears and is lost. It is not. After traversing perhaps hundreds of miles of subterranean passages, forgotten, unseen, it is still doing its work, and it rises again before it reaches the sea, and again makes new fields green, and beautiful, and bountiful. It required more than a thousand years to perfect the Scotch-Irish character. It is of a creation single from all races of mankind, and a creation not of one people nor of one century, nor even five centuries, but a thousand years of mingled effort and sacrifice, ending in the sieges of Derry, were required to present to the world the perfect Scotch-Irish character. If you would learn when the characteristics of the Scotch-Irish race began, go back a thousand years beyond the time of John Knox, and find that there was a crucial test that formed the men who perfected the Scotch-Irish character, after years and years of varying conflict and success, until the most stubborn, the most progressive, the most aggressive race in achievement, was given to the world. Let us go back to the sixth century, and what do we find? We find Ireland the birth-place of the Scotch-Irish. We find Ireland foremost of all the nations of the earth, not only in religious progress, but in literature, and for two centuries thereafter the teacher of the world in all that made men great and achievements memorable. For two centuries the Irish of Ireland, in their own green land, were the teachers of men, not only in religion, but in science, in learning, and all that made men great. She had her teachers and her scientists, men who filled her pulpits and went to every nation surrounding; and it was there that the Scotch-Irish character had its foundation; it was there that the characteristics became evident which afterward made them felt wherever they have gone. Those Irish were teachers of religion, and yet as stubborn for religious freedom as were the Scotch-Irish. Catholic, they often refused obedience to the Pope. They were men of conviction; they were men of learning. They were the advanced outposts of the progressive civilization of that day, and the cardinal doctrine of their faith, down deep-set in the heart, was absolute religious freedom, and they even combated the Vatican in maintaining their religious rights.

Then came the cloud that swept over the land, and that effaced this bright green spot from existence. Then came the barbarian from the isles of the Baltic. He came with the torch of the vandal and all the fiendishness of a barbarian, desolated the land, destroyed its prosperity, overthrew its minsters, razed its churches to the earth, and from that once bright green isle a land of desolation was made. The Irish of that day were not to be conquered in a generation; nay, not in a century. It was only after two centuries of desperate, bloody conflict, of sacrifice such as men to-day know not, that finally they were almost effaced from the earth. But it was like the stream that comes from the great mountains of the West, that had made the valleys beautiful which it had traversed, and then disappeared in the desert. The work of these men had perished and been overthrown for the time being, but their teachings were eternal, and they are as much impressed upon this audience now as they were twelve hundred years ago in Ireland. Then history tells how the province was finally laid waste, and, how, when it had ceased, by reason of its desolation, to invite any to it, the Scotch-Irish were invited to come to Ulster, and how there was literally founded the great people whose history and whose achievements we celebrate now. They had undergone persecution from King and Pope. Not until Pope Adrian and King Henry, Protestant upon the one side and Catholic upon the other, had united their arms, their schemes, and their statesmanship, was the land laid waste so that the Scots alone could rebuild the destruction which had been wrought. So great was the desolation, that prelates denounced Catholicism one day, and again praised it; the teachers at the holy altar abjured Catholicism to Mary and Protestantism to Henry. The church and state reeked with corruption. When there was universal demoralization, even at the very altar of the holies, then the Scots went to Ireland and settled in the province of Ulster, where the history of the race properly begins. They made the land again to bloom and blossom, and upon every hand was brightness and prosperity. They called a convocation of their clergy, and proclaimed their profession of faith, the same that you would proclaim at your altar to-night; and it seemed, at last, as though the angel of peace had visited the land, and that now there should be freedom to worship at the altar of their choice; that improvement, mental, social, religious, and material, should go hand in hand again, and that Ireland should become a place of plenty and of happiness. But scarcely had they established themselves, and proclaimed their faith, and restored prosperity for the desolation that they had found, when persecution again came, with the power of Church and State. These people were persecuted at their altars, in their homes, in their business, in all things; they were condemned as felons, and compelled to flee from their land. After a century of conflict such as we know not now, maintaining their altars and their homes and their rights, they seemed again to have been scattered to the four quarters of the earth. Again the bright mountain stream of education, religion, progress, and advancement seemed to have been swallowed up by the desert in utter hopelessness. It was then that John Knox came, and came as the long-concealed sweet waters from the fountain of religion and of education, having long been swallowed up by the desert of desolation and persecution, in all their splendor, pure as crystal, pure as heaven. Again the people were taught that the religion and the education of a thousand years before had not been lost; that there was one character of men, and one alone, in which was preserved eternally the truths of progress, of freedom, of religion; and finally, after conflict upon conflict, and sacrifice upon sacrifice, these men presented what I regard as the perfected Scotch-Irish character. At the siege of Londonderry, after twelve hundred years of education and teaching, and utter prostration under persecution of all the power of Church and State to destroy, the perfect Scotch-Irish character was presented to the world; and I thank the siege of Londonderry, because it was that which sent them to the new world. Then they came fleeing from home, from all which they loved, to the new world, as teachers of the inalienable rights of man to worship the living God as he shall choose, and maintain civil freedom as the highest right of God's created beings. They came, and they settled in Pennsylvania, the Carolinas, and Virginia; and it was the Scotch-Irish people of the colonies that made the Declaration of Independence in 1776. Without them, it could not have been thought of, except as a passing fancy. When the New England Puritan and the Virginia mixture of the cavalier and Scotch-Irishman sat side by side, and presented to the memorable Congress of Philadelphia the immortal document of the Declaration of Independence, they did not voice the views or convictions of Thomas Jefferson or John Adams; they voiced the teachings of the Scotch-Irish people of the land. They did not falter, they did not dissemble, they did not temporize, when a foreign government became oppressive beyond endurance. It was not the Quaker, not the Puritan, nor even the Cavalier nor the Huguenot nor the German; it was the Scotch-Irish of the land whose voice was first heard in Virginia. In the valley of Virginia was the first declaration of independence; not a formal declaration, but it was there that the smothered feelings of these people were first declared. Next, in North Carolina, at Mecklenburg, came the declaration of independence in form, and from the Scotch-Irish of that region. Next came the declaration of my own state, at Carlisle, Pa. There was the declaration made by the Scotch-Irish, that the colonies must be free from the oppressive hand of Britain. They had taught this, not only in their public speeches, they had taught it at their altars, from their pulpits, in their social circle; it was taught upon the mother's lap to the Scotch-Irish child; and it was from these, and these alone, that came the outburst of rugged, determined people that made the declaration of 1776 possible. They, and they alone, were its authors, and when they made a declaration, they meant to maintain it by all the moral and physical power they possessed. When a deliverance came from the Scotch-Irish—when they demanded that they must and shall be free, it was no mere diplomatic declaration; it was no claim to be tested and disputed and be recalled in season. When the Scotch-Irish of this land declared that the American colonies should be free, it meant that the Scotch-Irish blood was ready to flow upon the battle-field, that the Scotch-Irish arm was ready to wield the battle-ax, and that, come weal or woe, they meant to maintain the declaration with their lives. (Applause.)

I wish the truthful history of the Declaration of Independence had been written. It has not been done, and I am sorry that it will never be written, for the reason that it now can not be done. I wish that some other people, some other race than mine, had been in a position to write the true history of the Declaration of Independence. The Scotch-Irish can not write it, because in the writing they would make themselves immortal. There is no passage in history that tells you that, after the passage of this declaration by the Congress of the colonies at Philadelphia, two of Pennsylvania's representatives were recalled and retired for disobedience to the will of the people, and new men sent to complete the work. Need I tell you that these men were not Scotch-Irish? It was, perhaps, well for young American students, that they have not by history been told how the Continental Congress, even after passing the memorable Declaration of Independence, shivered at the consummation of its work; how men shuddered and hesitated at affixing their names to the document that would make them traitors to their King; and it was not until John Witherspoon, the

Scotch-Irish Presbyterian preacher, the lineal descendant of John Knox, rose in his place, with his venerable silvered head and earnest oratory, and declared that his gray head must soon bow to the fate of all, and that he preferred it to go by the ax of the executioner rather than that the cause of independence should not prevail, that the hesitating were made to stand firm, that the quivering heart beat its keenest pulsations for freedom, and made every man come up, one after another, and affix his name to the immortal document. What might have been the history of that day, if John Witherspoon had not lived, and had not stood there, as John Knox stood, centuries before, to present the teachings of religion, science, education, and freedom, from which could be drawn the inspiration, generation after generation, for twelve centuries? Had he not been there, I know not what might have been the record of that day. I only know, and rejoice for freedom and civilization, that John Witherspoon lived, and that, as ever, the Scotch-Irish ruled the great event of the day. How have they written their history amongst us? When the battle came for freedom, I need not tell you where they were. I need not tell you that, of the whole Scotch-Irish race on this continent, there was but a single exceptional community where there was not the most devoted loyalty to the cause of freedom for which the colonies fought; and these might have been patriotic if they had not been Scotch-Irish. They had given their solemn promise, upon parole and pardon, when condemned unjustly, and when it was a choice between freedom and death, and when their King had given them permission to settle in the new country, that they would maintain their loyalty to the King that pardoned them. This little community in North Carolina was faithful to its oath, and became apparently unfaithful to its liberty. This is the record of the whole disloyalty of the Scotch-Irish race in this country to the struggle for freedom, and this stands out with the stamp of Toryism; but it is made lustrous by the fidelity to the oath given to a King who had granted pardon.

As I told you when I began, I know not where to turn to tell you of Scotch-Irish achievement. I know not where to begin, where to go, or where to stop. Don't imagine, from what I have said, that the Scotch-Irish were all angels. They were very human. Dr. MacIntosh, in his address to you, summed up the Irish character pretty well in a single sentence. What were your words, doctor?

Dr. MacIntosh:

I said the Scotch-Irish kept the commandments of God, and every thing else they got to lay their hands on. (Laughter.)

Colonel McClure:

I want to get it from the mouth of the reverend doctor, because he knows them quite as well as I do. That was the truth of them. They were a thrifty people. In my own state they had a conflict with the Quakers. The Quakers concluded that Scotch-Irish immigration ought to be stopped, and in one of their petitions sent to the council of my state, they declared that the Scotch-Irish were "a pernicious and pugnacious people." They were in perpetual conflict. The truth is, the Scotch-Irish were ever upon the outskirts of civilization. The Quakers lived where they could live in peace. They were a lovely people, and we have the conviction that they founded Pennsylvania in peace. So they did. The truth is, they did every thing to aid warfare, and left the Scotch-Irish to fight it out. They would go amongst the Indians, and trade with them, and give them ammunition and firearms, because they were peaceful brothers, and the Indians would murder the Scotch-Irish, and the Quakers while dwelling in peace did great good in dealing justly with the Indian and getting him to kill the Scotch-Irish. They were in constant conflict. The Scotch-Irish entered the Cumberland Valley when the Quaker was scarcely outside of Philadelphia. They had gone to Fort Pitt, and settled in Western Pennsylvania, when the Quaker was dreaming of peace along the banks of the Delaware; and it was one perpetual struggle of noble daring and courage to maintain their homes against the Indians in that state. But the Quaker always protested, always complained, and in every possible way sought to limit Scotch-Irish immigration, or drive it from the state; and they did drive many from the state. Turn to South Carolina, and you will find settlements of Scotch-Irish from Pennsylvania, who took with them the names of Pennsylvania counties—Chester, Lancaster, York. Before the Revolutionary War they settled many counties on the borders, simply because they got away from the Quakers, who constantly complained of and criticised them. These Quakers made the truest charge they ever did when they said: "These men absolutely want to control the province themselves." Of course they did. There never was a Scotch-Irish community anywhere that did not want to boss every job around it, and of course these people in Pennsylvania wanted to control the colony. The Quakers wanted nobody but themselves. The Scotch-Irish were the pioneers of civilization, and wherever they went with their trusty rifles and built their log-cabins, there was the school-house, there was the little log church, for religion and education went hand in hand with the Scotch-Irish wherever they went, from the time of the Revolution until now; and what was true of Pennsylvania was true of every part of the land where they settled. They dominated, and that was the cause of complaint against them. They dominated, simply because in the nature of things it could not be otherwise. They were born and educated a thousand years as leaders of men; they were men of conviction; they were men of faith in religion, faith in God, and faith in themselves, and tell me why should not such a people at that day resolve that the land belonged to the saints, and that they were the saints?

Men have inquired whether there is not a decadence in the Scotch-Irish character, and men of thought and students of the race have at times hesitated to answer. Let me say that if there shall be decadence in the Scotch-Irish race, there shall be no conflicts worthy of the Scoth-Irish character to develop their grandeur and their heroism. (Applause.) Turn but back to the last great conflict between the North and the South, and there was not a man upon the battle field that was not made more heroic by Scotch-Irish leaders and Scotch-Irish soldiers. There would have been thousands fewer fallen in that conflict but for the pertinacity of the Scotch-Irish character and its influence throughout the whole American people; and after reading all of Grecian and Roman story, there is nothing in human history, there is nothing in all the conflicts of men, ancient or modern, that evidenced such matchless heroism as was shown by the blue and the gray that stands to-day lustrous over all the heroism of the earth as the heroism of the whole American people. Tell me not that there is decadence in the Scotch-Irish character. There is no decay, but there is no achievement to-day, because there is nothing heroic to achieve. He is foremost in the conflict, when the conflict is for the right. He is but a man as all men are, human, full of all its infirmities, but the grandeur of his character, fixed twelve hundred years ago, is to-day as perfectly true to its teachings as when Ireland, in her grandeur, was the teacher of the world. When these men fail in achievement, it is because there is nothing to achieve. However, they will be felt when the battle field is not to be found. When there are no conflicts in statesmanship, when the great issues have passed, think you that the Scotch Irish teaching is still and unheard and unfelt in civilization? No. When the tempest is still, and all is calm and beautiful around you, the dews of heaven make the flowers jeweled in the morning, and your fields green with the promise of future plenty. Thus with the Scotch-Irish character, in conflict grander than all; when every conflict shall have been won ; when free is the banner of faith, and liberty has triumphed, then, as gentle as the dews of heaven, will be felt the teachings of the Scotch-Irish in behalf of a civilization which has grown for centuries and centuries, until, in the fullness of time, will the Scotch-Irish character stand out grandest and most beneficent in all the achievements of men. (Applause.)

ADDRESS OF HON. BENTON McMILLIN.

Mr. Chairman, Ladies and Gentlemen, and Fellow Citizens:—I am happy to have the privilege of meeting and greeting you on this auspicious occasion. It is said to be well for a speaker who comes before an audience for the first time to, by some means, get into their good graces at an early moment. I am going to do that by announcing that I am too selfish toward myself and too generous to you to detain you long from the good feast that awaits you from the lips of one more eloquent than I could possibly be.

It is well for us to be here to-day, not simply because Scotch-Irish blood flows in our veins, for that of itself is a minor consideration. But why, my friends, are we here? It is to commemorate the deeds of a glorious ancestry, not because they were our ancestors, but because, by that commemoration, we may possibly instill into the young men, upon whom the responsibilities of government and the responsibilities of defending religious liberty are soon to rest, ideas which will nerve them to come up to those responsibilities with more of patriotic fervor and more of religious zeal than was possessed before the meeting of this assembly. (Applause.)

It was not my pleasure to be with you at the opening of this congress, as had been arranged, for the reason that I was from home in New York when the invitation reached me about the time of the opening of this assembly, and did not get back home so as to be here at the inauguration of the exercises. This I say in justification of myself. I am glad to come into your midst. I have heard much of this glorious land in which you live, and its unstinted hospitality; I had heard of the magnificent and fiery spirit of its sons; I had heard of the beauty and feeling of its daughters; but I can truly say, in the language of one of old, that the half had not been told. (Applause.)

I take another pleasure in coming here. It is the home of one of the purest patriots, one of the greatest friends I ever had, a man who Tennessee regrets and the nation regrets is stricken with affliction to-day, and for whom the prayers of all patriotic people ascend on this goodly morn; need I say that I speak of your own distinguished fellow citizen, General Whitthorne? (Applause.)

My friends, it has been said, in language more eloquent than I can command, that the history of the Scotch-Irish race is the history of the combat against physical force and the combat against oppression of the church by the state. I rejoice in the little blood that flows in my veins from that stock. I rejoice in the memories that cluster around the illustrious heroes that this country has had, and I am glad that it is impossible for the historian to omit from the pages of glorious deeds the actions of these thrice-glorious men. Suppose that they could be obliterated, what would you have? The conquest of Mexico by your own immortal Polk would be unknown, the defense of New Orleans by Tennessee's glorious sons would be unrecorded, the great intellectuality of Calhoun would be unknown to American youth as an inspiration to exertions, and that fierce and fiery appeal of a Henry to his countrymen to rush to arms would never have resounded down the ages to awaken every man with the love to be free. It may be truly said of the Scotch-Irish race what was said by Byron, the great poet, when he spoke of Corinth and said:

> "Many a vanquished year and age
> And tempest's breath and battle's rage
> Have swept o'er Corinth, yet she stands,
> A fortress, formed to freedom's hand."

So it is with the Scotch-Irish race. They stand to-day as they have stood through the ages and the centuries, defending freedom, proclaiming the freedom of the press, freedom of religion, and freedom of the citizen. Those three freedoms we come up to-day as Scotch-Irishmen to again proclaim the faith of their sons as it was the faith of our fathers. (Applause.)

A peculiarity of the Scotch-Irishman is that he is not the kind of a believer in freedom of religion which is described so graphically, and I fear so truly, by Artemus Ward, when in his book he praises his ancestry as follows: "The Wards is a noble family. I believe they are descended from the Puritans, that band of religious patriots who fled from the land of persecution to the land of freedom, where they could not only enjoy their own religion, but prevent every other man from enjoying his." That is the difference between the Scotch-Irish love of freedom and the love of freedom which he says characterized the Puritan. My friends, when I look around at the great country that is our common blessing to-day, I feel that on its account it is not amiss for us to meet here and commemorate the noble deeds by all races and in all ages. We have sixty odd million people in these United States. We have more Jews than Jerusalem, more Irish than Dublin, more Scotch than Edinburgh, more Germans than Berlin, and still have more than 50,000,000 of native born, American citizens, noble sons of noble sires from every clime and every country. Thus far we have got along reasonably well, but the time will come when the vast public domain, acquired by our ancestors, will not be here unoccupied as an inviting field in times of calamity and distress that may occur in the east and the south. My prediction is that it will then require all the patriotism of the patriot, and all the wisdom of the sage to correctly steer this government between all the breakers that will rise of anarchism on one side and socialism and the disposition to control by other than patriotic means on the other. It is characteristic of the Scotch-Irish race that in its ranks, so far as I know, there has never been found a single anarchist or socialist. On the contrary, there has never been found a single Scotch-Irishman that was not able to defy power and potentate, be he king or anybody else, who stood in the pathway of progress and of right. When I look around in this beautiful country, I rejoice that there is a considerable amount of Scotch-Irish blood in the southern states of the Union; and in what I shall say, it is not my purpose to deal with any part of my country except as a patriot talking of a part of the whole country, every foot of which is loved, and every foot of which every man of the South stands ready to defend. (Applause.) I don't recur to the past save for the lessons of wisdom and instruction and patriotism that it may give us. Twenty odd years ago there was not in all this land, from Kentucky to the gulf, hardly a single thoroughly fenced farm; our homes were desolated, our farms yielding nothing, our country depopulated. The same spirit that had characterized our Scotch-Irish ancestry, characterized the people of the South, and they have caused this country to bloom as the rose, until to-day it is hardly possible for a stranger to detect that the blighting hand of war ever fell upon it. I also speak the truth of history when I say that at the close of the late war there was eleven millions of people in the South, seven millions of whom could not have bought their kettle, and yet the coal that lights the streets of London is mined in Kentucky, and the iron that makes the screw to fasten down the coffin lids of the dead Englishman comes from Tennessee and Alabama, and is manufactured in Connecticut. Who is there that could have done more than this, more than Aladdin with his lamp? You men of the South deserve much; you were never discouraged in defeat. But a most potent factor in the rehabilitation of the South was its glorious women. When impartial history shall have been written, it may be truly recorded that she who saw disaster with a smile, who encountered defeat and poverty without any thing of encouragement; she who uprooted the thorn and planted the rose; she, the woman of the South, deserves the praise for what has been done; and she deserves the praise for keeping our young men in firmness and uprightness which alone should characterize a man made in the image of his almighty God. (Applause.) My friends, we have a glorious country, and the reason I rejoice that there is Scotch-Irish in my veins, is not simply because it is Scotch-Irish, but because it gives a little more grit and a little more resolution to see the right and to have the courage to do it, and be a better American citizen; for, after all, my greatest ambition is to be one of the best of American citizens. But I promised you in the beginning that I was not going to detain you. Complying with that promise, and thanking you for your kind attention, I give place to one who can more fittingly entertain you. (Applause.)

JOHN KNOX IN INDEPENDENCE HALL.

BY REV. JOHN S. MACINTOSH, D.D.

As we pace the story-laden Piazzetta of San Marco, we think with stirred souls of the ducal makers of Venice; as we sit toward sunset beneath the heavy shadows of the historic Campanile, we behold move past in stately progress the majestic makers of Florence; as we rest by the banks of the turbid Thames, we stand amid the crowding captains and statesmen, who have been the makers of our own ancestral Britain; and as we turn aside from the glare of broad sunlight and the din of the thronged streets into the cool shade and the sacred silence of our own dear hall of liberty, our common nation's hallowed home of freedom, we face the crown and glory of all these mighty men, the makers of our own republic.

But who made these makers of our land, we can not but ask, as we front our great dead once more? Whence came these souls of purest flame, whose glowing spirit fires blazed the new and broad pathway to rest and freedom, to happy homes and ever-enlarging power for the weary and the downtrodden from a score of the old world's packed and groaning serf-pens? Who were the sires of the fathers of our republic? Who breathed into them their quickening spirits; who flashed into their capacious hearts the impulsive inspirations; who unbarred for them the way to new life, new rights and duties? Question of deepest interest! Few studies so tempting as the studies of origins! What so enchanting as the search after the upper fountains of great world streams, the Niles and the Congos? Who, then, the sires of our fathers; whence their origin; what the fountains of these life streams that flowed together into the glorious tide of a new land of freemen?

Like most potent incantation works swiftly the question. And forms hoary and honored to us rise like Samuel's at Endor from graves of quiet dignity; and as these august ancients gird us round, forward with glad, bold, almost defiant cry of recognition and right filial pride start the Puritans, to show and claim as their all-honored sires, Milton, and Hampden, and Sydney, and Pym, and, greatest among the great, England's uncrowned Protector; and forward bound with Gallic eagerness the Huguenots to lay their reverent hands on Conde and Coligny, and Calvin and our own Lafayette; and forward stride with firm foot the Hollanders, pointing out majestically, and linking their descent with William the Silent and the sage De Witt, the dashing Egmont, and the fearless Van Horn; and forward come the Germans, and trace their blood to the Hohenzollerns and Saxon electors, and Luther, lordliest of them all. But amid these many gladsome and proud voices of childhood, and amid these bold, true claims upon the bluest blooded ancestry any land can show, one group has hitherto been strangely silent. Have these silent ones, then, no sacred obligations to grand ancestral dead? Have they had no divine preparations for their achievements through God-given and God-taught sires? Call they no Heaven-built man father? Are they the American Melchisedeks, kings verily by all mightiest proofs and world-wide confession, but kings without royal parentage? Nay, verily! But while Puritans have made this land, and as many more as they could reach, ring time and again with Mayflower and Mayflower's men and women and their glorious ancestry, while Dutch and Germans and French, and the sons of St. George, have long lifted trumpet tones of self-gratulation because of their great fathers, this silent, patient group, not the smallest in the land, not the weakest, as every battle field and place of state and church and busy life may prove, not the least laurelled, as shows the country's roll of honor, not the least trusty nor backward in danger's hours, nor giving fewest chieftains to the makers of this compacted empire of freemen—this silent band of proud self-repressiveness has hitherto said but little as to their own intellectual, political, patriotic patriarch, the high-towering soul of impulse, the new creative force, who under God has been the fountain and origin of their most marked qualities, their national and everswelling glory. Have, then, we Scotch and Scotch-Irish, for we have been the silent band, unorganized and unbound till this happy hour, have we no prophet? Can we call no seer as sire from honored grave, to say of him with reverent affection, "He is the soul of fire the Lord sent to stir the flames of new daring within our fathers' souls?" Strange if we, of all, had not! Looking round the portrait-lined walls of our hall of freedom, gazing on and studying with pious steadfastness, those strong, masterful, distinct faces from Witherspoon's and Henry's, round and round, faces that throw out into so rugged and characteristic boldness of relief, the Scotch and Scotch-Irish makers of this republic, we must feel it passing strange indeed, if no one grand, lone chieftain can be planted at the head of our clan, and with a fearless, intelligent pride, pointed out as noblest among the very noble—the peculiar and royal leader of a peculiar and royal race.

Peculiar and royal race; yes, that indeed is our race! I shrink not from magnifying my house and blood with a deep thanksgiving to that Almighty God who himself made us to differ, and sent His great messenger to fit us for our earth-task ; task as peculiar and royal as is the race itself ; I shame me not because of the Lowland thistle and the Ulster gorse, of the Covenanters' banner, or the Ulsterman's pike. If we be not the very peculiar people, we Scotch-Irish are a most peculiar people, who have ever left our own broad, distinct mark wherever we have come, and have it in us still to do the same, even our critics being judges. To-day we stand out sharply distinguished in a score of points from English, French, Dutch, German, and Swede. We have our distinctive marks ; and like ourselves, they are strong and stubborn ; years change them not, seas wash them not out, varying homes alter them not, clash and contact with new forms of life, and fresh forces of society blur them not. Every one knows the almost laughably dogged persistency of the family likeness in us Scotch Irish a' the warld ower. Go where you may, know it once, then you know it, ay, feel it forever. The typal face, the typal modes of thought, the typal habits of work, tough faiths, unyielding grit, granitic hardness, close-mouthed relf-repression, clear, firm speech when the truth is to be told, God-fearing honesty, loyalty to friendship defiant of death, conscience and knee-bending only to God—these are our marks ; and they meet and greet you on the hills of Tennessee and Georgia—you may trace them down the valleys of Virginia and Pennsylvania, cross the prairies of the west and the savannahs of the south, you may plow the seas to refind them in the western bays of Sligo, and beneath the beetling rocks of Donegal ; thence you may follow them to the maiden walls of Derry, and among the winding banks of the silvery Bann ; onward you may trace them to the rolling hills of Down, and the busy shores of Antrim ; and sailing over the narrow lough you will face them in our forefathers' cottier-homes and grey keeps of Galloway and Dumfries, of the Ayrshire hill, and the Grampian slopes.

These racial marks are birth-marks, and birth-marks are indelible. And well for us and the world is it that they are indelible. They are great soul-features, these marks. They are principles. The principles are the same every-where ; and these principles are of four classes, religious, moral, intellectual, and political.

Of the religious, the denominational, the confessional, I will not speak, for this is neither time nor place. While I am churchman of my church through and through, and to the last drop of my heart's blood ; while I would nail the blue banner of Presbyterianism to the very tip of the mast, and nail it there, and fight to death to keep it there, while I do not cease nor hesitate to claim for my church the truest apostolicity, the fullest catholicity, and the sweetest charity, all in its own place and time; but the place and the time for this ecclesiastical distinctiveness is not here, is not now.

On this common platform of a race's rally I hail as brother my Episcopal brother, Dr. Beckett, and my Methodist brother, Dr. Kelly, as eloquent on the platform as he was dashing and daring in the charge. I hail as brother all in whose veins runs the good old blood of loyalty and liberty, whether he be of Scotch church, or Anglican, or Latin. I hail all with gladness who come from town or hamlet, hill or glen, that lies any-where between Cork's green coves or far Loch Awe.

On broader lines than sect or party, than clique or section, we want to start and run this great brotherhood. We grasp hands all round; we stretch across a continent; we welcome all our kith and kin. Let there be no strife, for we be brethren.

And such I take it, from my conference with them, are the thoughts and desires of all the busy and able officers of this Congress. Such I know to be the aims and the wishes, heartfelt wishes, of him who is in very truth the father of our Congress, who first thought of it, who has wrought for it with that quiet, resolute energy so characteristic of our race, who has joyed in its triumphant and rising success, but who, with a self-sacrificing modesty, as noble as it is rare, has not suffered himself to be seen or heard in public, yet has been felt everywhere, and always for "sweetness and light," my dear friend, the Hon. Thomas T. Wright, of Florida; dear to me as the boy from Ballymoney, little moorland town of Ireland's Antrim, so closely linked to me and mine, but dearer far for his unwearying kindness and manly virtues.

The sectarian and the confessional topics I shall avoid, and of the moral I shall say naught except as involved in the intellectual and the political. With ourselves, as citizens and patriots and politicians, or rather statesmen, I would here exclusively deal, and then with the great personal historic impulse and force that lie behind us in our peculiar and royal citizenship and patriotism

As citizens, we are pre-eminently thinkers and politicians, that is, thoughtful patriots, who have an enlightened and conscientious policy for the guidance of land. In holding by and working out their intelligent patriotism, our fathers and brethren have ever demanded, have toiled for, paid, fought, suffered, and died for two all-precious boons, the school and the people's limitations of governmental control. Educated freemen we want to be, and educated freemen who shall say with sovereign authority, and will and strength backing up and enforcing our utterance, "thus far shall the ruler come, but no farther."

To us an enlightened public opinion is essential; a public opinion, not the haughty mandate of a despot, nor yet the bigot cry of any self-conceited separatist; and that enlightened public opinion immediately influential and operative; and, when duly formulated and expressed, final and mandatory. Hence, wherever our race is, and has been found, there, sooner or later, these three things are met: rational, right-built politics, regulated liberties, and representative government; or as a quaint, alliterative friend put it once, the pedagogue and the press, the pulpit, platform and parliament. Whosoever would sway us must give the reason, the whole reason, and nothing but the reason, and that the sufficient and the right. Our race is every-where hard-headed and firm-handed; we are a people of logic and law, of truth and reason, of rights and duties; we call for freedom chartered by highest and impartial law, and upheld by the conscientious convictions of the independent commonwealth; we work for the willing cohesion of self-respecting and brotherly freemen; we exact the bold and honest execution of the common law; we pride ourselves upon our sacred love of the old customs, "the use and the wont," so long as these are reasonable, just and useful; we admit changes slowly, but ours is a fearless acceptance of the new, if right, needed and practical. We have feelings, the "*perfervidum ingenium Scotorum,*" but it is "passion's steed curbed by reason's master hand." Not traditions, but truth sways us; but only truth that can be tested through and through, truth put logically, argumentatively, judicially. Not the haughty dictates of despotic arrogancy constrain us, but law; law being the voice and assertion of righteousness, righteousness being articulate, active, aggressive. Hence we seek truth that goes back to final truth; hence we labor for laws going back to supreme righteousness. Therefore, have we ever thought and sought that the moral should bulk both in the intellectual and the political. We wish the supreme code both in our schools and in our senates.

This union of all-ruling truth and right you may easily find in all our characteristic philosophy and religion, in our church and our conduct, in our politics and our patriotism. The tone we love best and bow before most readily is, "I speak as unto wise men—judge ye what I say."

Hence, the world has in the Scotch-Irishman a man as distinct from the Puritan as the Puritan is from all other men; and the Puritans of England and the Presbyterians of the Lowlands and of Ulster, were the two pillars of our national temple. As we enter the hallowed court of our country's sanctuary, and gaze upon and contrast this "Jachin" and this "Boaz," the pillar-man "established of Jehovah," and this other pillar-man "strengthened from on high," we see that while the Puritan believes in personality, the Scotch-Irish believes in partnership; while the Puritan believes in separation, the Scotch-Irish in representation; while the Puritan believes in individuality, the Scotch-Irish in equality; while the Puritan believes in independency, the Scotch-Irish in liberty; while the Puritan believes in experiment, the Scotch-Irish in experience; while the Puritan believes in the town meeting, the Scotch-Irish in the state house; while the Puritan believes in the congregation, the Scotch-Irish in the assembly.

And so up they rise, burly men of brawn and of brain, who say in the market, "A man's a man for a' that;" who say in the forum, "Give a reason for the hope that is in you;" who say in the commonwealth, "We be brethren, let there be no strife;" who say in the church, "Call no man master, for One is your Master;" and on the battle field, "No surrender," and "Keep your powder dry and trust in God;"—great, strong, kindly, true-hearted men—if at times a trifle grim and hard; men of reality, on whom their fellows lean; men believing in broad humanity, solid reason, free conscience, God-taught faith, and godly works showing forth faith; men fearing God, but no other.

That is how I think of them; that is how I have seen them in a score of strangely diverse lands; that is how they have met me as man and minister; that is how they have greeted and wrought with and helped me, by the old ingle, on the perilous glacier, in fire, and on flood, at the hospital bed and on the play-ground, when they have marched out to battle, and when they have laid themselves down to die, may the God that made them thus, their fathers' God and their God, bless, preserve, and keep them every-where!

So traditions and history show them from 1889 to 1776, from 1776 to 1688 to 1547.

But at that eastertide of 1547, you face a break, a vast, deep gap; up to that date and up to that garrison chapel at old St. Andrew's, where John Rough summoned out the God-sent maker of the newer and world-stamping Scotland, you never miss the one characteristic face, the one faith, the one force; but before that day there was no such Scotland, no such Lowland band of intelligent patriots, no call for common schools, and the broad equality of daring freemen, no concerted readiness to do and die for a free creed and a free country; while from that hour onward, these are never wanting, and they only strengthen, as the Scotch and Scotch-Irish multiplying from that creative moment spread themselves across the glad earth that welcomes them.

That hour and that gap are epochal. Such hours and gaps meet you ever and anon, as you steadily push your way down the historic pathway. On this side it is the polytheists of Ur of the Chaldees, on that the monotheists of the tents of Mamre; on this side it is the slaves of the Egyptian brick-kilns, on that side it is the jubilant freemen of the Red Sea; on this side it is the broken-hearted serfs of Spain, on that side it is the sturdy burghers of the Dutch Republic.

So 'twas in Scotland. There had been the "making" of men, but the men had not been made.

Suddenly the men are, and never henceforth disappear. No doubt there were antecedents; no doubt there was a long patience of divine toil; no doubt He who sees the end from the beginning had made His beginning far off in the dim distances of the race-movings and race-minglings. No doubt for over even twelve centuries, the older Scot, with his poesy and piety from Erin's isle, the roving Pict with northern daring, and the free-souled Teuton, had poured into the Strathclyde, there in turn to conquer and be conquered by the splendid British race of Arthur and his knightly band; and thus furnish the peculiarly rich and varied blood of our ancestors. But preparation is not product. Possibilities and promises are not active and victorious powers.

Here is my point of agreement with my friend Colonel McClure, and also my point of divergence from him. During twelve hundred and sixty years, the path is wending slowly to the Scotch, whom we know, and the Scotch-Irish, but the new man is not on the path.

You have the raw material, but not the finished work. It is the difference between the crystalline mass and the crystal itself. There in the great bowl you have the crystalline mass; shoot your electric bolt through it, you have another and a new thing, the true crystal, with its strange property and exact angles.

Up to that eastertide, 1547, your crystalline mass is gathering; then came the master-chemist, his hand shot the charge, and the crystal is.

I see Michael Angelo in the quarries of Carrara; his great far-seeing eye falls on a great block of fresh-hewn marble; the master pauses, then starts, and bids them send him that huge block. Now in his work-place I see the prince-sculptor walk up and down, his whole soul heaving with his thoughts and plans, beside him the raw material of the rough block, with its possibilities.

Now he works; the flaming spirit burns in his eager hands, and the creative soul passes through skilled, plastic fingers, into the dead, dull thing, from change to change it is carried by the artist's strength, till at last before the wondering world it lives—the Moses with the Law!

So do I see, before 1547, lying between the Grampians and the Dee, all across the historic Strathclyde, rarest raw materials, but after 1547 I see leaders of the world with the law of God in hand and heart.

The same, yet not the same. Name and fortune all changed. You stand at the Straits of Dover and look across. On each side there is the same geologic formation, the same old, rich chalk; but in between has burst the mighty tide of the sea, and on the one stands France, on the other Britain, with histories, and fortunes, and futures all so different.

And thus the race is in itself the same before 1547 as after, but there is a great gulf, and in between rolls one vast vitalizing tide of life. That separating, yes, transforming tide, was a man with such race-changing, and race-stamping force, as scarce another has owned and wielded.

The epochal gap is such at eastertide, 1547.

And in that epochal gap stands one great prophetic form, our ancestral seer. Before that Samuel of the later hour, you meet not our "school;" before him you see not our characteristic features of faith and freedom; after him you always do. And this lone, massive, formative man, sent by the Nations' King just as our motherland grew hot to whitest heat, and fit for the "crown-mark," is John Knox, at once our Moses and our Joshua, father of the school, father of chartered freedom, father of Scotland, of Ulster; yes, of us all! Here is the one man who, God-taught and God-fitted, taught our common family how to balance and harmonize the freeman's individual rights with dutiful and just submission, the supreme power of the people, with the support and recognition of constitutional rulers.

From exile and from bondage he came back to his native land in the darkest of her dark days, to find Scotland the enslaved province of a foreign and greedy state; to find no true people, no sturdy commons, no brave burghers; to find no constitution, no folk-made laws; to find no common schools, no free creed or free church; and he left behind him a steady, courageous, God-fearing nation in a freed land; a sturdy, truth-seeking, school-building, conscientious peasantry; a conquering, colonizing people, who guard righteous liberties and love their Bible, that divine Magna Charta of real freedom; who sing "Scots wha hae," or raise "plaintive martyrs" or "wild Dundee" amid the snow of Sutherlandshire and Canada, the Alleghanies or the Rockies; who build states beside the rolling Ohio or the floods of the gulf, and feel their strong hearts leap with gladness, here in the frosty blasts of

Minnesota, or there in the soft airs of Louisiana, here on the hills and downs of Virginia, or there in the vast wheat-fields of our West, as some familiar voice lifts up the old race words:

> "Breathes there a man with soul so dead
> Who never to himself hath said,
> This is my own, my native land."

Before Knox wrought and enstamped himself, our race had abilities; after him we have achievements; before him capacities, now careers; before him powers, now performances; before him strugglings, now success.

In long years of somewhat close historic reading and of sharp, interested studies of national departures and racial trends, I have found many a marked and self-impressing leader who, for some time, has made a nation wax and molded it at will; but then new fires came and a new stamp. But I have not found one such other case in profane history where a single leader has so deeply, pervasively, and permanently enstamped himself on a people who, of all folks, stand foremost among the self-asserting races.

Knox, under God, made the Scotch and the Scotch-Irish. All the race recall him; and the larger they are in characteristic build and features, the more obtrusive they are in racial majesties, by just so much the more do they reveal their great forefather's face.

His own quaint but invaluable history, McCrie's Life, Moncrieff's Studies, Cunningham's Lectures, and Froude's all graphic pages prove that Knox, first man of English speech, formulated, threw in covenant or charter form the balancing principles of individual independence and the authority of a constitutional government. His was indeed the earliest hand that penned any thing I can call a declaration of independence. He boldly taught broad and stirring Scotland these lessons, and put the generative words into clear writ, "The authority of kings and princes was originally derived from the people; that the former are not superior to the latter, collectively considered; that if rulers become tyrannical, or employ their power for the destruction of their subjects, they may be lawfully controlled, and, proving incorrigible, may be deposed by the community as the superior power; and that tyrants may be judicially proceeded against even to a capital punishment." Mark well these propositions; they are far-reaching; they are fruitful. They will appear and reappear; they are met constantly in Knox's preaching; they are written with large letters in his famous "Counterblast;" they are restated in his memorable answer to Queen Mary; they are set forth afresh in his declaration to Elizabeth;

they underlie all the Covenants; they are heard among the Lords of the Congregation; they were pealed across Scotland by the Covenanters; they were frequent maxims of Paden and Cameron, and Walsh, by Carrick's side, and the Valley of the Six Mile Water; they were battle words for the Ulster Volunteers; they survive to this very hour among the Presbyterians of Connor; they were fires in the heart of Patrick Henry; they were the familiar thoughts of John Witherspoon; they lie behind the war of independence; their spirit greets the world in our declaration; and, therefore, walks forth as master spirit their immortal author in the dear old hall of my native city. *Johannes Knox, semper virens, semper vivans!*

Observe well, the influence of this prophetic patriot was felt most at St. Andrews, through the long Strathclyde, in the districts of Ayr, Dumfries, and Galloway, the Lothians and Renfrew. There exactly clustered the homes which thrilled to the herald voice of Patrick Hamilton; there were the homes which drank in the strong wine of Knox; there were the homes of tenacious memories and earnest fire side talk; there were the homes which sent forth once and again the calm, shrewd, iron-nerved patriots who spurned as devil's lie the doctrine of "passive resistance;" and there—mark it well,—were the homes that sent their best and bravest to fill and change Ulster; thence came in turn the Scotch-Irish of the " Eaglewing;" thence came the settlers of Pennsylvania, Virginia, the Carolinas, Tennessee and Kentucky; and the sons of these men blush not as they stand beside the children of the "Mayflower," or the children of the Bartholomew martyrs. I know whereof I affirm. My peculiar education and somewhat singular work planted me, American born, in the very heart of these old ancestral scenes; and from parishioners who held with deathless grip the very words of Peden, Welsh, and Cameron, from hoary headed witnesses in the Route of Antrim and on the hills of Down, have I often heard of the lads who went out to bleed at Valley Forge—to die as victors on King's Mountain,—and stand in the silent triumph of Yorktown. We have more to thank Knox for than is commonly told to-day.

Here we reach our Welshes and Witherspoons, our Tennents and Taylors, our Calhouns and Clarks, our Cunninghams and Caldwells, our Pollocks, Polks, and Pattersons, our Scotts and Grays and Kennedys, our Reynolds and Robinsons, our McCooks, McHenrys, McPhersons and McDowells.

But the man behind is Knox. Would you see his monument? Look around. Yes! To this, our own land, more than any other, I am convinced, must we look for the fullest outcome and the yet all unspent force of this more than royal leader, this masterful and molding soul. Hither came the men most thoroughly saturated with the teaching of Knox, because of their very special training and experience in Ulster, on which most fertile theme time will not suffer me even to touch; here they met those singular, historic provocations that imperiously summoned forth into fiercest but still strongly ruled action the mightiest and most characteristic powers of their souls; here they had acute call and most magnificent reason to stride into justest battle for the very principles that were of all ancestral gifts the very dearest and most sacred; here they were given of the wise God and the most foolish George the field and opportunity to let stream forth floods of energy in the seeking of a new home of freedom; here they triumphed; here they won no second place in state and church, on bloody field and hall of legislation, on the billow and in commerce; here they hold their own, and grow and multiply, and give themselves fullest scope and sweep to the good of the common country, and their own honor and the glory of the God whom alone they fear. Carlyle has said: "Scotch literature and thought, Scotch industry; James Watts, David Hume, Walter Scott, Robert Burns. I find Knox and the Reformation at the heart's core of every one of those persons and phenomena; I find that without Knox and the Reformation, they would not have been. Or what of Scotland?" Yea! verily! no Knox, no Watts, no Burns, no Scotland, as we know and love and thank God for! And must we not say no men of the Covenant; no men of Antrim and Down, of Derry and Enniskillen; no men of the Cumberland valleys; no men of the Virginian hills; no men of the Ohio stretch, of the Georgian glades and the Tennessee Ridge; no rally at Scoone; no thunders in St. Giles; no testimony from Philadelphian Synod; no Mecklenburg declaration; no memorial from Hanover Presbytery; no Tennent stirring the Carolinas; no Craighead sowing the seeds of the coming revolution; no Witherspoon pleading for the signing of our great charter; and no such declaration and no such constitution as are ours,—the great Tilghman himself being witness in these clear words, never by us to be let die: "The framers of the Constitution of the United States were greatly indebted to the standards of the Presbyterian Church of Scotland in modeling that admirable document."

Never, then, to us of the Scotch and Scotch-Irish lineage race of resolute and orderly citizens, never let the name of Knox be other than battle-blast and household boast, nor his memory ought save inspiration—yes, consecration!

SCOTCH-IRISH SETTLERS IN SOUTH CAROLINA, AND THEIR DESCENDANTS IN MAURY COUNTY, TENNESSEE.

BY HON. W. S. FLEMING, COLUMBIA, TENN.

It is not my purpose, in this paper, to dwell at any length upon, or to magnify and extol the racial characteristics of the Scotch-Irish— nor to investigate the causes which led them to leave their homes in Scotland, and to find new homes in the province of Ulster, Ireland; nor to inquire into the motives, be they civil or ecclesiastical, which induced or impelled them to seek an abode in the then wilds of America. All this has been done and will be done by abler pens than I can wield, and tongues in strains more eloquent than I could ever dare to attempt. My humble purpose is to trace in brief the history and progress of one colony or society, more or less connected with each other by ties of affinity and consanguinity. And instead of entering into an elaborate discussion of or treatise upon the manners, customs, habits, and genetic characteristics of the race in detail, I will attempt to illustrate their distinctive traits of character by a very brief historic sketch of this little colony; for its history is that of many others, if not nearly all, who emigrated from Ulster to America. In the language of the Roman poet:

"Ex uno disce omnes."

From 1730 to 1734, this colony, the parent of one in this county of Maury, to be mentioned presently, migrated to Williamsburg District, South Carolina, of which Kingstree is the county seat. Of those who came during the above period were the following heads of families: James McClelland, William and Robert Wilson, James Bradley, William Frierson, John James, Roger Gordon, James Armstrong, Erwin, Stuart, McDonald, Dobbins, Blakely, Dickey, and perhaps a few others. In the last named year, to wit, 1734, John Witherspoon, of the same family with the distinguished signer of the Declaration of Independence, born near Glasgow, Scotland, in 1670, and who had removed to County Down, Ireland, came to Williamsburg, bringing with him his four sons, David, James, Robert and Gavin, and his daughters, Jennet, Elizabeth and Mary, with their husbands, John Fleming, William James (father of Major John James, of revolutionary memory and distinction) and David Wilson. All these colonists were from County Down, Ireland. They were all members of the Presbyterian Church, or reared and indoctrinated in its faith. Consequently one of their first cares was the erection of a house for the worship of God; and the present, known as Bethel Church, is the representative and successor of the original body constituted and established by them. In 1849 three of the original elders, to wit, William James, David Witherspoon, and John Fleming, died of a singular epidemic, known as the "Great Mortality," which ravaged the country, carrying off no less than eighty persons of the little township. For many of the foregoing facts I am indebted to a historical discourse delivered on the 120th anniversary of this church, in 1856, by Rev. James A. Wallace, its then pastor.

It is proper to notice another family or connection of Scotch-Irish, who, coming down from Pennsylvania through Virginia and North Carolina, settled in or near the "Waxhaws," in Lancaster District, South Carolina. These were the Stephensons, the Dunlaps, the Crawfords, Blairs, Fosters, and General Andrew Jackson's parents, who were nearly related to the Crawfords. I mention these, because both before and after the immigration to Tennessee they became connected by intermarriage with the Williamsburg branch. They were all of the same religious persuasion, and all of the John Knox type. During the War of Independence every man of these settlements capable of bearing arms was in the field on the side of liberty. There was not a "tory" among them in a district abounding with "tories."

In the address alluded to above Mr. Wallace says: "Among the descendants of the Irish Presbyterian colonists of the township, the name of 'tory' was unknown. 'Liberty or death' was the motto of every man; and it was the immutable sentiment of every heart." They mainly formed "Marion's Brigade," whose patriotism and deeds of daring have passed into song and story and become household words, lisped long after by their children, and inspiring with sentiments of chivalry the youthful minds of their descendants. With them were many descendants of the French Huguenots, those sterling Christian patriots, exiled by the revocation of the Edict of Nantes, united with them in one common faith, political and religious. Shoulder to shoulder stood these two distinct races, through all the terrible scenes of bloodshed and danger, battling for the same eternal principles of truth and liberty—"Man's heritage in the Church and man's heritage in the State." Simms says: "The people of Williamsburg were men generally of fearless courage, powerful frame, well-strung nerves, and an audacious gallantry that led them to delight in dangers. They felt that 'rapture of the strife' in which the Goth delighted."

They took part in every battle fought in the state of South Carolina, and some of them took part in the Battle of King's Mountain, the thunder of whose guns sounded the key-note of Cornwallis' dirge. Besides many minor engagements with British troops and tories, they participated in the Battles of Eutaw, Cowpens, Monk's Corner, Fort Motte, and Georgetown. But I must not dwell longer upon the patriotism and gallantry of this people in the old Revolution. Their record is without a stain—their escutcheon untarnished.

And now let us trace for a brief space some of their descendants, and follow them to this state and to this county. If this course will in any way illustrate the Scotch-Irish character, then the attempt will not be without profit. This account deals with the people of a settlement, known as "Zion's Church," all of them Scotch-Irish—an offshoot of the Williamsburg colony—a swarm from that as the parent hive—always regarded as a peculiar people, more so formerly than at present; peculiar in its intermarriages within itself, so to speak; peculiar in its systematic and thorough instruction of the young in the Westminster Confession and the Shorter Catechism; peculiar in its rigid observance of the Sabbath, such as no shaving, no chopping of wood, no cooking except the drawing of coffee, no dinings, no visiting except of the sick, upon that holy day; peculiar in the religious instruction given on Sundays to their slaves, of whom they possessed a very large number; peculiar in their very exalted standard of honesty and morality; peculiar in their entire exemption from all legal prosecutions involving crime or moral turpitude. Many, if not most, of these peculiarities are, or were, common to the Scotch-Irish race, but not to those outside of it.

About the 25th of March, 1805, James Armstrong (my maternal grandfather), Moses G. Frierson, James Blakeley, and Paul Fulton, with their respective families, emigrated from Williamsburg, South Carolina, being members of Bethel congregation, under the charge of Rev. James White Stephenson, D.D. After six weeks of laborious travel they reached the vicinity of Nashville on the 8th of May, 1805. In the fall of the same year they removed to the neighborhood of Franklin, Williamson County, Tennessee, where they rented temporary habitations for themselves, and also secured places for some of their friends and relatives, who proposed to follow them the ensuing year.

Accordingly, on the 6th of March, 1806, the following, with their several families, left their native homes in South Carolina to seek their abode in the wilds of Tennessee and join the four families who had preceded them, and with whom they were closely connected, to wit: John Dickey, Mrs. Margaret Frierson, Mrs. Jane H. Blakely, Samuel Frierson, Thos. Stephenson, Wm. Frierson, Wm. I. Frierson, Samuel Witherspoon, Elias Frierson, John W. Stephenson, and Mrs. Mary Fleming (my paternal grandmother), with her four boys. They were singularly blessed and providentially favored in their long and tedious journey by reason of the clemency of the weather, the low stage of the many water-courses they had to cross, the facility for obtaining food and provisions in abundance along the way, and their entire exemption from disease and death, although attended by a large number of slaves. This company reached their friends in Williamson county about the middle of April, 1806. True to their religious training and habits, they soon resolved to meet every Sabbath for the purpose of reading the Scriptures, and of prayer and praise. They accordingly erected a stand, where they spent most of each Sabbath in religious exercises. In the fall of 1806 they received a visit from their old pastor, Dr. Stephenson, who remained long enough to preach on several occasions. Soon they resolved to purchase land suitable and sufficient for a permanent settlement. A part of General Green's 25,000 acre grant was selected as the most eligible and desirable they could find. This lies in Maury county. The next question was whether it could be bought and titles could be secured from Green's heirs. Accordingly a messenger was at once dispatched to their home on Cumberland Island, off the coast of Georgia, near the mouth of the River St. Mary, to ascertain whether a purchase could be made, and if so, to pay the purchase-money and have the title papers executed. Captain George Dickey, one of the colony, undertook the apparently perilous journey, through the tribes of Indians then settled along the Tennessee and Chickamauga Rivers and the mountainous regions of North Georgia. The response was favorable for a sale, which was soon effected. Eight square miles, lying in oblong shape, were purchased at $3 per acre, the total amount being $15,360. This purchase lies in Maury county, its nearest boundary line to Columbia, the county seat, being about five miles west of that city.

This purchase lay in an unsettled, wilderness state at that time, a few scattering habitations in remote parts of the county—probably not one upon the entire Green survey. The county had not as yet received its name; no settlement to be found, dating back as far as a year; the whole face of the country densely covered with cane, so that in but few spots here and there could a man see fifty steps in any direction around him. Wild game abounded, such as wolves, bear, deer, and turkeys.

On a given day every able-bodied man, with as many men slaves as he could spare, was present on the land so purchased, at a designated spot, for the double purpose of dividing the land and of erecting a large log-house, to serve as a house of public worship. This church or meeting-house was built as near the center of the purchase as possible, regard being had to the procurement of water. This was not a matter of much difficulty, as the tract abounded in springs of water of excellent quality, as does the entire country.

Upon assembling, some proceeded to survey the land and lay it off into lots or smaller tracts, to suit families, while others were engaged in getting out timbers for and in constructing the church building. In less than one week it was finished, and the land divided into suitable shares or sections. Then each returned to his home and family in Williamson county, about thirty miles distant, to make preparation for his removal.

Think what a people this was; not a cabin was built, nor a move made in the direction of home and individual comforts, until a house for the worship of Almighty God was first built. In the fall of 1807, most of the little colony returned to their new purchase to rear temporary huts or cabins for their families; and early in January, 1808, a general move was made to their new homes and cheaply constructed habitations. Their labors were now arduous. Provisions must be hauled thirty miles in midwinter, along narrow, newly-made, muddy roads; the dense cane must be chopped out and the ground cleared for cropping. All these things required the closest attention, as well as untiring industry.

Soon after their removal, they began to hold services in their log church or meeting-house. Remarkable punctuality characterized their attendance on divine worship. The utmost unanimity, unaffected friendship, and cordial hospitality prevailed among them. They were yet without a pastor, or "stated supply," yet they never failed to keep up sermon reading, singing, and prayer on the Sabbath. This state of affairs, however, did not long continue, for, in April, 1808, there was an addition to their number in the arrival of Dr. Stephenson, their former pastor, Dr. Samuel Mayes, Robert Frierson, and Joshua Frierson, all from the same church in South Carolina. Dr. Stephenson, who was from the Waxhaw settlement, had been pastor of this people for some fifteen or twenty years. A sketch of his life may be seen in Dr. Howe's " History of Presbyterianism in the Carolinas."

These last immigrants, at first, rented farms for a year or two in Williamson county. One of them, old Mr. Robert Frierson, being a very old man, died, and on his death-bed requested that his remains should be taken to the new settlement, and be buried in the churchyard there, which was done, and so he became the first solitary tenant of that sacred spot.

In the spring of 1809, Dr. Stephenson, having married Mrs. Mary Fleming, who, with her four boys, had already come to the country, as before stated, removed from Williamson county, where he had rented for about a year, to the Zion neighborhood, and became at once what is termed "stated supply." An incident is related of him, that occurred during the war of the Revolution. In one of the battles, I do not remember which, but fought desperately, either at Eutaw, the "Cowpens," or Fishing Ford, as he had his gun to his face, and was in the act of firing, a ball from the side of the enemy struck his gun near the lock and severed the barrel from the breech. At the instant a comrade fell dead by his side, and he instantly seized his gun and continued the fight.

This settlement possessed a large number of slaves, and in proportion to the whites had a much larger number than any other settlement in the county, and probably in the state. For many years they had been brought over from Africa to Charleston, and their ancestors had been large purchasers. These slaves were, without exception, kindly treated and cared for, both as regards their temporal and spiritual interests, and the slaves loved their masters. They became, when converted, members of the same church, worshiped with them, by having their own particular seats assigned to them, and partook of the sacraments with them, but not occupying the communion-table at the same time. I do not remember any more impressive and touching sight to my youthful mind than to witness them (the communicants) come down from the galleries, where they always sat during service, and march up the two aisles in the body of the church, with a white elder at the head of each column, singing as they went to occupy the seats around the long-extended table, just before occupied by the white communicants.

Soon after Dr. Stephenson took charge of the church the session concluded that a certain number of their body should employ a portion of each Sabbath in catechising and instructing the young people of the congregation. The plan succeeded admirably in familiarizing them with the larger and shorter catechisms.

In the beginning of 1811, the permanent white members of the congregation, young and old, male and female, numbered about one hundred and forty. Of course, the number of communicants was much less, not exceeding probably thirty or forty, and this was a very rapid increase. It may not be out of place to state that in this year (1811) a presbytery was for the first time constituted or organized. Its style was "The Presbytery of West Tennessee," and was held at Bethsaida, on Fountain Creek, in Maury County. Dr. Stephenson was made moderator, and Dr. Duncan Brown clerk. The other ministers present were Rev. Messrs. Blackburn, Donald, and Gillespie.

In the spring of this year the congregation resolved to provide ways and means for the erection of a brick building as a church. The work and materials were distributed among the members in the proportion of their taxable slave property; and on the 5th of August, 1812, the corner-stone of this grand old church was laid. In the summer and fall the walls were carried up, and in the spring of 1813 the house was ready for preaching, and was accordingly so used.

Of these men it might be truly said, what their hearts designed to do, their hands, with all their might, pursued.

Here we might close the early history of this church and congregation, but I must be permitted to add that, within a few feet of this old church building, a new church edifice was erected and received as finished on the 20th of March, 1849, being the same now standing, and in which the congregation now worship. It is built of brick, large, commodious, and well appointed.

Of the ministers who have had charge, from the beginning to the present time, are the following, in the order in which they officiated, to wit: James White Stephenson, D.D., who served them about forty years—some sixteen in South Carolina, and about twenty-four in this church. He died January 6, 1832. James M. Aornell, a native of New York, was elected to succeed him, January 9, 1832, and died March 4, 1850. Rev. Duncan Brown, quite an old man, filled the pulpit from time to time till the call of Daniel G. Doak, who was elected as "stated supply," June 20, 1850, and on account of ill-health resigned his position in 1855. Rev. A. A. Doak, father of Editor H. M. Doak, was then called, but remained only a short time, less than a year, as now remembered. Rev. I. Tilghman Hendrick, son of Dr. I. T. Hendrick, formerly of Paducah, Ky., was elected pastor October 1, 1857. In a few years he died, and upon his death the pulpit was supplied by various ministers—as Rev. C. Foster Williams, Rev. William Mack, D.D., and perhaps some others, until Rev. S. W. Mitchell was called, who filled the pulpit for several years, and until his recent resignation in the fall of 1888. A call has been made and accepted by Rev. Mr. Kennedy, who will enter shortly upon his duties as such minister.

Very few of that congregation, who reached the age of responsibility, have ever neglected to unite with the church; and I may be allowed to say I can now recall but three or four instances in which any male descendants of these fathers have left the church; but, I am happy to further say, that in these few instances they have shown themselves consistent, efficient, useful Christians.

From this congregation as a mother hive, her children have, from time to time, swarmed, so to speak, and formed colonies or settlements in all the Gulf States; and wherever they have migrated, they have carried with them the faith of their fathers. From this stock, I venture to say, there have sprung a greater number of ministers of the Gospel of the Presbyterian faith than from any other in the United States. It may be interesting to some to know who they were and who they are.

I will first give the names of the ministers who are the direct descendants of the original colonists and founders of Zion Church, without regard to chronological order: W. Vincent Frierson, deceased, of Pontotoc, Miss.; W. Vincent Frierson, Jr., of the same place; John Stephenson Frierson; John Simpson Frierson, late deceased, and W. J. Frierson of Columbia, Tenn.; Jerry Witherspoon, Nashville, Tenn.; T. Dwight Witherspoon, Louisville, Ky.; S. Reese Frierson, deceased, Starkville, Miss.; Jno. C. McMullen, Chester, S. C.; Rev. Fulton, S. C.; Thomas R. English, Yorkville, S. C.; W. D. Heddelston of Kentucky; then Robert Gayle of Mississippi and A. I. B. Foster of Tennessee. These two became and now are Methodist preachers. In all there are fifteen ministers, thirteen Presbyterian and two Methodist, descendants of the original colonists.

This estimate does not embrace the three brothers, David E., Edwin O. and M. L. Frierson, whose father did not immigrate to Tennessee, nor David E., Jr., son of David E., located in Lewisburg, W. Va. If these are added then we would have nineteen from this family connection. All these were descendants of Scotch-Irish Presbyterians, who emigrated from County Down, near Belfast, Ireland, to Williamsburg District, South Carolina, from 1730 to 1734.

Of the ministers, who intermarried with some of the colonists, their daughters, grand or great-granddaughters, may be numbered James White Stephenson, D. D. Duncan Brown, D.D., James M. Arnell, J. Tilghman Hendrick, C. Foster Williams, S. W. Mitchell, and Thomas A. Hoyte of Philadelphia. All these preached in Zion at different times, and the last mentioned three still survive.

Then there were Thomas R. English, Sr., deceased, of South Carolina; James P. McMullen, deceased, of Alabama, who fell in battle at the head of the regiment of which he was chaplain; M. C. Hutton, of Alabama, and L. R. Amis, of Tennessee. All these intermarried with descendants of these colonists, the last named being a Methodist preacher, quite young and promising, in all eleven of these, added to the nineteen, give us thirty.

Four of these early colonists were soldiers in the war of independence, to wit, Dr. Stephenson, James Armstrong, Dr. Mayes, and David Matthews. This entire connection of people, or rather their ancestors, were all Whigs in that war, and fought under Greene and Marion and at King's Mountain. They or their descendants fought under Jackson in the War of 1812–14. They were fully represented in the Seminole War of 1837. In the war with Mexico, in 1848, her sons stood before the walls of Monterey, and their blood stained the plains of Buena Vista. In the late war, their bones lay scattered on nearly every battle field of the south. At the tap of the drum, at the call of the bugle, they have always been ready, without compulsion, to gallantly respond.

So it seems that rigid instruction in the Calvinistic or John Knox faith of their Scotch ancestry was not inconsistent with their ideas of a lofty patriotism.

From this little colony of Presbyterians, or rather their descendants, Tennessee has had some dozen of representatives in her legislative halls, one speaker in the state senate, one United States senator, one judge on the supreme bench of the state, two chancellors in Middle Tennessee, several editors, besides many very eminent lawyers and skillful physicians.

Last of all, but not least, I have never known or heard of one of their descendants being convicted of or charged with any capital or penitentiary offense, or any less offense or misdemeanor, involving moral turpitude or degradation of character.

The record thus given of this, the oldest Presbyterian church in Maury county, is worthy of preservation, and may be viewed with pride and veneration by every descendant, however remote they may be removed from the home of their fathers, or wherever in this broad land Providence may have cast his or her lot.

www.ingramcontent.com/pod-product-compliance
Lightning Source LLC
Chambersburg PA
CBHW020817230426
43666CB00007B/1046